STRUCTURE

ANDREW PLOTNER

All views expressed in this book are the sole opinion of the author and do not in any way represent the views of the Department of Defense or the Department of Justice.

Copyright © 2019 Andrew Plotner

Book Cover by Najdan Mancic

All rights reserved.

ISBN: 9781074311711

Structure

"The dogmas of the quiet past are inadequate to the stormy present. The occasion is piled high with difficulty and we must rise with the occasion. As our case is new, we must think anew and act anew. We must disenthrall ourselves, and then we shall save our country." -Abraham Lincoln 1862

CONTENTS

	Introduction	ii
1	The Structure of Capitalism	Pg 1
1.5	Review Section	Pg 23
2	Defending the Labour Theory of Value	Pg 26
3	Structure of International Exploitation	Pg 35
4	Obtaining/ Maintaining International Exploitation	Pg 41
5	Use of Force in International Exploitation	Pg 48
6	How we Support and Propagate International Exploitation	Pg 69
7	Exploring the Circulation of Capital	Pg 76
8	The Structure of Crisis	Pg 93
9	Relating the Exploitative Systems	Pg 105
10	Political Change Without Economic Change	Pg 110
11	Manufacturing the Red Scare	Pg 117
12	Is Growth Without Exploitation Possible?	Pg 127
13	Hurdles to Transition	Pg 136
14	Policies to Structurally Overcome the Hurdles	Pg 144
15	Structural Policy Goals: Social Security & Taxation	Pg 152

16	Structural Policy Goals: Energy	Pg 158
17	Structural Policy Goals: Necessities & Healthcare	Pg 173
18	Structural Policy Goals: Infrastructure	Pg 181
19	Structural Policy Goals: Education	Pg 185
20	Structural Policy Goals: Criminal Justice	Pg 196
21	Structural Policy Goals: Direct Democracy	Pg 208
22	Final Word: Infinite Game	Pg 217
	Acknowledgment	Pg 221

INTRODUCTION

Ever look at the world around you and question the most basic of its functions? Wonder how, or why something operates the way it does? For example, maybe you have been standing in the shower and noticed how little drops of water skid atop the wet tile as if they were rolling. Perhaps you have asked the question as to why that is.

By asking that question you begin the path to discovery. You learn that when a droplet falls, there is a cushion of air trapped beneath it and the surface of the water. That it isn't until this cushion is pushed out that the droplet can coalescence with the water below. That the reason droplets form on vibrating water is because of the formation of peaks and valleys. That those peaks and valleys alternate and seemingly catch the falling droplets like one would catch a water balloon in such a way to prevent it from bursting. That once caught, the vibrations of the water continuously renew the presence of air underneath preventing coalescence from occurring, and as a result, creates the phenomenon witnessed in the shower. I find that process of discovery to be absolutely amazing!

These questions allow you to see the world differently. To see colors as different energies of light, to see table salt as being frozen, or to know that the vast majority of the things around you are mostly empty space.

Cultivating that mindset is the intent of this book. To get you, the reader, to think, and analyze. To provide you with a different perspective that makes you question what you already know. To focus this mindset toward the betterment of society. In cultivating this new perspective, we will explore the functions of the Capitalist foundations, the flaws that come out of those foundational observations, and what is needed to address them. By providing you with these perspectives, you can begin to question for yourself and come to your own conclusions.

The last thing I want from anyone who reads this book is to parrot the arguments I make. My goal is the questioning of basic foundations we take for granted. To create a mindset that allows for a new way of viewing how we talk about politics and economics. To change the discussions from those of finite goals to that of an infinite pursuit. Science pursues knowledge and truth above all else. It never stagnates because it always seeks to question. Progress is ever moving forward.

"Complacency is the deadly enemy of spiritual progress. The contented soul is a stagnate soul." - Aiden Wilson Tozer

Science, you see, plays the infinite game. As such no matter how many setbacks it receives it marches forward unrelentingly. We must apply that same spirit, that same principle. To every aspect of our lives, our community, our country, and our world. We must find our own infinite game, find the ideal and push forward, never ceasing, never stopping, never becoming complacent. So, with that introduction out of the way. Welcome to my perspective on the Foundations of Capitalism and the Need for a Democratic Economy. Welcome to **Structure**.

Tips

<u>Not one for Economic analysis?</u>

If so, you might consider Chapters 1, 2, 3, 7, 8, and 12 as "dry" chapters. I recommend reading Chapter 1.5 first and moving on to chapter 3. Save the above chapters for the very end.

      a. Reading this way will allow you hear about the end goals advocated for first. The above chapters merely present the argument for why the goals advocated for are structurally necessary.

<u>Browsing the book?</u>

I recommend Chapters 10, 13, and 19 as chapters to read to whet your appetite.

CHAPTER I
THE STRUCTURE OF CAPITALISM[1]

To understand why our society has such high levels of inequality, one must first understand Capitalism. Though many applaud it as the most exceptional system, they seem to neglect the concept of improvement. That once identified, flaws and problems need correcting. In this way, the glorification of Capitalism appears to have taken a near-religious aspect to its defense, unwilling to receive criticism, reluctant to improve. This book intends to explore the systematic structure of Capitalism and expose the origins of the flaws and contradictions contained within it. Let us begin with the first step toward understanding these flaws. Let us start with the commodity; Something we are all familiar with and utilize daily. The commodity will be our primary tool with which we will begin our investigation into this system called Capitalism.

The Commodity:

This book is a commodity; your computer is a commodity; anything you use and have bought is a commodity. But what exactly does that mean? Is money a commodity? Some say that wealth is the accumulation of commodities, but by what definition does that statement rest?

To continue, we must first define it. We can view a commodity through the use of its quality or quantity to satisfy a desire. We can say that a commodity must have an origin. What did it take to create it, in chemical terms what energy constitutes its mass? Much like any matter in existence, which you can break down into its basic building blocks: electrons and protons.[2] The same holds for the commodity; you can break it down to its principal components: Nature and Labour.

---

[1] Wealth of Nations by Adam Smith / Capitalism by Anwar Shaikh / Das Kapital by Karl Marx

[2] For example, a table is made of wood, wood is made up of plant-based cells, those cells are constructed of atoms of carbon, oxygen, hydrogen, etc. Each individual atom is constructed of the same material, protons, electrons, and neutrons, neutrons simply being a proton and electron as well. Both those consisting of energy itself. Thus, everything in the universe can be simplified to the very basics, and understanding the building blocks is what allows us to understand the whole.

It is no secret that anything you look at in a store was produced at one point or another. That production consisted of Human Labour, tools, and raw materials. Those tools were constructed of raw materials and Human Labour as well. Therefore, everything utilized in the production of a commodity can be simplified down to Nature and Human Labour.

We can say that a commodity must have a Use Value. The Use Value is a part of the commodity itself and is independent of the Labour that went into creating it. It doesn't matter if a hammer took 30 seconds to make on a production line or 100 hours to make by hand; it contains the same Use Value within it.

Thus, we see the two factors that make up a commodity, that it must be produced, and have a use.

Now, we will take it a step further; it deals with the exchange, or rather the concept of it. For an exchange to occur, Value must be present. We see already the two categories that can give a commodity its Value: production, and Use. We have also split production up into Nature and Human Labour.

Starting with Nature. Indeed, from your own experience, you recognize that Nature is valuable. But where from does it ascribe its Value? Does it get its Value from its Use? If so, then is Nature useful without Human Labour? Certainly, Nature grows trees and produces oil, but without Human Labour to harvest that Nature, it has no Use Value in the market. It is true that trees produce oxygen and that it is of immeasurable Use to us, as are other qualities of Nature, but that Value has no place in the market and hopefully never will.[3]

For this reason, Nature's Value in the market comes from the Use Value it brings to the market itself. That being the Labour that can be done on it so that it may be useful to others. This reveals the exciting duality of Value: Labour Value, and Use Value.

A modern-day example to show the duality of Value is with the fidget spinner. When it first came on the market, it was merely a ball bearing with three plastic protrusions that would spin freely and easily for a while. Its price was relatively high for what it was. It had a novelty attraction to it, but once it was on the market for a while, people realized that it was easy to produce. More producers arose, and competition increased. Thus, the market had to adjust the pricing from Use Value (satisfying a desire) to Labour Value (what it takes to make one).

This duality of Use and Labour make up the Value. And therefore, identity and definition of a commodity in our society.

---

[3] If president Scroob ever figures out how to bottle and sell air, we better hope Lonestar and Barf are there to save the galaxy from the evils of Spaceballs.

This is essentially where Neoclassical Capitalists end the explanation on how society attributes Value to commodities. But by doing so they end up tricking everyone into missing an important relation, there is more. To have an exchange rate, a price if you will, you must have something about the commodities be equal. Looking at the duality of Labor and Use we can discern which is qualitative and quantitative. The Use Value is the qualitative relationship and the Labour Value the quantitative relationship when you place them in exchange with another commodity.[4]

Exchange:

Since qualities of two commodities are not similar the Use Value does not lend itself to explaining exchange value. However, the quantitative relationship of Labour does. As an example, let's look at the purest form of exchange, one commodity for another; Commodity for commodity (C-C).

Example:

- We will attribute the Value of 1 hammer to being worth that of 100 nails.
- We shall say that you, already possessing a hammer of your own and an extra, need the nails but do not have any.

To trade for nails, you must find someone who has them and has a use for your extra hammer. The Use Value of a hammer and nails themselves are entirely different though. They differ qualitatively in the Use they are going to serve and quantitatively in their Labour Value to each other. The quantitative is, thus, how price should represent Value.

The trick Neoclassical Capitalism plays comes about by saying that the utility is where the Value lies. That the Use Value dictates the price you are willing to pay for something, and this desire then shows up in the market in the form of price. But price and Value are not the same. This is a crucial point. Price is not value, it is merely an indicator of it, and when price and value are not in equilibrium inequality arises.

---

[4] "The Value of a commodity, or the quantity of any other commodity for which it will exchange, depends on the relative quantity of Labour which is necessary for its production, and not on the greater or less compensation which is paid for that Labour". -David Ricardo, it's incredible how blunt Ricardo is in this statement. Right off the bat, he lays the groundwork for Exchange Value and Use Value. He states clearly that it is Labour which gives Value to the commodity but that the compensation to the Labour which produced it, is Valued differently. We will see how this valorization of Labour is accomplished later, and the implications it brings.

When you utilize Use Value as the means for exchange, the Use Values of two people will never be the same. This leads to one person working to produce something to trade for another thing that has less Value than what they produced due to their need for it. What this means is that one person is getting the shaft. The more they need something, the more Use Value they have for it, and the more inequality in the transaction they are willing to suffer to obtain it. That inequality is the difference in Labour performed by the two parties; one did more Labour than the other.

Use Value, is absolutely necessary for the exchange to occur. Without both parties gaining a Use Value, the exchange wouldn't happen.[5] Proponents of Capitalism say that pricing exchange in this way is mutually beneficial and therefore not predatory, but that is just sleight of hand logic that ignores the greater lie by focusing on a smaller truth. Both parties may gain a Use Value from the exchange, but that does not stop it from being predatory since there is an imbalance in the Labour Value of the exchange. It ignores that an equal exchange of Labour Value will still result in a gain of Use Value. This is one of the inherent flaws of Capitalism; that it lends itself to predatory exchange. Let's re-affirm this with an example.

Example:

Because all commodities have Use Value and Labour Value attached to them, this inevitably leads to the accumulation of Labour Value by one party of the transaction. This power imbalance is precisely how every job today functions:

1. I the employer have money which is a Use Value to you, you need this to survive in our economy.

2. Your Labour is a Use Value for me, so I need it as well to run my business.

3. Because I, as the employer, have many more people eager to fill your spot, my Use Value for you as an individual, is low.

4. Thus, I will pay you based on my Use Value for your Labour instead of its actual Labour Value.

5. You will accept this unequal exchange because your Use Value for the money is substantially greater. To have some money is better than to risk having no money at all.

---

[5] In all chemical reactions, there must be sufficient energy present for it to occur. Without energy, no matter how big the desire, the reaction will not take place. In this scenario, energy is the Labour that creates the product and the desire for the product is its Use Value.

That is exploitation, plain and simple. You exploit Value from your employee to obtain more for yourself based on the threat of hiring someone else who will work for that lower wage.[6] If you paid them their Labour Value, this would not be an issue, but that is not the design of the system. It is designed to say "see they are free to make their own choice, and that is what makes this system perfect. They wouldn't choose this if they didn't like it." little do they realize their "choice" is the same as that given by Jigsaw to his victims, a choice between bad and worse.

This current system defines Value as Use (or utility). However, Use is only the desire for a commodity and is separate from its Exchange Value. The Value itself is the Labour it took to create it. In all chemical reactions, there must be sufficient energy present for it to occur. Without energy, no matter how big the desire, the reaction will not take place. In this scenario, energy is the Labour that creates the product and the desire for the product is its Use Value. This stance is known as the Labour Theory of Value and was originally created by Adam Smith and further perpetuated by David Riccardo and Karl Marx. However, defining value in this way created a problem for Capitalism as Karl Marx's analysis showed how predatory Capitalism was under this definition of Value and how futile its perpetuation was so long as equality and freedom was the economy's objective. As a result, the economic proponents of Capitalism had to abandon the Labour Theory of Value to try and defend it. This resulted in absurd arguments against the Labour Theory of Value, arguments which had to completely abandon the foundations that Adam Smith put forth. Two common analogies given to thwart this theory are the mud pie example, as well as the water and diamond example.

The mud pie example goes that if you spend 100 hours making a mud pie, then its Value should be enormous. But this argument neglects two things, first that a commodity must have a Use Value to be considered a commodity and second that the law of supply and demand are still in effect. Surely 100 hours did go into it, but, was there a demand for mud pies? Most likely not, so this argument's premise to start with was absurd. Productive Labour is only applicable if it is meeting a demand by creating a supply, put another way, if it has a Use Value.[7]

---

[6] Many individuals claim that you cannot run a business without Profit, this is true in a sense, but you must first define what Profit is, and second where it comes from. Profit is the accumulation of Labour Value from all Labour that has gone into the product. It is unknown before the sale. If we are to make profit non-exploitative then after sale profit must be divided out appropriately to the contributors or reinvested democratically with the permission of those who created that value. If it is taken by the Capitalist for their own personal gain, that is theft, it is the denial of ownership to the producers of the value that they themselves created.

Socially Necessary Labour Time

The second argument is the water and diamond analogy. That if someone stumbles upon a diamond, they have done very little work to obtain the Value. But somehow it is worth more than water, and surely since water's Use Value is higher than that of a diamond, then it should be more expensive. They argue that since it isn't, the Value must come from utility (desire). But this argument conveniently skips over the concept of Socially Necessary Labour Time. That is, it skips over the fact that the market works off of supply and demand. Since the supply of diamonds is much less than that of water. If another person were to go and try to find a diamond, they would undoubtedly spend many hours or days in that attempt. Thus, the social average of Labour it takes to get that diamond is what determines supply. Typically, it is far easier to get water than diamonds. Which is why diamonds are more expensive, I.E the Labour it requires to bring them to market is far greater; however, let's say that water was just as scarce as diamonds. That is, the supply of water and diamonds is equal. You can search for water for 20 hours and find a gallon, or you could search for diamonds for 20 hours and only find one. Which is then more expensive? If priced in Labour Value, they would be the same. If priced as they are in our current system, Use Value comes into the equation and influences price. Therefore the water becomes more expensive, the reason being is that its Use Value is higher.[8] So we see that in the Labour Theory of Value, we have the demand defined as the Use Value of a commodity, while we have defined the supply as the Socially Necessary Labour Time that it takes to produce it. If the Use Value is high and the amount of Labour it takes to produce the commodity is also high, then the price is high. If the Use Value is high and the amount of Labour it takes to produce the commodity is low, the price will also be low. That is because, in the Labour Theory of Value, use only serves as the activation energy necessary to allow a transaction to occur.[9] In Neoclassical Capitalism however, it plays a role in the price.

---

[7] This also gets into socially necessary Labour, but we will cover that in the next example.

[8] When supply and demand equal to each other, price and Value are equivalent. The Value is derived from the Labour that goes into a product. However, when supply and demand do not equal each other, the Use Value is used to influence the price. This is to say; the natural Value of a commodity is its Labour Value. The influence of Use Value on price is what creates Profit, whereby that Profit is derived from the in-balance in the Exchange Values of the commodities being traded and results in the loss of Labour Value by one party compared to the other.

[9] If you want a specific commodity to be produced and you have an extreme use for it. Does that bring the commodity into existence? No. Therefore only having a Use Value for something does not bring it into existence. You must provide the Labour to bring it into

Labour Power

There are many different kinds of Labour, all with different degrees of skill, intensity, and monotony. No Labour is any better than another, and all Labour can be thought about abstractly. Again, what exactly do I mean by this cryptic statement?

Just as no superpower is superior to any other, it is a person's affinity to it that dictates how well or how poorly they use it. Same for Labour, depending on a person's affinity for it depends on how accepting they are of doing it and how proficient they are at it. Take, for example, the doctor whose skill and intellect are top notch. His Labour may or may not be very intensive. Contrast the doctor than with a garbage truck driver and a landscaper. All require varying degrees of intensity, commitment, work ethic, monotony, etc. We will call this time, intensity, skill, effort, and monotony required to do Labour, Labour Power. Why then does the doctor hire the landscaper, and why then do both pay for the garbage truck driver? Why not do the work themselves? Again, affinity and acceptance of the Labour Power required for a given task are why.[10]

Should the doctor not wish to do the work of the landscaper or drive his trash to the dump he/she must then decide how much of their Labour Power (which they have an affinity for) is worth the Labour Power of the others (which he/she doesn't have an affinity for). If the landscaper charges too much, the doctor may soon as well decide that his Labour Power would suffice to accomplish the job. However, by accepting an exchange rate, they accept the trade-off that the other person's specific Labour Power is worth a certain quantity of their own Labour Power. This valorization process is what we call Abstract Labour. It is the valorization process based on quantifying your work with someone else's.

Thinking about an exchange in this way fits in nicely with the exchange environment we are familiar with already. This is because the exchange itself hasn't changed; it only altered the valorization process of the exchange. It is no longer use-based as neoclassical proponents will argue but Labour-based. Let's continue.

---

existence. When you exchange two things of equal Labour Value, you each obtain a commodity that is worth the exact same but has a Use Value higher than that of what was traded away. This is how the exchange is mutually beneficial in a non-predatory way.

[10] Perhaps one of the biggest reasons is time. Should the doctor enjoy his work as a doctor or at the very least has become conditioned toward being able to do his job as a doctor that particular job is what gives him the most Value for his time.

Should you as a landscaper go to the doctor and pay $2000 for a procedure, and the doctor turns around and hires you for $2000 to pour five cubic yards of concrete for their new patio, you have just performed an exchange. Let's make this easy and say the doctor used $1500 worth of equipment in his testing and running the procedure, and he charged for his Labour Power $500. You as the landscaper required $1600 worth of materials and tools and charged $400 for your Labour Power. In effect, both parties have decided that the Labour Power of landscaping is 4/5ths the Value of the doctor's Labour Power. We can thus take this a step further and declare that both are measured in the form of Abstract Labour. Abstract Labour being the socially average amount of time, intensity, effort, and monotony required for a particular task. Aka, Abstract Labour is Socially Necessary Labour Power and Time for a given task.[11]

To cement this idea, let us do a thought experiment. Imagine you are the landscaper. Think of what levelling a yard, hauling the dirt, digging the holes, pinning the weed guard, arranging the bricks, planting the bushes, and laying the sod would require. Now imagine your current work, whatever it is. Think of all the time, energy, and effort the landscaping would take and compare that to your current job. How many hours of your current job would that landscaping job be worth? This valorization process is the concept of Abstract Labour. It is the understanding of the Socially Necessary Labour Power required to accomplish a task in comparison to your own Socially Necessary Labour Power. That is what exchange is. It is the exchange of your own Socially Necessary Labour Power for that of another person's in the form of a commodity.[12] Let us take a moment now and examine Waged Labour and how that fits into this.

Waged Labour

Like Migi provided Shinichi with the proper abilities for both to stay alive amidst all the Kiseiju. The employer too provides his workers with tools and raw materials so that both may survive amongst the competition.[13] What this

---

[11] Socially necessary is the key here. Though it is not explicitly mentioned, the socially necessary portion refers to the competition-based price finding mechanism of Labour Time, which Smith did an excellent job of dissecting.

[12] Paul Cockshot does a fantastic video dissecting the objective way in which you can determine Socially Necessary Labour Power between industries utilizing I/O tables.

[13] Kiseiju (parasyte) is a Japanese Anime where all the Kiseiju have come to earth and have taken over human hosts. They do so by controlling the brain. While the human is technically alive, their existence is reduced to that of a tool for the parasites. The human's sole purpose is that of increasing the prosperity of the Kiseiju race. Migi, who was a Kiseiju

means is that both the employer and the Labourer must be invested and cooperate for a business to grow in a proper exchange environment. But the existence of waged Labour has alienated workers from the value of the products they produced. To realize the importance of this alienation we will look closely at Adam Smith and utilize his understanding of exchange. From that understanding we will pinpoint the moment where the exchange begins to go awry, and from there move forward on examining the problem posed by waged Labour.

Let us start with the classical origins of the Theory of Relative Price, as Smith does with the rude and early state, and build up from there.

The rude and early state (competition between producers)

We have:

- a market of private producers
- Mobility of producers from one sector to another in search of the highest income.
- The producers here own the means of production (entrepreneurs, aka their income depends upon selling the products they make)

We have a situation where the income of producers relies on the price of what they are selling. If you have two sectors (sector being a catch-all for anything different: location, commodity, etc.) and one sector is getting a higher price, aka higher income per hour worked, the freely mobile producers will move into that sector. This shift increases the supply in that sector and lowers its price. That has the effect of decreasing the supply in the other sectors, thus increasing its price. This movement creates a balancing act, but a balancing act where prices somewhat equalize and thus, income/hour also equalizes.

Since incomes per hour equalize through the price, then the price must be proportional to Labour Time. That is Adam Smith's starting point, which is

---

who failed to take over the brain of the host human must now survive while sharing the decision-making capabilities with his human. Should his human die he would also, so he becomes attached and must work with Shinichi to survive as all the Kiseiju who have fully taken over their hosts view the pair as an anomaly that must be destroyed. The symbolism to Capitalism is quite strong in that the relationship between employer and worker is a top down structure. The employer is the dictator, and the employees are merely tools for the employer's own survival. This is, unfortunately, the reality as the Capitalist is a class of employers who have fully taken over and view their workers as nothing more than an unwelcome expense that is a necessity. The way the structure should be formulated is that of the Migi/Shinichi relationship where both realize they need the other and thus work together, both making decisions, taking risks and reaping benefits.

that prices are proportional to direct and indirect Labour Time, and it is this proportionality that moves the market.

The question that we must ask is what causes prices to deviate from this proportionality with Labour Time. That is to say that if Labour Time goes down and the price doesn't change, then it is no longer proportional and therefore deviates from the fundamental understanding of Adam Smith's Theory on Value and Price.

To find this deviation, let's complicate the rude and early state.

Let's add private property into the means of production.

- Where you have the entrepreneur who:
    - Rents out a place of work from one sector
    - Buys materials from another
    - Adds Value through his work creating a product
    - Sells that product for an income
- What we find is that the addition of private property does nothing to change the prices from becoming un-proportional to Labour Values.
- You take the gross income and divide it out.
    - If you make $10 for a product and after division ends up paying yourself $4 and $6 to rent and materials then your income for that amount of time you worked will still stay proportional to the price.
- All the addition of private property did was increase the price; it did not change proportionality.

What then happens if we look at the competition? Theoretically the rules of competition do little to change this proportionality between Price and Labour Time either because of mobility in the markets. But, let's imagine a situation to confirm this.

There are two sets: Set 1 is getting 15 dollars an hour and Set 2 is getting ? dollars an hour. Because the producers are the entrepreneurs, their price is income.

- Set 1 is paying $3/hour for rent and $2/hour for materials, then that with the $15/hour Labour gives us a price of $20.

[10]

- If set 2 is paying $5/hour for rent and $3/hour for materials and selling for $20, then their getting paid $12/hour for their Labour.
- This will cause a shift away from set 2 into set 1. Lowering the supply in set 2 and increasing the supply in set 1.

This will adjust the price of all the factors involved.

- In Set 1 rent and materials will increase slightly due to more demand while the income/hour decreases due to more supply, i.e. incomes are related to sales, more supply means less market share in this case.
- The exact opposite will occur in Set 2, prices of rent will decrease due to less demand and an increase in income/hour due to less supply.

In effect, we see that Labour Time is still proportional to price. Since all sectors operate in the same way you need not worry about the rent sector, the materials sector, or the consumer's sector. Each is maintaining the above situation of supply and demand for their own benefit; thus, their sectors operate similar to the Labour sector.

We still have yet to find the deviation from Price and Labour Value though. Let's take the next step forward and introduce a class separation. The two previous examples are all entrepreneurs; the producers work for themselves. Now we will add workers to the economy and as a result we have added a new class, the Capital class. The critical setup here is that once again the division of Value added must be divided up equally among all sets.

We now have Capitalists and Workers. You can combine all the other sectors like materials, rent, and tools into the raw materials sector. These sectors all operate on the same principle this current example does. You then separate the employers into the Capitalist division and the Workers into the Labour division. So long as the division of the Value added (Labour Value) is equal among all sectors (equalization of wages) there is no reason for prices to change should Supply and Demand remain constant as well.

What does this mean? Well, everything is made up of Labour and Capital, which means materials in one sector are made up of materials and Labour from another sector. Those sectors are made up of materials and Labour from yet another sector, so on and so forth. So long as the division of Profits to Labour and Capital are constant in each sector, and the supply and demand of each sector are constant, the prices of each sector will not change.

Let's take Nature and do some work onto it and sell that product for a set price. Let's also pick an arbitrary ratio for Capital to Labour division of

Profits: 60/40.[14] Profit defined here as the difference between the price the product sold for, and the cost of its production. The Capital owns Nature and gets 60% of the Profit generated. The Labour done gets 40% of the Profit. If the supply of Nature goes down, then more work is required to achieve the same quantity as before, and the price increases proportional to the Labour done. If Nature becomes exceptionally plentiful or productivity increases, then less work is required to achieve the same quantity and therefore, supply increases, which drives the price down. All the while that same relationship is maintained at 60% to Capital and 40% to Labour Profit division.

Next, that sold Nature has work performed on it. The product of this work is then sold. The Profit of the sold object is divided 40% to the Labourer and 60% to the Capitalist who purchased the Nature. Another Capitalist then buys that sold product and combines it with other purchased products which are further combined with Labour and sold for a final price. The Profit generated is split up to 40% Labour and 60% Capital. This process continues for every product. Notice the role Profit plays in this example. The very existence of Profit means that Capital has yet to pay itself and has yet to pay Labour.

What we find with this analysis of the market is that since products get their Value through the work done on them, then the price should be proportional to the wages paid to Labour. This proportionality is the Profit's Capital/Labour ratio that must be maintained for the price to not deviate from the Labour done, which is the relationship that is present in Adam Smith's rude and early state. Let's look at an example of this ratio.

Example:

Let's use metal and wood to make a hammer.

- We will say the price of wood harvested from Nature is $10.
- Then we'll take that arbitrary 60/40 ratio and say those working on cutting down the trees get $4, and those who own the trees get $6.
- The one who buys that wood pays $10 for it and then has work done on it.
- They cut it and shape it into handles for a hammer.

---

[14] In Smith's Rude and Early state, the producer was both the Capitalist and the Labourer. His was garnered by the Profit from what he sold. That Profit was determined by the price of his product minus the cost of the materials that went into it. Since Capital and Labour are splitting the Profit in the rude and early state, that relationship MUST be maintained into further complications for the rude and early state to mean anything at all.

- The $10 worth of wood transformed into 20 hammer handles which then sell for $20.
    - The ratio maintains that Capital pays $10 for the wood and splits up the Profits 60/40, so Capital gets $6 and workers get $4.
- Let's now look at the price of the hammerhead.
- The price of iron ore harvested from Nature is let's say $20.
    - Those working on mining the ore get $8, and those who own the mine get $12.
- The ore itself is sold for $20, and the one purchasing it then pays workers to Labour on it to turn it into 20 hammerheads.
- The hammerheads made from the purchased ore are then sold for $40 — $20 for materials, $8 for Labour and $12 for Capital.

In this setup, the lockstep of Labour and price is absolute. However, the exact Value of Labour is unknown; we only know that it is 40% of the Profits that will go to Labour. What does that mean? Well it begins to mean something when we place competition into the mix.

If we add competition (two hammer producers) and keep the Capital/Labour ratio constant with one enterprise where the price of a hammer is $7 and the other where the hammer is $5, then the $5 hammer will sell more unless you have good advertising or better-quality material for the $7 hammer. However, both increase the product's Labour, thus the price increase. But if the two are of the same quality and have had the same amount of Labour done to them, then competition will level the price out and determine the cost of Labour. Mobility of workers from one to the other in search of the highest wage will level out the price. The price will settle around the $6 mark per hammer. That's a $3 Profit after materials, so $1.20 per hammer goes to the workers. We now have a market-determined Value for the Labour it takes to produce a hammer.[15] In this case, price and Labour Time remains fixed.

Now, let's introduce a bit more complexity into this thought experiment — an increase in productivity among the mining industry.

- Let's say innovation in mining happens and the cost of producing the ore drops from $20 to $10 per 20 hammerheads worth of iron ore.

---

[15] This price finding mechanism is the determiner of socially necessary.

- The mining of the ore dropped by half due to a reduction in the amount of work through innovation.

Let's now look at the effect this has on the next sector, the one who takes the mined ore and produces hammerheads from it.

- That mined ore must still have work done on it to make hammerheads.
    - That work is still the same amount of work as before: $8 per 20 hammerheads.
    - What has changed is the Capitalists portion of the Profit, from $12 per 20 hammerheads to now being $22 per 20 hammerheads due to the reduced cost of purchasing the ore.
    - STOP RIGHT THERE!!!

This change has altered the Profit's Capital/Labour ratio and has, therefore, divorced us from the fundamental principles that were present in the rude and early state. It is no longer 60/40 but instead 73/27. Since prices are attached to Labour, and the price of the hammerheads has the embodied Labour of mining within it. That mining Labour has diminished, and the price of the hammerhead should have diminished as well. The reason for this is the rule of competition that Smith lays out. The sellers of hammerheads will compete with each other, and that will alter the end price. Which will settle right around the established Capital/Labour ratio that compensates them appropriately for their Labour Time. But notice that the deviation of the price to the Capital/Labour ratio has still occurred. Let's remind ourselves of why this deviation suddenly occurred.

What is occurring is that each sector will pick up the Labour Value of all the sectors that make up its composition. Any changes to those sectors will cause a change in the ones above it. A hammer will be influenced by the wood sector, the iron ore mining sector, the hammer handle producing sector, and the hammerhead producing sector. Any changes in those sectors will influence the final sector. A change in the price of a lower sector will cause a change in the price of a higher sector. This change in price will, therefore, influence the Capital to Labour ratio and cause a deviation of price from Labour Time to occur, now why is that?

Notice in the first examples of the rude and early state the producer benefit from their own production. Now with the introduction of Waged Labour, the Capitalist benefits from the producer's production. What used to be the wage paid for the entrepreneur's Labour is now split between Capitalist and Worker with the introduction of Waged Labour. That split is where we need to pay attention.

Consider for a moment, a situation where ten workers are in the mining sector. If productivity doubles in the mining sector, there need only be five workers working the same number of hours, or 10 workers, working half as many hours to generate the same quantity of product, or even keep the same number of workers working same amount of time to generate double the product if the demand is there. Regardless, because the supply of your ore has increased, the price will decrease because the market knows that an increase in supply means a reduction in Labour Power needed. The price will fall. But do the Profits fall? Highly unlikely, as the demand is still there.

The market will continue to purchase what it needs. If you are working a full day for 20 hammerheads worth of iron ore and the market needs 100, you will be bought out and paid for a full day of work. If your productivity increases fivefold, the market will still purchase all of your ore. If your prices don't change, then your Profits can only increase with more productivity. What this means is that even though productivity would increase fivefold, the workers are still all working full days and getting compensated the same as they were before, but it is now a smaller percentage of the Profits. Is it right that only the Capitalist should prosper from ingenuity in another sector? Indeed, the worker hasn't done anything else and is working just as hard as before. Opponents use this to justify not increasing wages, but is that not valid for the Capitalist as well? Why set up a system, so one class is systemically privileged over another?

Let's look at another angle. What if the market only needs 100 and you can produce 200 a day? Well, the Profit rate is still there, half a day of work is all that is required to meet the market's demands. The increase in productivity has served to lower the hours and the Socially Necessary Labour Time needed of the workers. By only making 100 you are meeting market demand, and your Profit rate is steady. If your workers are being compensated the same 40% of the Profit as they were in the rude and early state, then their time working has been halved, while their pay and the Capitalist's pay hasn't changed. The only thing that has changed is the amount of work needed to meet market demand. But the Capitalist will say "wait a minute, you could also reduce the number of workers by half to meet the demands of the market and have the remaining Labourer's work full days". But this would need to lead to a doubling of the remaining workers' pay if the Profit to wage ratio were to be maintained.[16] Put another way since half the number of workers is getting the same cut of the Profits their wages need to be doubled to stay proportional

---

[16] The remaining workers are doing twice the Socially Necessary Labour Time that is necessary for their pay. Later we will see how this act revalorizes money (remonetizes Labour) by redefining Socially Necessary Labour Time, which affects Abstract Labour evaluations which then affect consumption and leads us toward Crisis.

with prices. That is only true if we want to keep the principles of Adam Smith's rude and early state, though.

Let's contrast that with the current way in which the markets operate to find out where Price and Labour deviate. I am sure you have already realized.

The current system would say that if 100 are needed and we can produce 200 in a day with ten workers then let's cut half the workers out since their production is not needed. The Capitalist then says "you are doing the same work that you were before so you will get paid the same as you were before, and (even though I am doing even less than I was before since I have fewer people to manage) I will take a larger percentage of the Profits for myself."

This re-monetization of Labour Power is the mechanism by which Capital makes its Profit, and destroys the relationship between Labour and Price that existed in the rude and early state. Capitalist's Profits come through the stealing of the workers share of that Value-added, which remains unknown and unrealized until its sale is complete and the market decides its value.

This mechanism is then sold to us precisely through the idea of Use Value. The Use of 10 workers has reduced to 5, and hence, the Value of Human Labour diminishes by half. Since the perceived Value of Human Labour diminishes by half. The wages paid to the totality of the Labour are also reduced by half. But this is done by viewing the Value of the Labourer through their Use and not their Socially Necessary Labour Value.

The truth is that the Use Value of 10 workers has diminished to 5, but the Necessary Labour required of those five remaining workers has now doubled. Therefore, the wages paid to those five remaining workers should also be doubled, not remain the same. By having the wages remain the same, the Capitalist reduces the portion of the Profits set aside for those wages by half and therefore increase the Capitalists share of the Profits. The Profit's Capital/Labour wage ratio has thus been altered, and it has occurred at the same time as the deviation from prices to Labour Time.

Again, the maintaining of the Profit's Capital/Labour ratio is crucial to upholding Adam Smith's understanding of the rude and early state, and it is precisely Marx's analysis which points out how the organization and operation of the economy become predatory after proceeding from that rude and early state. The contradiction is that the workers and Capitalists sharing of the Profits was the foundation of the rude and early state, but in later iterations of more complex markets that sharing of the Profit is abandoned for the idea that workers are a set cost and that the Capitalist is the sole owner of the Profit.

Let's take a look at the arguments for and against each side.

The standard argument for the Capitalist owning and reaping a more significant share of the Profits, that 73/27 ratio from our earlier example, is that the Capitalist took a risk. What about the workers? Why should the worker's wages increase if the cost of materials decreases? What is the argument for that?

There are two:

First is that workers also take a risk as their pay is dependent upon sales just like the Capitalist. Put another way. The Capitalist takes a risk with their money; the Labourer takes a risk with their time.

The second argument is since the Labour Value added determines price, and if the price of material has decreased in another sector then there is less indirect Labour input into your product; therefore, the price should be lowered. By not lowering the price you are in effect re-monetizing Labour's worth. Because Price and Labour Value must remain proportional as shown in Smith. By not changing the price, you are redefining the Labour's worth, and by redefining the Labour's worth without changing the wages paid to Labour, you are instead stealing Profit from the Labourers and increasing the Capitalists share.

That is why the Capital/Labour ratio is so important. If it isn't maintained, then this little sleight of hand where Labour is re-monetized and the wages remain constant will occur over and over again, each time increasing the inequality of the system. It is theft plain and simple. We can see the real-world effect of this by comparing real wages with productivity increases.

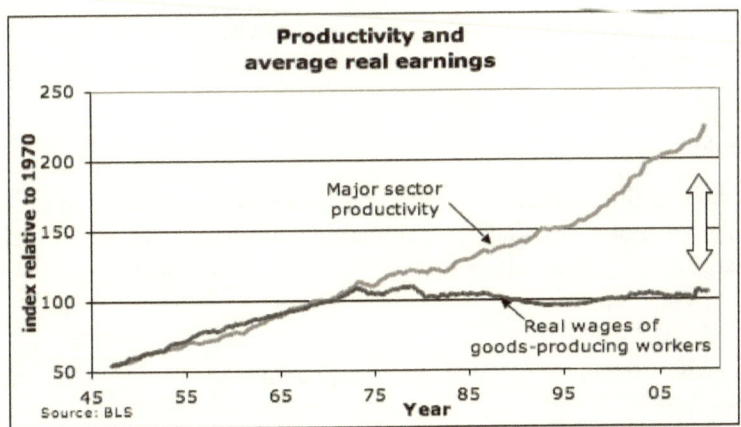

The structure of the system simply does not lend itself to maintaining this ratio, in fact, it is impossible, and we will show why in later chapters.[17] The

---

[17] Specifically, Chapters 7-9

goal of the system is to increase Profits, while the sole decider of those Profits is the Capitalist. Inequality is designed into the very structure of the system and is unavoidable so long as Profit ownership by the Capitalist exists. Profit is the reason why Capitalism is and always will be prone to self-destruction. A constant process of stealing Value from the Labourers for Profit, laying off the Labourers for Profit, manipulating the price for Profit, all ultimately undermining the very consuming class of the economy until inequality becomes rampant and the system collapses underneath a series of its own short-sighted, self-destructive, Profit-based decisions.

This structural imbalance leads us to Marx's Labor Theory of Crisis.[18]

Labour Theory of Crisis

Companies do not act rationally; the temporary Nature of the employers that govern the company is what governs their behavior. A CEO is not interested in the long-term prosperity of the company... well, not as much as keeping their job anyway. Shareholders are individuals who have little interest in the company and care more about dividends, and they are the ones who elect CEOs. This practice means the decision to hire or fire CEOs is company Profitability. This job insecurity incentivizes CEOs to make short term decisions that benefit shareholders by rapidly increasing Profits, padding their own pockets before the company must face the music and when those poor decisions hit the fan, the CEO has already left with a nice paycheck while the company has to deal with the backlash from those poor decisions.[19] But let's not look at this one particular structure. Let's look at "proper" companies, ideal companies operating in an ideal way. Let's abandon the reality of Capitalistic companies and instead go off the ideal Capitalistic company. You will see it is the underlying structure, not the individual behavior that leads to these crises.

Example:

Let's take a few companies. All are competing for market share in a sector. We will not allow them to purchase each other as we see in reality, but instead, force them to compete in a "true free market fashion".

Well, what happens. You have each company trying to produce hammers.

---

[18] Expanded upon heavily in Chapter 8.

[19] This is exactly how Donald Trump's Atlantic City Casinos failed. He made millions, everyone else was left with the mess.

Structure

- One produces the hammer for $10 (A), the other for $7 (B) and another for $5 (C).

- The one producing for $10 (A) is using suitable sturdy materials and their hammers last a long time, but the increased cost of the raw materials forces the price to be high. The one for $5 (C) uses cheap materials, and the $7 (B) uses average materials.

- After some length of time market share is determined and it comes to the knowledge of the $7 (B) and the $10 (A) companies that the $5 (C) hammers are vastly outperforming them.

- To compete, they must adapt. To do this, they begin the process of innovation.

- The $7 (B) hammer company decides to copy the business model of the $5 (C) hammer company and purchases cheap materials too and manages to copy the price of the $5 hammers.

- The $10 (A) hammer company takes a different approach. They use the materials that the $7 (B) company was using but create an automation process that allows them to be more productive.

    o They fire half of their workforce due to the increase in productivity and can sell the hammers for $4 undercutting their competition.

- (A)'s hammers being of higher quality and cheaper allow them to capture a large portion of the market share. This more substantial market share brings them massive Profits.

- Bewildered, the other two companies set off to discover this automation process and after a while can copy it, thereby cutting their workforce in half and allowing them to sell their hammers for $2. The Company selling the $4 (A) hammers now mimics the cheap materials of the other two, and all three are selling hammers for $2 now.

But what has this served? It has created a situation where each company is now making less Profit than it was before. This reduction is called the diminishing rate of Profit and results because Profit is derived directly from the amount of Labour that goes into a product.

- $M^P = C^C - M^{I+W}$ [Profit = Price - Cost of Production (investment + wages)]

- $C^C = M^I + C^L$ [Price = Initial investment + Labour Value]

- $M^P = (M^I + C^L) - (M^I + M^W)$ [substitute in Values]

- $M^P = C^L - M^W$ [Profit = Labour Value - Wages paid to Labourer]

If you reduce your Labour force for short term Profit, once the rest of the sector has caught up to you, your market share is reduced back to the steady state. With the reduced market share, the price is now lower than it was before and your Profit is also lower because you have fewer workers from whom you can take Value.[20]

Put in a more concrete way if you are paying workers $10/hour, and you have ten workers who are reaping you $200/hour in Value, your Profit is $100/hour.

Now if you decide to get super Profit (which is short term Profit achieved through an increase in productivity where Profit is derived directly from the firing of workers to lower price and increase market share) Then let's use the above example to see what happens.

Super Profit

You increase productivity 100%, you then fire half of your workers and lower the price of your product by 50% simultaneously putting you below what your competitors can match. Let's say before you had 30% market share, and now you have a 60% market share. Your Profit increase would be calculated from you paying $50/hour for your 5 workers and pulling in $200/hour due to increased market share.[21]

That's great! You are making more Profit now. But this is a short-term game, others will discover the automation process as well and before you

---

[20] This theory of the diminishing rate of Profit is correct, but it has some caveats attached to it. Those caveats deal with the mass of Profit. Reality doesn't work like ideal systems; those three companies would surely not survive the transition from a $10 hammer down to a $2 hammer. This would cause fewer companies to be in the market place and therefore, more market share to be captured. This leads to a balancing act. The rate of diminishing Profit can be counteracted by achieving a larger market share. That is if you have $100,000 making 1% return a year vs $1,000 making 70% return a year. The 1% rate of Profit is undoubtedly vastly diminished compared to 70%, but your mass of Profit is still higher ($1,000 vs $700). This is how companies can stave off crisis caused by the rate of diminishing Profits; by permanently capturing more of the market share via forcing competitors out of the market. Acquiring more market mass by reducing price, so the number of customers increases to offset the loss, or by performing mergers and acquisitions. The downside is that these decisions tend to lead to monopoly and reduce consumer purchasing power.

[21] The important lesson here is that increasing productivity is necessary to stay competitive ---it reduces the rate of Profit---it only leads to an increase in the mass of Profits if the market share increase can be maintained, otherwise total Profit mass will fall

know it your market share is back down to 30% as they have copied your process and competition has brought the price back down to the social average. But now you are paying $50/hour for work, and only pulling in $100/hour from sales. Your Profit went from $100 before to now only $50.

Some rather significant increases in doubling and halving existed in these examples. Real world operates more in the realm of small percentages, but over time, they add up precisely to the effect you see above. This innovation leads to a never-ending game of cat and mouse between increasing productivity, firing workers, increasing market share, and having competitors catch up.

The only way to stop this process is to either eliminate your competitors which is what we see through the formation of monopolies or duopolies through mergers and acquisitions. Or to not fire your workers in the first place and be content with current Profits and not chase after super Profits.

However, the latter will never happen since the name of the game is Profit, and you are rewarded based on Profit, and harmed if you do not chase it. Sacrificing others for your self-preservation is the natural outcome of such a structure, which prevents Capitalism from ever reaching an equilibrium, and making the very notion of equality an impossibility.

Grow or Die

Why can't Capitalism reach equilibria? Capitalism must constantly grow. The reason for this is built logically into the structure. The rule is that an individual Capitalist must continue to grow or face extinction. The reason for this is that if a Capitalist takes that Profit and says "I am satisfied with it", other Capitalists whom he is in competition with will increase productivity to increase their market share and eventually swallow him up, he must respond in kind by doing the same thing, just to recapture his previous market share and stay competitive. Therefore, continual growth is survival, hence the term if you're not growing, you're dying. But this very process is what undermines Capitalism itself.[22]

These periods of increased productivity and super Profits lead to tremendous gains for investors. But when every sector participates in this, more and more workers are thrown out of work. Which means the consuming class loses more and more purchasing power. Even though the prices of goods are getting cheaper, the consuming power of the populous is decreasing at the same time, meaning more and more people struggle to get by.

---

[22] These competing rules of Capitalism are known as contradictions. David Harvey has an excellent book called the 17 contradictions of Capitalism.

This makes intuitive sense. If money achieves its Value from the Labour that goes into earning it, then the money is directly proportional to the amount of Labour performed by the consuming class. If you cut the work, then you cut the amount of money being earned and moving in the economy. Less money moving means fewer purchases are taking place. This loss of velocity is why even though the prices halved, consumption has not doubled. This slowdown is because the wealth of the workers who make up the consuming class have also diminished by half. Therefore, there is half as much money able to be moved in the market.[23]

This diminishing has only served to sacrifice overall economic growth for short term financial gain. As this process continues sacrificing more workers for Profit, the money that would have gone to them and recirculated back into the economy will instead go to the hoarders of money, the Capitalists. Where it will sit idle due to their inability to maintain the same amount of consumption that the masses have.

This fall in the rate of Profit eventually leads to massive inequality amongst the workers and the Capitalist, as well as infighting amongst the Capitalist as the Capitalist business owners must deal with Capitalist investors who see a diminishing rate of return. As investors pull money from businesses those businesses begin to fail. Capitalists begin to cannibalize one another as they fight for more Profit, all the while more workers lose their jobs and the economy comes crashing down until faith in the system can be restored. A government entity usually does this, for if it was indeed a free market and the government did not exist, it is at this point all the exploited workers would surely grab pitchforks and torches and hunt the heads of the Capitalists. Therefore, the state is necessary to protect the Capitalists from their own greed. [24]

---

[23] This is a simplified view of what constitutes the velocity of money, but the primary structure and result is still extremely valid.

[24] This dives into a whole separate topic that will be covered later dealing with the role of the state and the impossibility of the free market.

CHAPTER 1.5
REVIEW SECTION

Let us do a very quick review as to what was covered, and give some common critiques one might experience when attempting to explain this to others.

We start with a **Commodity** which is anything that has been produced through **Nature** and Human **Labour**, and has a supply and demand. It obtains its **Value** through the **Socially Necessary Labour Power and Time** that goes into producing it. This Value is what is represented in the market through **Exchange**. We see that there are two types of exchange: **CMC** and **MCM'**. Where the majority of people in a Capitalist system are workers who sell their Labour as a commodity to gain money, who then use that money to purchase other commodities which they need to live. The Capitalist works off the MCM' principle where they use their money to buy a commodity to then sell it for more money. This is the cornerstone of **Exploitation**. Where the following shows how that "more money" comes to be:

- $M^P = C^C - M^{I+W}$ [Profit = Price - Cost of Production]

- $C^C = M^I + C^L$ [Price = Initial investment + Labour Value]

- $M^P = (M^I + C^L) - (M^I + M^W)$ [substitute in Values]

- $M^P = C^L - M^W$ [Profit = Labour Value - Wages paid to Labourer]

The exploitation occurs due to the unequal power distribution amongst the Capitalist and the Labourer. Capitalist owns the end product which when sold means the Capitalist owns the Profit. As a result, this puts Profit and wages in direct competition with each other. The systemic effect of this can be seen when **Competition** comes into the picture. Capitalists compete with each other for market share. This drives the prices of their products down to the Socially Necessary Labour Time it takes to produce them. The Capitalists in order to gather a larger **Market Share** must try to lower the prices of their goods beyond that of their competitors.

You can only take so much away from the worker before they refuse to do the work for the **Wages** offered, so you must lower cost of production in other ways. This is achieved through introducing an increase in **Productivity**. This productivity increase can be through automation, process improvement, or better tools and equipment. The result is that you can produce the same you were before in less time. That time difference correlates to the amount of Labour you no longer have to pay for. This results in a diminishing of the work force since all those "excess" workers are no longer needed. As a result, you still pay the remaining workers the meager exploitative wages you were paying them before, but you also get to take the laid off workers wages and add them to your Profit.

At the same time since you have increased your Profit you can now afford to lower the price of your product in order to obtain a larger market share. This leads to **Super Profit** as you have undercut your competitors by a price they cannot yet match and you are obtaining the same Profit rate or greater that you were previously. This is thanks to the wages of the workers that were let go, plus whatever the differential is between the rise in market share minus the drop-in price equates to.

For a short period, your company thrives, however competition still exists. The competitors will figure out your trick and copy you, thus bringing the price of all goods back into an equilibrium. This means that the Socially Necessary Labour Time of that good has fallen and your market share is back to what it was before. However since your market share is back to where it was before, the price of your good is cheaper than what it was before and you have less workers from whom to exploit, thus, your Profit rate has actually fallen.[25] This recurring theme is what is referred to as the **Falling Rate of**

---

[25] Again, rate has fallen in the ideal world where competition is always present, but in the real world the falling of a company's real Profits can be staved off through an accumulation of market share by eliminating competitors. This does little to stop the crisis though, since you are still gathering more and more money into the hands of fewer and fewer individuals. Remember that money is the mode of exchange which means that it must be circulating for the market to work, if it funnels up to fewer and fewer people, then there is less in circulation and the consuming class must then ration their money to fewer and fewer sectors, this leads to crisis in those sectors who are now losing market share and therefore Profit as a result.

Structure

Profit and is the underlying mechanism of the **Theory of Crisis** that explains why every 6-10 years we experience a recession and every 60 - 80 years we experience a depression. This mechanism is:

1. Productivity increase (good)

2. Reducing workers to increase Profits (bad)

3. This lowers consuming class purchasing power (bad)

4. This leads to less consumption and a lower mass of Profits (bad)

5. This causes an economic slowdown/recession/depression (bad)

6. Equilibrium is restored after price and value synch back up (good)

CHAPTER 2
DEFENDING THE LABOUR THEORY OF VALUE

This section deals with common and specific critiques you will find that are utilized to dispute the Labour Theory of Value. It is followed by a significant excerpt from Marx with an accompanying discussion.

Most Common Critique Against Labour Theory of Value:

1. The Labour Theory of Value is false; it is Utility that creates Value

One might try to point to exchange and say that Value is represented by whatever the customer is willing to pay. This is fair; however, it must not be forgotten that the customer has obtained their money through their own work. Therefore, whatever amount of money they are willing to part with for that commodity is the amount of their own Labour Time they are ready to give up for it. As a result, the price of a good or service is still the social average of Abstract Labour that is willing to be traded for it. This concept of Abstract Labour results in the fact that the Exchange Value is still represented in Labour Time for Labour Time. Do not let "utility" confuse and divorce you from the dialectic that is Labour and Value. And do not allow one-off situations detract from the understanding of a market, supply and demand, and the Socially Necessary Labour Time. Just take a step back and calmly analyze the parts of the argument given that can be traced back to their origins. For example, let's look at an Arbys inside of an airport vs an Arbys outside of an airport, and how the Labour Theory of Value can be used to explain the differences in price despite the same Labour being performed.

Arbys in an airport is not the same market as Arbys outside an airport. There is more demand in the airport and less supply; therefore, it is a different market than outside the airport. The prices reflect the social average of Abstract Labour of that market. The customers are willing to part with more of their own Labour Value since the supply of food is lower. Comparing two different markets is a fallacy as supply and demand are different; however, that does not stop our analysis. It can be noticed that the employees inside the airport are paid the same as those outside the airport. This is because the Capitalist will seek to pay the Labourers the lowest wage they will tolerate.

Profit rate has nothing to do with their wages as they have already been suppressed to the maximum the workers will allow. Since those workers do not live in the airport and expend their money in a market other than the airport market, they tolerate the wages they get. Beware this trick of utilizing two markets, especially ones where the Value of a product is the same in both, but the prices are different. For this example, in particular, markets like an airport, where consumers and workers live in a separate market but are forced for a short time to purchase in this one.

It is important to note all these distinct differences and how they relate to one another. Knowing these will allow you to navigate any false criticisms given to the Labour Theory of Value.

Supply - the amount of a commodity that is being produced for the market.

Socially Necessary Labour Power-The average amount of skill, intensity, effort, and monotony required to produce a supply

Socially Necessary Labour Time- the average amount of time that the Socially Necessary Labour Power needs to produce the supply

Exchange Value- The Socially Necessary Labour Time in a commodity. It is the comparison of Labour Value you performed to make your money with the social average of Labour Value that produces a product.

Abstract Labour- The intuitive process of converting Labour you perform to the Value of Labour in a commodity. The Social Average of Labour Power and Time play a part in our formulating the value of Abstract Labour.

Price- The Social Average of Abstract Labour in terms of money, can be lightly or heavily influenced by Use Value in markets of low competition. It is the market indicator of Socially Necessary Labour Time. Can be artificially controlled through false scarcity (supply) and consumerism (demand). It is the money form of Exchange Value but does not dictate actual Value within a commodity, it merely informs the market of it.

Demand - The amount of desire there is for a product.

Use Value - The amount of Use one gets from a commodity, its existence is necessary for the exchange to occur.

Exchange - The act of trading Exchange Values to gain a Use Value, be it in the form of Labour itself, of money obtained through Labour, or in the form of a commodity created by Labour.

Value- Is Labour itself. Every commodity comes from Nature and Labour, Nature existing freely and Labour being the Value that is imparted unto Nature to change it into something that can enter the market.

Specific common critiques:

2. Nature is inherently valuable without Labour:

This argument states there is a person selling berries at the bottom of a hill, while at the top of the hill, berries grow wild. The fact that the person selling the berries can sell them at all proves that Nature is valuable. This argument neglects the fact that for a product to enter the market, Labour must be done to it. If something such as berries garners a price in the market, they get their price from the Labour done to them to bring them to the market. I.E. walking up or down the hill, and picking the berries. If the demand is significant and supply mediocre, then people will have to do more Labour to acquire the berries needed to meet the demand. The berries will become scarce, and people will need to either search harder for them (more Labour) or begin to cultivate them (again more Labour), aka the market price increases either way. To assume that berries fetch a high price naturally is absurd. If the supply is greater than the demand, why would anyone pay a high price for berries when they can go walk up the hill and pick their own? It is more practical to perform their own Labour instead of using the market to make the exchange.

-This argument neglects the application of supply and demand.

3. The mud pie or large pit argument:

This argument goes that if a lot of Labour goes into a task or product that doesn't necessarily mean that the product is valuable; Products like mud pies or digging a large hole. This is in fact true, but it doesn't negate the Labour Theory of Value. This argument neglects that under the theory for a commodity to exist, there must be a demand for it, I.E. it must have a Use Value. The supply that meets that demand gets its Value from the Labour done. Simply doing Labour for the sake of doing Labour when there is no demand is pointless. This is an insanely silly argument and intentionally disingenuously.

-This argument neglects the existence of Use Value. It also avoids the proper application of supply and demand.

4. Excessive exertion:

This argument goes that if a worker spends years creating a product, such as writing a book by hand vs using a computer. That the Value of his product is far less than the Labour that went into it. This argument fails in its understanding of Socially Necessary Labour Time. That is for a commodity, the Value is determined by the social average of the Labour that it would take to create that product. It also neglects supply and demand. Its Use Value is the same as that of one produced by a computer. So, the Socially Necessary Labour Time is far far lower than the Labour put into handwriting the book.

This argument is merely an iteration of the previous one where a misunderstanding of Use Value as well as the concept of Socially Necessary Labour Time.

5. Non-exertive effort:

This is the diamond in the rough example. If someone finds a diamond by luck, they have performed little Labour but garnered lots of Value. Again, like the previous example, this is a misunderstanding of Socially Necessary Labour Time. Sure, the individual got lucky, but the Value of it in the market is a result of the supply and demand. The supply is low, and the demand is high. Should someone try to find their own diamond, the Labour performed would be close to the social average of the Labour it takes to find a diamond. That social average, which is the work necessary to produce the supply, is what gives Value to the diamond.

This is a misunderstanding of Socially Necessary Labour Time.

6. Unequal ability:

This argument says that if two Labourers produce at different skills, then their Value is not the same. This is actually a proper observation. Indeed, if one carpenter can make a table in 7 hours and the other can make it in 8 hours, and if they are of similar quality, then they have achieved similar Value by doing two different amounts of work (I.E they have different Labour Power). Again, however, Socially Necessary Labour Time is the Social

Average of the Labour Power in the market that it takes to produce a table, and that is where Value is derived. If the Social Average of Labour Power produces a product in 7.5 hours, then that is the Socially Necessary Labour Time. An individual worker who is more skilled will get more Value for their Labour Time than the less skilled one due to the difference in their Labour Power. This results again out of supply and demand. The demand for a product is more than a single individual can produce, and as a result, the supply comes from many individuals. The Value of the supply is thus the social average of the Labour that it takes to produce the product.

This argument misunderstands Socially Necessary Labour Time.

7. The argument for incentive:

This argument goes that performing Labour is a disutility in itself. If the economic gain from Labour is the same Value as the Labour performed, why do the Labour at all? This argument neglects the difference in Exchange Value and Use Value. Exchange Value is the Socially Necessary Labour Time that goes into producing a product. The Use Value is the need you have for that product. By performing Labour and creating commodities that meet demand but also which you don't need, ensures two things. 1. That you will be able to sell those commodities. 2. That you will be trading away something that you have a low Use Value for, for something that you have a high Use Value for. If you make tables and you already have a table, then those tables you are making are of little Use to you. You make them because there is a demand in the market, and you can sell them for money which is of high Use Value to you. Money which other people had to work for. Thus, you are trading away the Labour Time it took you to make the table for the Labour Time it took the customer to make that money. This is the concept of Abstract Labour. The Value of that transaction therefore is solely dependent on the Socially Necessary Labour Time it takes to create the supply.

This argument misunderstands Use Value and Exchange Value.

8. Unequal uses of purchased goods:

This argument tries to say that the Value of a good is dependent upon the Utility of the good. That is to say its Use Value. It is undoubtedly true that if two consumers both buy the same product but get different uses out of it, then the product has different Use Values for those consumers. For example, a guitar purchased by a musician and a guitar purchased by a musically illiterate person both are bought at the same price, but the Use each gets out of it is different. But this doesn't change the Exchange Value of the commodity, which is determined by the Socially Necessary Labour Time it takes to produce the supply. Use Values are what influence demand and allow for an exchange to occur. The guitarist's Use Value is that he gets to play it. Perhaps, the musically illiterate person merely likes to look at the guitar, and that is the Use they get out of it. Regardless of whatever the Use is, the exchange that occurred was still at the socially necessary Labour Value for that commodity.

This argument misunderstands that Use Value and Exchange Value are separate...if anything it is an argument against Utility, not for it.

9. Unequal Prices of goods:

This argument goes that if a person has two bottles of water and is dying of thirst. The may consider selling the second bottle at a very high price while refusing they sell the first at any cost. This argument neglects Use Value. As exchange will not happen unless the individual who is making the exchange gains a Use Value from the exchange. Since the person in this critique would die if he sold the first bottle, of course, nothing he gets would be of Use to him. This, however, does not change the Exchange Value of the bottle of water. Just because one person Values something at an extremely high cost doesn't matter. Their opinion does not affect the Socially Necessary Labour Time it would take to produce the same bottle. It merely means that this person is not a part of the market. To try to force him into the market while ignoring other sellers means you have willingly reduced your supply of a material to a single individual. The amount of Labour this individual would have to perform given his state is astronomical, thus the very high price.

This argument misunderstands supply and demand as well as Use Value.

Every single one of these objections stems from a misunderstanding of supply and demand. What their relationship to Use Value and Exchange Value is. And how those have relationships to Abstract Labour and Exchange, the relationship of Price and Value, and how all relate to Socially Necessary Labour Time.

Below is an excerpt from Marx Capital. Vol. 1. Page 677 & 678:

"It is not Labour, which directly confronts the processor of money on the commodity market, but rather the worker. What the worker is selling is his Labour Power. As soon as his Labour actually begins it has already ceased to belong to him, and therefore cannot be considered to be sold by him. Labour is the substance and the imminent measure of Value but has no Value itself. To say it has Value itself is a tautology... In the expression Value of Labour, the concept of Value is not only wholly extinguished but inverted, so it becomes its contrary an expression as imaginary as the Value of the earth. These imaginary expressions arise nevertheless from the relations of production themselves. Classical political economy borrowed the term, the price of Labour, from everyday life without any criticism, and without ever asking how it is this price was determined. Soon recognized the changes in the relation of demand and supply explained nothing with regard to the price of Labour or any other commodity except those changes themselves, i.e. the oscillations of the market price above or below a specific mean. If demand and supply balance, the oscillation of prices ceases. All other circumstances remaining the same. But then demand and supply also cease to explain anything. The price of Labour at the moment when demand and supply are even is its natural price. Determined independently in relation to demand and supply."

Utility promoters will love to point to price and try to use price as the proof that Labour is not Value. That the price is whatever someone wishes to pay for it. That one person may get more Utility out of a commodity than another, so they are willing to pay a different price to obtain it. This is all true, but it neglects the intrinsic Value that is present, it tries to focus on the perceived Value.

The Intrinsic Value is whatever it took to bring that thing into existence and whatever it will take to bring it into existence again. The perceived Value is what someone believes it is worth. That is, what did it take to make it, what Use will I get from it, and how much of my own Labour am I willing to trade away for it. Notice that at the end of the day, it is the Labour of the commodity. What it took to bring something into existence, and the Labour of the money that is being traded. Perceived Value has a subjectivity to it, and that is Use Value. A person's Use can vary from a necessity to a want.

Since price is what informs the market of the Labour that went into it. If the price is not reflective of the Labour, in cases like the airport where the price is used to take advantage of necessity. The perceived Value doesn't change, but the need for that item does. If you are stuck in an airport and don't want to buy an $8 Arby's sandwich, then you are going to go hungry. Tough shit if you got a 5-hour layover. The customer reluctantly pays the price. This can be proven by the fact that you know airports are overpriced yet you still pay. This shows that your perceived Value and the price are not in sync with each other. Every time you spend money for something and reluctantly do so, you recognize that the price and the Value are not in line with each other. This doesn't change your needs; however, it is precisely by this method that price while the indicator of Value in the market is not tied to Value itself. This is the trick utility plays; it relates Price to Value and says that the Labour Theory of Value cannot be correct since prices fluctuate and change. However, the fact remains the Intrinsic Value of an item, i.e. that which it took to create it, is the same regardless if you are in an airport or not. As a result, the Value is the same, it doesn't matter if the price is different.

The above quote answers this by analyzing supply and demand. If you equalize supply and demand in all markets. The price does not fluctuate. Commodities reach a fixed price with each other. Utility goes out the window because everyone who wants something has it available to them. As a result, the price becomes the actual Value of the commodity. Where then does Value come in? The answer is Labour. Value is the Labour it takes to create something. This is what Marx calls natural price. Utility explains price wonderfully in an economy where supply and demand don't equal each other. This is excellent explanation-wise, but it sucks in actuality since it hides the true Nature of exploitation in exchange by making it feel natural and giving it an explanation. This is precisely the reason we must divorce price from Value at this point. Because when supply and demand equal each other, Utility is unable to explain price at all. Natural price can only then be explained by Labour that goes into it, aka its Intrinsic Value.

This reveals a trick of Capitalism. That supply and demand can never reach equilibrium. Because the M' means that the price must be higher than the cost of production, that is, it must be higher than the Value that it took to create the commodity. The living Labour performed on the raw materials, and the dead Labour performed to create the raw materials. As a result, the price is always slightly higher than the Value so that the Capitalist can take a chunk for themselves. This, when placed in the market, creates havoc. Price is supposed to inform the market of a commodities Value; this means consumers will compare the Value of their money with the Value of the commodity through the price. As a result of this, a worker who creates a commodity that has a price of $10, put in $5 amount of work on $4 worth of raw materials to create a product whose Value is $9. The price though is $10, so when another worker who has done Labour receives $10 in compensation, he goes into the market and buys that commodity for $10. The premise being CMC, which means the worker (assuming here this singular worker represents the entire market) has deemed the Value of his $10 worth of Labour to be equivalent to this commodity priced at $10. This means $4 goes back to the dead Labour that went into the commodity, and the other $6 is what is considered the Socially Necessary Labour Time it took to create the product.

Notice here how the worker did work that had the Value of $5, but after the market transaction, his work was Valued at $6. Though he did not make that extra dollar. This has an implication because when price does not reflect the real Value of a product, a constant re-monetization of the Labour that goes into that product occurs. Abstract Labour must be informed to be relevant and when it is informed in a way that does not represent the Value accurately re-valorization occurs. But it is not Labour that is being re-valorized, because Labour is Value itself. You can't re-Value Value. What you are instead doing is re-valorizing the money that is used to purchase the Labour. Thus the Labour is being re-monitized. This means that in each cycle as Labour is slowly exchanged for Profit and prices are slightly higher than the Value that goes into the commodities, the Labour Value of money decreases. This means the Labour you could buy with a dollar before is less than the Labour you can buy with a dollar now. This is what leads to inflation.[26] This is the problem with the perception of Value. That when supply and demand are not equal, and the price does not correctly inform Abstract Labour, the Value becomes unknown.

---

[26] There are two types of inflation. Inflation caused by equilibration and hyperinflation. Inflation caused by equilibration occurs when someone perceives that the purchasing power of money in the system is changing. In response, they will raise prices a little to try and make sure the goods being sold bring in the same amount of purchasing power as they did before. Hyperinflation occurs when the number of essential goods is not prevalent to meet society's needs. Necessary being defined here as goods that maintain the current quality of life. Because the supply is low and the demand is high, its price rises and will continue to rise until the supply meets the demand. This is why hyperinflation is mainly a commodity thing, not a money thing. Having massive amounts of money flood into an economy will not lead to hyperinflation. At least not as long as there are enough essential goods to meet the demand created by that influx of money. Inflation by equilibration will occur instead. By flooding the market with money, you have just re-monetized the Labour Value of the money. That is not the same type of inflation because it will "equilibrate" itself after a while. Hyperinflation cannot equilibrate until either the goods meet the demand or the population dies out and begins to lower the demand.

CHAPTER 3: STRUCTURE OF INTERNATIONAL EXPLOITATION

Before continuing on to how Capital circulates and by what exact mechanism crisis form, it is vital to first understand the concept of international exploitation. This will help cement ideas presented in earlier chapters as well as introduce concepts necessary to understanding the circulation of Capital.

The objective of international exploitation is the exact same objective as domestic exploitation. To increase Profit as much as possible. Companies look to international countries as an opportunity to acquire cheaper resources and cheaper Labour. We saw this during the period of colonialism, and the same principle is practiced today. Companies export Labour overseas to lower the cost of Production.

How is this done, or by what mechanism does it occur? Within any society, society grows and prospers through the work done to improve it. When you operate within the confines of a society, you have a set geographic area containing a defined number of people able to work and then purchase the commodities produced. This structure of a defined workforce acts as resistance to Price and Value from straying too far apart. Your consumers are your producers in other words. When this is the case, the previous section's exploitation structure is the method by which people are exploited. To the Capitalist, this is a barrier. Ideally, they would be able to sell something which cost them nothing to produce. However, when the workforce is constrained, that is, the number of producers and consumers are relatively constant, driving the price of Production and price of wages to zero becomes significantly harder. To get around this, you export your Production to another location. Preferably one which is less economically developed and whose standard of living is so low that the cost of maintaining that standard of living is minuscule.

This is what leads to international exploitation. It is the exploitation of workers or resources outside the boundaries of your consuming class. It is no different than the slavery system of America. Slaves performed the work, you paid the bare minimum to allow for their continued survival, and then you sold the commodity to your consuming class.

The biggest problem that exists with this system is the stagnation of growth it creates in the exploited area. When a company moves into an area with a low quality of life, it pays wages just high enough to meet that quality of life or barely exceed it. This has the consequence of simultaneously restricting that population to that low quality of life. Any improvement to the quality of life for the exploited population will lead to a loss of Profits realized by the company due to wages having to rise to meet that new quality of life standard. This suppression is done both intentionally and systemically.

Intentionally this is done through economic control of the country through debt, and outright control over the government, which we will touch on in depth in the next chapter. Before we can understand the reason for the intentional ways, we must first understand the systemic ways. To understand this, we must look at how a community can grow and how it can stagnate.

A community grows through the reinvestment of Labour into itself. First, you are a community with nothing, not even tools. You make everything by hand. Suddenly through lots of work, someone develops a hammer, another a saw. Those hammers and saws are sold back into the economy. Their presence increases the efficiency of other sectors. This frees up the total amount of available Labour in the society. Before what would take you two days to collect a ton of firewood, now you can do the same amount in a day through the use of the saw. This means that you have an extra day to devote to another task, such as farming. This continuous cycle of reinvestment of Labour back into the economy is how communities grow. Here is an equation you can use:

$$\%Growth = \frac{Final - Initial}{Initial} * 100$$

Where "final" is the total amount of product at the end of the year. And "initial" is the total amount of product at the beginning of the year. This is how modern economics defines growth anyway. However, I believe it is slightly wrong. Not all products are useful and contribute to growth. As we just went over, the growth of a society is dependent upon the reinvestment of its Labour. But not all Labour if reinvested leads to growth. For example, food. If you flood society with food, do they grow? Not necessarily. Food, however, is essential to society as it allows for survival. Thus, we will term this type of Labour, Necessary Labour. There are other types of Labour, such as the Production of art, which is Luxury Labour. This type of Labour can increase the quality of life but does little to help it progress from where it currently is. Another kind of Labour is Wasteful Labour, Labour which has been done and produced a product, but that product goes unused, food that expires or is exported are examples of wasted Labour.[27] The last type of Labour is Productive Labour. This is Labour that is reinvested back into the economy to increase the efficiency of the economy. Production of tools in the above example served as this type of Labour. We can define this Labour as commodities whose Use Value serves to reduce Socially Necessary Labour Time and which has contributed back into the economy a reduction of Labour Time greater than what it took to create it.

We now have the essential terminology necessary to determine what growth is. Using the same equation as before we just need to change how Final and Initial is defined. Final is defined as the total amount of Productive Labour at the end of the year, and the initial is the total amount of Productive Labour at the beginning of the year.[28]

This allotment of different types of Labour is how international exploitation works. With the buying of land, you prevent the local population from being able to utilize all their resources, i.e. the land that you own. If you own a large portion of land in such a way that the remaining resources available to them are barely enough to provide the minimum necessary for producing Necessary Labour products, then you have pigeon-holed them into stagnation. Since there is not enough land to go to everyone, the remaining

---

[27] You can perform Wasteful Labour by exporting the goods out of your country. While it is Wasteful Labour it does not mean it is pointless Labour, you can use the income from the exported goods to then import Productive Labour, i.e. a commodity that leads to an increase in productivity. Should this happen, Wasteful Labour becomes Productive Labour. The opposite too can happen, you can sell a tractor for food, that is a loss of Productive Labour. Wasteful, Productive, Necessary, Luxury only refers to the end result on how that Labour was utilized, and how it impacted the economy.

[28] Productive Labour actually only being productive dead Labour. Living Labour cannot be productive by this definition since it can only contribute to the productivity of society in the form of a commodity. Productive living Labour becomes encompassed within the commodity during Production. It is, therefore, unnecessary to measure the productive living Labour of society and instead only have to measure its productive dead Labour, otherwise, you are double measuring. If a worker puts in 10 hours to create a hammer and that hammer goes into society to increase the productivity of someone. The workers 10 hours of productive living Labour is now encompassed within the hammer. The hammer represents a Value of 10 hours. If its contribution to society regains more than 10 hours of Labour Time back through productivity increase, then it is contributing to the growth of that society.

portion of the population must find work elsewhere to survive. That work comes from the company. They pay wages low enough to allow for the workers to purchase just enough Necessary Labour to survive (i.e. food, shelter, water, clothing).[29] This means that at the end of the year, most if not all Labour being performed is Necessary Labour or Wasteful Labour with only minute amounts of Productive and Luxury Labour being performed.[30]

How does this happen? Well, every society of people has enough Labour Power to grow continuously. Even a society of one will create tools to make their daily tasks easier to perform. The trick to international exploitation is to lower the domestic Labour to a level below the Necessary Labour needed for all. The closer the available Labour is to the minimal level of Necessary Labour needed for survival, the more chance there is that zero growth will occur that year. This is done through the exportation of Labour Value. All Labour performed by the workers for that company is being exported away. This steals the total amount of Labour that is being put back into the country. That is to say, all Labour performed for an international company is Wasteful Labour.

We should stop here and clarify that Necessary Labour should not be viewed as a hard line, but more as a zone. You can survive off of a potato a day, but you will eat more if you can. This means that Necessary Labour has an upper limit and a lower limit. The lower limit is absolute starvation, the upper limit is excessive consumption. The goal of international exploitation is to keep the population closer to the lower limit than the upper limit. If the amount of available Labour approaches the upper limit, then individuals will start to sacrifice performing Necessary Labour in favor of Productive Labour. This will lead to an increase in the quality of life and thus lead to a shift in the lower limit of wages that workers will be willing to accept. This shift cuts into the Profit margin of the Capitalist corporation.

---

[29] If you control the countries, utilities & natural resources even better for the exploitation of that population.

[30] If large amounts of land are unable to be purchased to achieve the stagnation effect, then wages from the company are given to be just a bit higher than the living standards. This removes workers from the population to then work for the company because it is the best option for them. Since all products of the company are exported, none of that Labour performed is Productive Labour, this slows the ability of the country to grow. The best option for the individual, in this case, is not the best option for the society as it allows the individual to survive, but it stagnates society. This is how structural violence works. Hiding the large second and third order determinants behind a small first-order benefit.

It is precisely this reasoning which debunks the argument that "sweatshops are good". While it is true that you are paying them a "wage" that is higher than what they could earn otherwise. This is a misnomer since the Labour that is remaining in the country is not enough to cover the upper limit of the Necessary Labour needed. That is because all those who are receiving a "wage" are having their Labour exported out of the country. Which means the only thing they can buy is the Necessary Labour that remains. If they were not working for the sweatshop, there would be enough total Labour to cover the societies Necessary Labour requirement and the leftover Labour could be diverted into Productive Labour that would lead to growth.

It should also be noted that international exploitation both benefits and hurts the home country in which the goods are being exported to. It benefits the home country by importing cheap Labour Value. It hurts the home country because it increases the reserve army of Labour. When a country exports itself abroad, it lowers the number of jobs available in the home country. When the number of workers exceeds the number of positions available, the workers are pitted against each other for jobs, and the reserve army of Labour is used as a threat to force acceptance of lower wages. This has its own flaws domestically. If a factory moves production abroad, that towns reserve army of Labour skyrockets. Job competition rises and wages become more exploitative. This reduces the towns consumptive power which means they are now spending a larger portion of their consumption on Necessary Labour and as a result less on Productive Labour thus limiting domestic growth.

As we saw in the first chapter, Profit comes directly from what is not paid to the worker. Obviously moving your company overseas and paying pennies on the hour for Labour increases Profit. But it also reduces the purchasing power of your home market in the long run. This leads to the same fundamental flaw presented in the Theory of Crisis. That is, for a short while you will experience super Profit, but when competitors catch up, your market share will drop back down to what it was before. That is, unless you can somehow prevent that by reducing competition. Even if we go so far as to say it won't and the two companies maintain their market share and therefore never influence each other to cut-price. All it takes is one company to experience a reduction in Profits from a previous year which is going to happen because by increasing the reserve army of Labour you have reduced the purchasing power of the country. This will result over the next several years in a decline of total sales. That decline has the same effect on the CEOs and shareholders as losing market share because it results in less Profit this year than the year before. As a result, it is taking us right back to crisis.

Structure of International Exploitation

What happens if international exploitation is not able to prevent the growth of the international country's economy, or if a company moves to a country which is protecting its people and ensuring the growth of its economy? Nothing new happens. The above reduction of Profit that will occur simply happens faster. This can be seen in China. Super cheap wages but over the past couple decades the living standard of the people there have been rising increasingly fast. As a result, wages paid by international corporations must rise along with other local wages. This leads to a reduction in Profits seen, the lowering of prices to increase market share, and the super Profit game coming to an end with the final result moving us closer to crisis since the purchasing power of the home market has fallen.

To summarize this chapter, international exploitation leads to an increase in the reserve army of Labour domestically and stagnates the international country whenever possible to protect Profits. It does so by exporting Labour Value out of the country which prevents the country from ever having enough total Labour Value left within it to meet the need for Necessary Labour as well as have enough left over to devote to Productive Labour.

CHAPTER 4: OBTAINING/MAINTAINING INTERNATIONAL EXPLOITATION

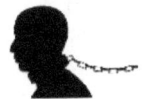

Now that we have looked at the structure and intent of international exploitation. Let's look at some real-world examples to show it in practice. It is important to note how extreme this section will become. Historically our principles, values and human life itself have meant nothing in the face of Profit. That is the ugliest truth of Capitalism. It is one we must learn. While Capitalism is exploitative at home, it is even more so abroad. To even begin, we must first start with history.

Let's start with settler colonialism, most know of this as the "Scramble for Africa" where colonization was motivated by the desire for resources. The subsequent exploitation of the African people would leave a lasting impact on the native inhabitant's freedom, and the ability to escape their new role. If you have read the Heart of Darkness, you know the atrocities that were present.[31]

But settler colonialism wasn't just Africa, and many forms are still present to this day. United States, Western Australia, Canada, and Palestine are all examples where the Government used land allotment as a legal way to take possession of indigenous peoples' land. They are still being oppressed to this day, forcing assimilation upon them, driving them ever further from their lands, and breaking promises and agreements whenever Profit is involved or hindered.

Let's look at our own history to outline the process that Settler Colonialism takes. It has a name, called primitive accumulation. It starts with

---

[31] "Anything approaching the change that came over his features I have never seen before, and hope never to see again. Oh, I wasn't touched. I was fascinated. It was as though a veil had been rent. I saw on that ivory face the expression of somber pride, of ruthless power, of craven terror--of intense and hopeless despair. Did he live his life again in every detail of desire, temptation, and surrender during that supreme moment of complete knowledge? He cried in a whisper at some image, at some vision--he cried out twice, a cry that was no more than a breath: The horror! The horror!" — Joseph Conrad, Heart of Darkness

the dispossession of people from their land. This allows for the occupying power to obtain a natural resource or acquire favorable land for themselves. This was accomplished in America via the removal and relocation of Native Americans into reservations. The Government facilitated this with the passage of the Indian Removal act of 1830. But this wasn't the first time Indians were removed from an area. In fact, many who were present in the south at this time had already relocated there from the North. So why be transferred again? Well, it just so happened that in 1828 Gold had been discovered in Dahlonega Georgia. In true Colonialist fashion, the Government of the United States went back on its word to not touch the land the Natives were living on. The language of the act is "negotiate" however, that was far from the case. Thousands upon thousands of Natives were forced from their homes and sent west simply so resources could be stolen from the land they resided on, and Profit could be made. This resulted in the Deaths of 12-50% of the individuals who were forcibly relocated. Exact numbers, unfortunately, do not exist. This would later come to be known as the Trail of Tears.

This relocation wasn't the last, and the practice continued as the new land they were relocated to was also found to be Profitable. In 1851 the treaty of Ft. Laramie declared a large swath of land to the west as Indian Territory. The U.S constitution holds that treaties are to be considered the supreme law of the land; however, this didn't stop Capitalism one bit when gold was discovered in Colorado.[32]

"I saw the bodies of those lying there cut all to pieces, worse mutilated than any I ever saw before; the women cut all to pieces ... With knives; scalped; their brains knocked out; children two or three months old; all ages lying there, from sucking infants up to warriors ... By whom were they mutilated? By the United States troops ..." -John S. Smith, Congressional Testimony of Mr John S. Smith, 1865

This led to violent retaliation in the west as America pursued its concept of Manifest Destiny. Indians were forced to relocate once again and then, Gold in California. This led to the famous California genocide, estimates range from 16,000 to 100,000 native Americans killed. While attempts were made such as the Dawes Act of 1886 to provide protection to the Natives, at the same time, it stripped them of their Culture and identity by turning communally held land that belonged to the tribe, to individually owned land held by members of the tribe to "civilize" them.

---

[32] Sand Creek Massacre: On November 29, 1864, seven hundred members of the Colorado Territory militia embarked on an attack of Cheyenne and Arapaho Indian villages. The militia was led by U.S. Army Col. John Chivington.

It is important to note that this theme of "barbaric" and "uncivilized" was a common justification for the stealing of land from indigenous people all throughout the world. Fortunately, however, the world seemed to be growing a conscience, and settler colonialism was starting to be viewed for what it was: Evil. This led to a shift in the way Colonialism was performed. Unfortunately, it only mutated into the form by which it is still performed today. Through Economic Colonialism.

In Economic Colonialism, it is the companies and not the Government who steal land and resources while simultaneously exploiting that countries people. Mostly the most Profitable parts of settler colonialism could be continued in a legally sanctioned way, allowing the companies to hide behind a legal curtain and Capitalist jargon to defend their actions.

"Settlers have rewritten histories, have created a legal system that justifies their rule, and have normalized a racist and unjust socioeconomic system" -Gerald Taiaike.

What are some common themes we see, and how is this Economic Colonialism carried out, maintained, and protected today?

How this is conducted today is through the farce of foreign aid being utilized to indebt countries into financial slavery through the use of structural adjustment programs (SAPs). In the book Confessions of an Economic Hitman, John Perkins recalls his own story of how he was recruited to be an Economic Hitman and how he utilized these programs to turn countries into debtor nations. Effectively making them slaves to their creditors. His role was to make economic predictions as to the effect a massive loan from the World Bank would have on some target country. He was trained to produce statistics that favored the loan being granted and showed massive increases to the economic prosperity of the target country as a result of said loan. The money from that loan was then given to the country who turned it immediately over to international firms like MAIN, Bechtel, and Halliburton to perform the work on modernizing the country. The problem is that this leaves the state with massive debt and if the prosperity predicted never comes (which it never does) then the country is left fighting just to pay off its debts. In essence, it becomes a slave to the nations who control the World Bank.

"EHMs provide favors. These take the form of loans to develop infrastructure—electric generating plants, highways, ports, airports, or industrial parks. A condition of such loans is that engineering and construction companies from our own country must build all these projects. In essence, most of the money never leaves the United States; it is simply transferred from banking offices in Washington to

engineering offices in New York, Houston, or San Francisco. Even though the money is returned almost immediately to corporations that are members of the corporatocracy (the creditor), the recipient country is required to pay it all back, principal plus interest." — John Perkins, <u>Confessions of an Economic Hit Man</u>

But it need not be the cloak and dagger hitman who performs this.[33] It is built right into the system. You have a corporation which looks to convince countries to take out huge loans that are then to be given to that very same corporation. The goal of the corporation is simple, convince both the bank and the country to give and take as big a loan as possible and lie and manipulate as best you can to get them to believe you. Once the credit is issued its a massive payday for the company. Since they lied, the country straddled with the debt is unable to pay it off since prosperity never came. This leaves the countries who divvy out these loans, places like the United States, in a position of power over the 3rd world country. This power is then utilized to exploit the country for favors and natural resources.

"If an EHM is completely successful, the loans are so large that the debtor is forced to default on its payments after a few years. When this happens, then like the Mafia, we demand our pound of flesh. This often includes one or more of the following: control over United Nations votes, the installation of military bases, or access to precious resources such as oil or the Panama Canal. Of course, the debtor still owes us the money—and another country is added to our global empire." — John Perkins, <u>Confessions of an Economic Hit Man</u>

It is in these ways that the most powerful Capitalist countries secure their natural resources and secure their cheap Labour. By saddling countries with debt making it so that all excess income they earn is forced to be paid as interest on that massive debt. Debt that they can never hope to pay down.

---

[33] There is a 3rd world development initiative from the world bank termed structural adjustment. It is headed by the International Monetary Fund and requires certain reforms to be present before approval. These reforms are preconditions before receiving financial assistance or adjustment loans from the IMF and subsequently from any western banks as well. These policy reforms include trade liberalization, export promotion, privatization, and a reduction in government spending on social welfare and subsidies. These stipulations only serve to keep the country in poverty while simultaneously benefiting America and other creditors - based on the article "Structural Adjustment, a Major Cause for Poverty" by Anup Shah & "IMF induced structural adjustment programs and women in Ecuador" - Saadatmand 2008.

Let's look at an example to cement the legitimacy of these claims. We will look at Ghana, which is lauded by the International Monetary Fund (IMF) as one of its shining successes. To spoil the reveal, the IMF only looks at meaningless statistics. In areas where it truly matters, areas like poverty levels, improved living conditions, and promoting economic growth by relieving indebtedness, it has failed greatly.

Ghana[34]

The IMF argues that the best way toward economic progress is through the opening up of markets, following the neoclassical line that this will alleviate poverty and will reduce the gap between rich and poor. The conditions they force upon the countries who are to receive these loans include trade liberalization, export promotion, privatization, and a reduction in government spending.[35] Ghana having implemented these reforms received its loan from the IMF who now claims it is a success. But why?

The IMF makes these claims because the SAPs did turn around the overall economic performance of the nation.[36] It reduced the inflation in Ghana from 73% to 13%, it expanded the industrial capacity from 24% to 46% and helped eliminate external payments and begin building up official gross reserves. This helped improve Ghana's world standing and make it more attractive to bring Capital into the country.

This all sounds great...but they are just numbers, they do not tell the story of the people. Ghana is but a name on a piece of paper, and those numbers are but the Profit of foreign companies raping the natural resources and Labour Power of the people within the borders of that country.

---

[34] Conditional Development: Ghana Crippled by Structural Adjustment Programmes - Aramide Odutayo

[35] The argument here is that it drives competition since local industries have access to purchase imported technology. The hidden fact is that they must also now compete with all of the producers of the world who have had a head start and can provide the same products for far cheaper driving those industries out of the market.

[36] This is a misleading statistic, though. If you bomb a city and rebuild that city, you show a massive spike in GDP and GNP, which are typical indicators of economic performance. But is that city better off? Has it grown? If anything, it is now behind by whatever amount of time it took to rebuild. It is not about whether or not the country has spent a lot of money. It only matters whether or not that nation has actually grown.

"The questions to ask about a country's development are, therefore: What has been happening to poverty? What has been happening to unemployment? What has been happening to inequality? If all three of these have declined from higher levels, then beyond doubt, this has been a period of development. If one or two of these central problems have been growing worse, especially if all three have, then it will be strange to call the resulting development, even if [GDP] doubled."-
Dudley Seers, U.N Economist

Other criteria to look at beyond poverty, unemployment, and inequality is what about the people's access to medicine, water, electricity, and freedom from debt? The IMF conveniently neglects to include these vital statistics in its analysis of whether or not a country it has made a loan to is successful.

The IMF will tout that Ghana experiences a 75% increase in their minimum wage in the first 3 years of the SAP implementation. However, when you look at the underlying fees they had to pay just to survive we see that the price of water increased by 150-11,000% depending on the area, Electricity cost increased by 47-80%, and health fees rose by close to 1,000%.[37] These price increases quickly took over the wage increase leaving the poor hurting for basic necessities more than they had previously.

What about the rate of poverty did it decrease as a result of the IMF SAP? You would certainly think so reading over their numbers. Reality is that no, it did not. Poverty remained at roughly the same levels as it had before the SAP. A large part of the reason why is that the 6 billion given for agricultural reform was mainly spent on the cocoa industries. The ones owned by foreign companies who export the product out of the country. Only a select few Ghana natives benefit from this policy. They are the ones pointed to as examples of prosperity, but the truth is that over 70% of Ghana's agricultural farmers are in non-cocoa producing regions. This policy only served to increase the wealth gap in the country.

Is Ghana the shining example of SAP success? Did the SAP achieve its stated goals: that by opening up the markets to free trade it will reduce poverty and the wealth gap, that it will help the country prosper? The answer is a resounding no. It created a country that is now enslaved to debt and whose natural resources and Labour Power is exploited by the countries few elites and the international corporations. Sure, the numbers look better, but the people do not, how can you call that progress? How can you call that a success?

---

[37] Anyinam, "Spatial Implications of Structural Adjustment Programs in Ghana," 455

Structure

This is not to say the intent of SAPs is terrible, the idea of building up the infrastructure of a willing nation is lovely. However, when that buildup comes as a result of a loan in a Capitalist system which seeks Profit above all else, it is easy to see how given the systems structural setup this financial slavery works perfectly with the goal of international exploitation within that system. The companies get to increase their own productivity, get to improve their own standard of living and get to do so while suppressing the living standards of the population guaranteeing them more substantial Profits. But what happens if one of these nations disagrees with this and fights back? That is what the next chapter is all about.

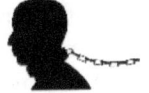

CHAPTER 5
USE OF FORCE IN INTERNATIONAL EXPLOITATION

Anytime you force your will upon another, there will be friction. Managing this friction is essential for the perpetuation of Capitalism. This is because it is always the minority exploiting the majority. Sometimes the conflict happens before exploitation has even begun, as a resistance to the coming exploitation. Sometimes the resistance rises up after the exploitation has started and must be squashed back down. Sometimes the resistance wins and sheds the exploiters and as a result, need to be fixed through external means. Still other times the resistance won't give the exploiters a single chance and must be utterly crushed as a warning to others. All of these situations will be explored. To do so, I will be offering 4 examples of this: Cuba, Guatemala, Iran, and Libya. But keep in mind that the list of nations whom these stories apply far exceed that.

Cuba

We as Americans like to think Teddy Roosevelt, and his Rough Riders are the reason for the end of the Cuban colonization by Spain. The reality is far grimmer. The rebellion had already been going on for three years by the time the U.S intervened. When we did, the war had basically already been won since Spain was utterly exhausted. The rebellion started in 1895 and was organized by José Martí. Martí emphasized that the Cuban rebellion had to achieve complete and total victory, anything less would lead to a U.S. intervention. First of Cuba, then the rest of the Americas. His exact quote was

> "to prevent, by the independence of Cuba, the United States from spreading over the West Indies and falling, with that added weight, upon other lands of our America." -José Martí

Unfortunately, he died in May of 1895 shortly after initiating the rebellion back in February of that same year. His collaborators Maximo Gómez and Antonia Maceo took over and had some successes against the Spanish. Unfortunately, Maceo was killed at the end of 1896. The Spanish after consistently losing brought in a new, stricter commander and more forces. In response to this Gómez began to fight a strictly guerilla-style war. Spain tried in 1898 to end the rebellion, agreeing to let Cuba become a self-governing state within the Spanish Empire. But Gómez refused this offer and instead continued the war. The war was of high interest in America. In the spring of 1897, William McKinley, supported by midwestern business interests, succeeded the anti-imperialist Grover Cleveland. While McKinley had considered Spanish rule to be a blight on Cuba, he was more fearful of the prospect of the Cubans governing themselves. McKinley worried that an independent Cuba would not be kind to America's business interests or do Washington's bidding in regards to trade routes. He was right to worry; Cuban rebel leaders were promising that once in power they would launch social reforms starting first and foremost with land redistribution. This scared American businessman who had more than $50 Million invested on the island. This led the U.S. to start a vast propaganda campaign and some historians even speculate, execute a false flag by sinking the U.S.S Maine. This allowed the U.S. to gain the sympathy of the public and declared war on Spain in April of 1898.[38]

Many economic factors went along with the U.S desire for the war. The U.S. needed to ensure its sea routes to Panama for the construction of their grand canal there. Cuba and Puerto Rico were critical players in assuring the protection of those sea routes. Then, of course, there was protecting the land of the very businessman that helped get McKinley elected. After the declaration of war, U.S victory was easily achieved. Thanks to the years of work put in by the rebels who were fighting for their freedom.

It is crucial to note that during the war, Spain had sought a peaceful resolution. They offered the Cubans the ability to rule themselves so long as they remain a part of the Spanish empire. The Americans were given a chance to aid in these discussions. As historian Samuel Eliot Morison concluded years later "Any president with a backbone would have seized this opportunity for an honorable solution." This would have saved lives, but not money. It would

---

[38] The sinking of the USS Maine on 15 February 1898 in Havana harbor was initially believed to be caused by a mine that exploded next to the ship. This was utilized to rouse anti-Spanish sentiment in the United States, which helped catalyze the Spanish–American War. In 1911 an initial study of the Maine's wreckage was conducted, but no findings were found. In 1976 however, a team of naval explosive experts re-examined the wreck. They concluded that the likeliest cause of the sinking was the spontaneous combustion of fuel coal stored in a bunker which led to an internal explosion. Due to this finding, some observers believe that the blast was a false flag meant to anger the U.S. populace and justify our entrance into the war. Cuban politician and former director of the national library Eliades Acosta claims that "powerful economic interests" in the United States were probably responsible for the sinking of the Maine.

have denied the United States its $50 million in land and its access to the sea routes. Those could only be won by conquest. That conquest is precisely what we did.

Cuba refused to let us onto their island for the longest time, but a Senator Henry Teller from Colorado was able to win over one of the generals. He did this through the passing of an amendment that declared:

"The United States hereby disclaims any disposition or intention to exercise sovereignty, jurisdiction, or control over said island, except for the pacification thereof, and asserts its determination, when that is accomplished, to leave the government and control of the island to its people." -Teller Amendment, 1898

This amendment was later tossed aside as just another lie with the passing of the Treaty of Paris followed by the Platt amendment. President McKinley placed the cherry on top of this backstabbing by declaring that the United States would rule Cuba under "the law of belligerent right over the conquered territory."

The Treaty of Paris, which ended the war, allowed the U.S. to take over Cuba, Puerto Rico and the Philippines as significant prizes just as Martí had feared. This led to the American Military Occupation of Cuba from 1899-1902. Attorney General John Griggs told the vice president of Cuba's provisional government that the U.S. Army in Havana was "an invading army that would carry with it American sovereignty wherever it went." Cubans were indignant, having fought for their freedom for 3 years just to be under the control of another imperial power. They continuously cried out for their freedom, and they did not go unheard. There were calls within the U.S., including Congress, for Cuban independence. However, Senator Orville Platt introduced legislation to the effect that the U.S. would retain the right to intervene in Cuba in the case of "domestic political instability". It also called for the leasing of a naval base in perpetuity. This became known as the Platt Amendment. It was merely a way of laying the legal groundwork for economic colonialism. Should Cuba ever do anything that goes against U.S commercial interests, then the U.S has the legal right to intervene. America made sure to incorporate the Platt Amendment into the very constitution of the Cuban people in June of 1901 in Havana, but not without protest by the people.

"Havana was in turmoil on the night of March 2. Torchlit procession delivered a petition of protest to General Wood at the Governor's palace. While another crowd of demonstrators sought out the

convention delegates and urged them to stand firm in their opposition to American demands. Similar demonstrations occurred on the following night. Outside the Capital, municipal governments throughout the island poured out a flood of protest messages and resolution, while public meeting were epidemic. On the night of March 5, speakers told the precession in Santiago that if the United States held on to its demands, the Cubans must go to war once more." -David F Healy, <u>The United States in Cuba, 1898-1902: Generals, Politicians, and the Search for Policy</u>

The delegates of the convention had a choice to make, accept the terms, or heed the warnings of America's threats. Which were that if the constitution were not approved, then even harsher conditions would be forced upon the Cuban people. Later in a private letter, General Wood, the last military governor of the United States occupation of Cuba wrote: "There is, of course, little to no independence left for Cuba under the Platt Amendment."

This decision was utterly hated by the Cuban people and bred such resentment that later when Fidel Castro came to Cuba. His one promise was that the Cuban people would never again live under the thumb of the United States. He governed based on principles he learned from Guatemala. The next country we will talk about, which is why despite his dictatorship like style, he was still accepted by the mass of the Cuban people. Because even he was better than being ruled by America. It was our own short-sighted economic interests that made us as a nation abandon our ideals of democracy, and produced hatred for America within Cuba. Capitalism, the pursuit of Profit abroad and the maintenance of economic colonialism are what laid the groundwork for such hate against us. We sacrificed people's lives, their freedom, our principles, and later on down the line our national security, all in the name of short-term Profit.

Guatemala

For Guatemala, we will first start with the origins of the United Fruit Company. As we look at how this company achieved its power and maintained its dominance, know that this same story applies to Columbia, Costa Rica, Panama, Honduras, and Nicaragua as well.

The United Fruit got its start in 1871 with the construction of a Railroad in Costa Rica connecting the city of San Jose to the port of Limon. The way the Costa Rican Government got this money was from the bank of London who was charging them a 7% interest rate on the loan. They were unable to meet the payments, and the owner of the Railway project, Minor Keith, made a deal with the Costa Rican government. That he would negotiate with the bank of London and reduce the interest from 7% down to 2.5%. In return, they gave Keith 800,000 acres of tax-free land and a 99-year lease on the railroad.

It took them 19 years to complete the 25 miles of railroad. Unfortunately, it did not bring in very much money. But he did have a ton of new land, which he used to start experimenting with growing bananas. He began shipping them from Limon to the United States, where they proved to be extremely lucrative.

He eventually made similar deals with Panama and Columbia to acquire large swaths of land. In 1899 Keith's finances caught up with him, and he merged with the Boston Fruit Company who dominated the banana trade in the West Indies. This created a new company, the United Fruit Company, which Keith was the Vice President of. In 1904, Keith signed a contract with the President of Guatemala, Manuel Estrada Cabrera, that gave the company tax-exemptions, land grants, and control of all railroads on the Atlantic side of the country.[39]

For the next 50 years, the company ruled ruthlessly and exerted its power over Central America. This ruthless control included murdering strikebreakers, hiring terrorist groups, controlling media outlets, spreading propaganda, propping up repressive governments, and more. One such event can be taken from Columbia. Which served as an example to every other country in the region of what would happen if they too tried to push back against the United Fruit Company. In Columbia when workers of the United Fruit Company organized a Strike on Nov 12 1928. Their demands were simple: 8-hour work day, signed contracts, and a 6-day work week. They were immediately labelled as communists and radicals by the Colombian Government, U.S Embassy, and American Corporations. On Dec 5th and 6th in 1928 in the town of Cienagawa, the massacre of 3000 workers was carried out. All this sanctioned by the U.S. Secretary of State who threatened military action on Columbia if they did not uphold the interests of United Fruit. Below is an excerpt from a Department of State Cable.

---

[39] Manuel Estrada Cabrera, he was a strong ruler, who modernized the country's industry and transport. But only by granting concessions to the American-owned United Fruit Company, whose influence on the government was felt by many to be excessive. Estrada Cabrera used increasingly brutal methods to assert his authority such as armed strike-breaking, and controlling or at the very least manipulating the general elections. He retained power for 22 years through these controlled elections (1904, 1910, and 1916). Until he was forcefully removed from office when the national assembly declared him mentally incompetent, and he was jailed for corruption.

Structure

> "I have the honour to report that the Bogadar representative of the United Fruit Company told me yesterday that the total number of strikers killed by the Columbian military exceeded one thousand." -Bogota embassy to US Secretary of State, January 16, 1929

It was apparent to all countries that reform was impossible so long as the government was controlled by the corporations. This is why when Jacobo Arbenz was democratically elected president of Guatemala in 1951, talks had already started in the United Fruit Company and Washington on how to get rid of him. His Platform consisted of Social reforms modelled after his idol, Franklin Roosevelt. In the United Nations Arbenz often voted with the American position. He was a leader trying to emulate the American structure to bring prosperity to his people. His reforms involved expanding the right to vote, giving workers the ability to organize, legitimizing political parties, allowing public debate, and land reform. But in trying to achieve this, there were two policies which the American corporations and government could not allow. First, he took the European approach toward political parties, this meant that in the height of the red scare, he permitted the existence of a communist party. But Eisenhower and John Foster Dulles were far too narrow-minded to let that slide. Even though Arbenz was not a member of the communist party, had no communist in his cabinet, and personally believed them to be far too radical for his tastes, it didn't matter. He allowed them to exist, so he had to go.

His second policy they couldn't stomach was the land reform program. Less than 3% of the landowners held over 70% of the land. Put in stats with the populous, less than 1% of the population held over 70% of the land. Arbenz's policy was simple, any uncultivated land would be sold to the Guatemalan Government and then given to the poor. United Fruit alone had over 500,000 acres of unused land. Arbenz's justification for the forcible sale was simple. The ancestors of that land were forcibly removed by the Spanish colonization. After colonization ended, the land was allowed to remain in possession of the remaining gringo colonizers. These gringos whose property and wealth gave them power which they used to control the government and give power to foreign companies. They did this by selling off land and resources to corporations to enrich themselves while utilizing their social connections to control elected officials. Arbenz said that was wrong, that the resources of the country should benefit the people of the country. But he felt at odds with taking away property that people were using, no matter the history behind it. So Arbenz limited the land reform to just the unused land. He even turned over all of his own properties to the poor. This didn't stop United Fruit or John Foster Dulles from labelling him a communist and embarking on a CIA overthrow of his democratically elected government.

CIA documents show that they hired a small band of mercenaries from Honduras against Guatemala. They were quickly turned back. They then embarked on utilizing the very democratic principles Arbenz was so proud of to undermine him. They used the free press, the many fringe political parties he legitimized, and the public discussions he encouraged. The CIA went to individuals in each of these areas and began paying them to spout falsities about Arbenz. Even with all that negativity, the public opinion was not swaying away from Arbenz. The CIA then resorted to purchasing rioters and used the media they controlled in the country to film portions of it. This film was then taken back to America to be played as propaganda against the "Communist government of Guatemala" so that public support in America could be gained. Even with all this, a movement within Guatemala never grew to oust Arbenz. Instead, the CIA had to create one. Using their own planes, they bombed the capitol causing Arbenz to flee, allowing their own puppet to take power via the CIA's coup d'état. [40]

It is important to note that during this time, Che Guevara was in Guatemala watching all of this unfold. He hid in the Mexican embassy until it ended. Meeting up with fellow rebel Fidel Castro afterward to discuss what he learned. Having seen what happened to Arbenz, Che told Fidel that what led to Arbenz downfall was his acceptance of democracy. It allowed America to attack him from every side and create a false perception of unrest that gave them legitimacy to invade. They knew that when they finally freed Cuba, that they could not allow such tools as the free press or public discussions to exist. Or else the same thing would happen to them.

Getting back to Guatemala, the puppet dictator that was installed was the one chosen to be the face of the assault on the capitol, Carlos Castillo Armas. The people of Guatemala were, of course, not happy. Many still supported Arbenz and knew that it was the rich and powerful who were behind his ousting. Miguel Mas Rodas was one such farmer who was helped by Arbenz's policies.

"If you ask me, he wasn't a corrupt president. The problem was the rich and powerful came together against him because of his land reform that helped the peasant's situation. It meant those who owned plots of land and didn't cultivate them would lose them, and it would be given to those who had nothing." -Miguel Mas Rodas, Guatemalan Farmer

The fallout of this decision by America was that their puppet dictator was just that, a dictator. He upheld the interests of the United Fruit Company, but

---

[40] The CIA operation is known as Operation PBFORTUNE.

he repressed and killed his people to do it. This led to a massive Civil War that lasted over 30 years and killed more than 200,000 people. Many of which were just civilians.[41]

So why all the bloodshed? Hundreds of thousands of dead, democracies toppled, all so that one company could continue to sell bananas cheaply and make a Profit. Once again, Capitalism places Profit over democratic principles and human life.

IRAN

A Similar story has played out in Iran as well. This one started off with British colonization. Through that system, British corporations came to control all of the Oil that was coming out of Iran. In fact, since 1901 a single corporation, the Anglo-Iranian Oil company, basically managed and owned by the British Government, held a monopoly on the extraction, refining, and sale of Iranian oil. This was held up into the new century via economic colonialism. A deal was struck with the monarch at the time, which led to Britain only having to pay 16% to Iran for everything they earned. Auditing never happened, so whether or not this was actually upheld is another contentious point in Iranian history. The Profit acquired in 1950 alone by the Anglo-Iranian oil company was more than it had given to Iran in the previous half-century.

It was during this time of massive Profit for the company that nationalism and anti-colonialism began to spread across Iran. A huge democratic uprising was taking place, and one idealistic Iranian was at the front of it. Mohammad Mossadegh. He rode the wave of populism into the democratically elected position of Prime minister in the spring of 1951.

Mossadegh was a European educated aristocrat in his late 60's and believed profoundly in creating prosperity for Iran and honoring its people's wishes by upholding a democratic political system. At the time Iran was set up much like Britain. They had a Monarch and a Parliament with a prime minister. However, it was the Monarch who held power in Iran. This meant that for democracy to prevail, Iran had to arrest power from the monarch,

---

[41] United Fruit ended up becoming Chiquita. To this day there is still unrest and guerrilla fighters trying to win their freedom in the area. Chiquita hired their own mercenaries during the civil wars and still today they hire terrorist groups to protect themselves from and silence their opposition in the violent environment which they have created. This was proven in court in 2004. The company was guilty of hiring terrorist groups such as the AUC. Unfortunately, all they received was a slap on the wrist.

How We Support and Propagate International Exploitation

Mohammad Reza Shah. He and the Parliament were successful in that endeavor. Their next task was to follow the will of the people which was "take back the resources of our country and use it to grow our own prosperity", not those of Britain. Both houses of parliament voted unanimously to nationalize the oil industry. One broadcast went so far as to say:

> "All of Iran's misery, misfortune, lawlessness, and corruption over the past 50 years has been caused by oil and the exploitations of the oil company." -Stephen Kinzer, Overthrow

Britain was furious, but Mossadegh was cunning, he simply stated he was following the example of his fellow democratic countries. He pointed to Britain's recent nationalization of their coal and steel industries as justification. It was not like Mossadegh stole the plants and equipment either; Britain was compensated for all lost property. But this wasn't enough for them. They sought help from their allies, mainly America. They cried communism and asked that America help them. America agreed to help under the condition that once Britain was back in control, they would get a 50% cut of the Profits. This is after all the deal America had set up with other colonizing countries in the surrounding areas. Britain refused.

They spent the next year attempting to bribe Mossadegh, assassinate him, and even considered launching a military invasion. President Truman, however, upon learning of this stopped them. Britain resorted to blockading off Iran and preventing them from selling their oil.

Britain, during their colonization, had procured several military officers, journalists, and religious leaders loyal to them. They planned to overthrow Mossadegh using the very democracy he set up. Mossadegh learned of this though and closed the British embassy in Iran on October 16 1952. This thwarted the plot. With covert options prevented and military intervention being blocked by President Truman, Britain looked like they were finished. That is until two weeks later when Americans went to the polls and elected Dwight D. Eisenhower as president.

Almost immediately, the CIA approached Britain with a proposition. An agent of theirs in charge of the middle east, Kermit Roosevelt, had a plan.

> "What they had in mind was nothing less than the overthrow of Mossadegh. Furthermore, they saw no point in wasting time by delay. They wanted to start immediately……As I told my British colleagues, we had, I felt sure, no chance to win approval from the outgoing administration of Truman and Acheson. The new Republicans, however, might be quite different." -Stephen Kinzer, Overthrow

In fact, the British were so eager to move forward with the plan they didn't even wait for the inauguration of Eisenhower. Instead, they sent one of their intelligence officers, Christopher Woodhouse, to talk directly with Dulles. They knew he would be on their side if they presented Iran as a communist sympathizer. It was no secret that Dulles was paranoid over anything communism. All they had to do was frame the proposal in a way that suggested to Dulles that Mossadegh was leading his country toward communism. At which point it would be a done deal.

Unfortunately, that proved to be true... even though there was only a small communist party in Iran called the Tudeh who wielded zero power. If any homework had been done, they would have known that Mossadegh abhorred Communist doctrine and rigorously excluded communists from his government. The political label of communist was merely a mask utilized as justification. The original decision to carry out the coup by America was solely based on economic gain. Historian James A. Bill later wrote this in regards to Dulles decision making process. That he saw fighting communism and protecting multinational corporations as interrelated and mutually reinforcing.

"There is little doubt that the interest in oil played a huge part in the American decision to assist in the overthrow of Mossadegh. Although many have argued against America's interest in Iranian oil. Given the conditions of excess that prevailed, Middle Eastern history suggests that the United States had always sought such access, glut or no glut.... Concerns about communism and the availability of oil were interlocked. Together they drove American policy of direct intervention." -James Bill, The Eagle and the Lion: The Tragedy of American-Iranian Relations

With the approval of Dulles, American CIA operatives were free to intervene. Under their plan, America would spend $150,000 to bribe journalists, editors, Islamic preachers, and other opinion leaders to "create, extend, and enhance public hostility, distrust and fear of Mossadegh and his government." They would then hire thugs to carry out "staged attacks" on religious figures and other respected Iranians, making it seem Mossadegh had ordered them to. Meanwhile, one of British military contacts, General Zahedi, would be given a sum of $135,000 to "win additional friends" and "influence key people." Also, an $11,000 per week budget was to be created to bribe members of the Iranian Parliament. On "Coup Day", thousands of paid demonstrators would march on parliament and the paid members were to vote to dismiss Mossadegh.[42] If he resisted, then General Zahedi would arrest

---

[42] This plan was known as Project Ajax

him. At this point the Corporation friendly monarch was but a figurehead, but once this plan succeeded, he would be placed back in power. This plan was happily approved by John Foster Dulles. Other members of the CIA who actually held principled beliefs harshly disapproved. One of them, Roger Goiran, chief of the CIA station in Tehran, went so far as to quit so that he would not be a part of it. At the passing of approval for the plan, Mossadegh popularity with his citizens was at 97%.

Perhaps thanks to that popularity someone who was involved with the Coup had warned Mossadegh of the plan. It was able to be thwarted, and that led to the arrest of Colonel Nassiri, a commander of the imperial guard. Kermit Roosevelt was annoyed that his plan failed but had not given up. He had built up good relations with some of Tehran's street gangs through his bribery and paying for demonstrations. Kermit called two agents in and asked them for their help. He wanted them to set off riots around the city. To his surprise, they denied him. He offered them $50,000 each, and they still said no. He then threatened to kill them. To this, they gave their help. That week violence descended upon Tehran. They went around assaulting people, destroying property, starting fires, all while yelling the words "Long Live Mossadegh and Communism!"

Mossadegh refused to utilize the military to stop the riots believing in the democratic process. He sent police out to the street to quell the violence, not knowing that many were being paid by Roosevelt. The cops joined in on the violence and only made it worse. It got so bad that even the Communist party came to Mossadegh pleading to be armed. They did not want imperialist powers to take Iran over and return it to being just another puppet state. To this, Mossadegh replied, "If ever I agree to arm a political party, may God sever my right arm!"

With the intended effect achieved, Roosevelt resumed the original plan and chose August 19th as Coup Day. On that morning thousands of demonstrators descended demanding for Mossadegh's resignation. As Tehran fell into anarchy, General Zahedi came upon the Radio and declared that he was now the lawful prime minister by the Shah's orders.

It comes as no surprise that the Iranian people did not take the rule of the Shah kindly. For the next 25 years, the Shah continued to rule with the backing of the American empire. Now to his credit, he did attempt some progressive reforms, nowhere near Mossadegh, but he did try. However, the damage had already been done. The sovereignty of the people was stolen, and regardless of what he does, America will always be seen as the root of any problem that faces them. This is why while America was rewarded economically short term, we were damaged in the long run in terms of both life and safety. Let me explain how.

The Anglo-Iranian Oil company was renamed British Petroleum and resumed its old monopoly. Only now, America got 60% of the Profit, whereas the remaining European companies only received 40%. Had Britain just accepted Mossadegh's initial offer, they would have come out farther ahead than they were now. And without creating all the second and third order effects. Those effects were far-reaching. In the name of short-term Profit America destroyed the only democratic flower blooming in the middle east and replaced it with a hated dictator. The dissenting voices could not speak publicly and had to retreat to mosques and religious schools where they listened to ever increasing extremist ideology from the clerics until finally, it sparked in the summer of 1977, gaining full steam by 1978.

"The US intervention alienated important generations of Iranians from America and was the first fundamental step in the eventual rupture of the Iranian-American relations in the revolution of 1978-79." - James Bill, The Eagle and the Lion: The Tragedy of American-Iranian Relations

This was the heart of the revolution, led by the extreme cleric who was the movements guiding figure, Ayatollah Ruhollah Khomeini. He led angry crowds through the streets of Tehran, crying out "Death to the American Shah!". After just a few months, the United States Embassy was seized, and American Diplomats were taken as hostage. For many in the west, this was the start of Iranian-American relations. This is also why many Americans view themselves as the victims and Iran as the aggressors. But for the Iranians, America was the "Great Satan", and since it was the American Embassy who staged the Coup, it was the first target to prevent that possibility from ever happening again. A former militant stated "Such was our fate, we were convinced at the time it was irreversible, but now we knew, we had to reverse the irreversible."

But this wasn't the end of the impacts our intervention in Iran caused. It led to similar uprisings all throughout the middle east. Most importantly, from our perspective in Afghanistan, where religious movements started to form and groups were moving about. Some of these groups were very anti-Soviet and began to move around Russia's southern border. Russia responded by sending military presence to Afghanistan to protect itself and its people from these extremist factions. This freaked America out even more as it was still in the height of the cold war. In response, the CIA armed and trained a local operative to combat the Russians in Afghanistan. That operatives name,

Osama Bin Laden, and we know the rest of the story from there. Or at least that is one telling of the history. It's actually far worse.

In 1998, in an interview with the Parisian publication Le Novel Observateur, Zbigniew Brzezinski, an adviser to President Carter, admitted that he had been responsible for instigating aid to the Mujahideen in Afghanistan which caused the Soviets to invade. In his own words:

"According to the official version of history, CIA aid to the Mujahedeen began during 1980, that is to say after the Soviet army invaded Afghanistan on 24 December 1979. But the reality, secretly guarded until now, is completely otherwise. Indeed, it was July 3, 1979, that President Carter signed the first directive for secret aid to the opponents of the pro-Soviet regime in Kabul. And that very day, I wrote a note to the President in which I explained to him that in my opinion, this aid was going to induce a Soviet military intervention." -Zbigniew Brzezinski, Advisor to President Carter

Brzezinski justified laying this trap since he said it gave the Soviet Union its version of Vietnam and helped cause the breakup of the Soviet Union.

"Regret what? That secret operation was an excellent idea. It had the effect of drawing the Russians into the Afghan trap, and you want me to regret it?" -Zbigniew Brzezinski, Advisor to President Carter

The reality is that a fundamentalist uprising that occurred was due to our own actions. We destroyed a democracy then Capitalized on it by starting a war in a separate nation. All so we could Profit and cause problems for another country whom we disagreed with ideologically. Our actions led to the needless deaths of roughly 1 to 1.8 million. Of course, that wasn't the end, this only served to hurt the United States in the long run. The ones whom we backed ended up being a significant threat to our own national security later on.

What would the Middle East look like today, had we not intervened? Britain had already failed, and there was a thriving democracy in the Middle East. Perhaps other countries would have followed suit. Instead, that entire area has become a quagmire, and a breeding ground for anti-American terrorists and we give our populous explanation like, "they hate us because of freedom", or "we are doing them a favor, and they welcome our intervention." These are half-truths at their very best, and outright lies at their worst. The truth is that pursuit of economic Profit has once again destroyed a democracy, lead to the deaths of thousands of people, and undermined our very national security.

LIBYA

We could talk about Iraq, but I feel recent history has already proven to most people that was a war for oil. One which we were lied into it and that it was completely unrelated to the very reason the public was thirsting for war. No, it doesn't need to be explored in depth. That example is too plainly obvious to see how human life and national security were sacrificed for Profit. Instead, I want to focus on Libya, which is hardly ever viewed in an economic light. Many people still believe we went over there because of "Human Rights". I hope that it has become abundantly clear that "Human Rights" is just the new buzzword that has replaced "Communism". It is code for pillage and plunder with no regard for future consequences. That the target's real crime is threatening U.S economic interests.[43]

What did Muammar Gathafi do to incite the wrath of America? I'm not going to go into how he was overthrown, we have already seen the "how" play out twice in the examples given. To understand why, let's first look at Gathafi's policies before he suddenly became such an evil character.[44]

Gathafi came to power in a military coup ousting the monarch Sayid Hassan in 1969. The military coup was accomplished with very little violence, and the rulers were deposed with no harm to their bodies. It was so bloodless in fact that it earned the term "White Revolution". Following this, he expelled all Italians (their colonial rulers) from Libya. His promise to the people "Freedom, Socialism, and Unity." He imparted his own brand of socialist theories to accomplish this. He called it Jamahiriya or "State of the Masses."[45] It was a participatory form of democracy with literally hundreds of democracy halls built to allow the people to vote on issues directly. There was a total of 2,000 people's congresses, based on the ancient tribal association of the people. And nearly the entire country did show up and meet in the democracy

---

[43] That is not to say human rights violations don't occur, just that we are hypocritical in our stances of what we tolerate. It has become merely a political tool for garnering support for some economic adventure that we would like to take, but one in which the public opinion would be against it.

[44] The official story is that Gathafi fired on protesters in the streets of Benghazi and that he committed air strikes against rebel forces who started a Civil War. Yet to this day the claims that Ghaddafi killed his own people has yet to be substantiated. Even defense secretary Robert Gates said, "we've seen no confirmation whatsoever."

[45] An article titled "Gathafi's Libya was Africa's most prosperous democracy" - Garakai Chengu, Harvard's De Bois Institute of African Research.

halls to discuss international, domestic, and local affairs. In this structure, the masses held economic and political power. He would then take those policies the people voted on and implement them. This resulted in himself having little control over policy but quite a bit of power over execution. It was in this capacity of leading and executing the nation's strategy that leads many of his opponents to call him an evil dictator. Because they only saw him, they claimed the direct democracy form of government was never used. But independent journalist interviews with his people suggest otherwise. Just looking at his policies over the years makes it hard to draw anything but the conclusion that he listened to his peoples wishes.

Libyan policy was highly anti-imperialistic, supported Arab and African unity, and resulted in the massive improvement to the quality of life of the Libyan people. Oil was nationalized, and its Profits used to invest billions in African development and were even used to discover water in the Sahara Desert. A green revolution was started to develop farms in the middle of the desert. This was intended to make the Libyan people self-sufficient in food by the end of the decade (infrastructure today is valued at 7 trillion). They spent billions to ensure not a single Libyan was without a home. Libya provided free healthcare, education, and electricity to its people. Petroleum was given to citizens at insanely low prices ($0.56/gallon). Profits from it were even deposited right into the bank accounts of every citizen.[46] Libya also had its own state bank that would give interest-free loans to citizens, and that carried no external debt. Even mothers who gave birth were given money to help out with child expenses, roughly $5,000 worth.[47] I personally find it hard to believe that he was a ruthless dictator and that the political structure of the system was a sham when policies like these were being passed and acted upon.[48]

This is not to say that he was a saint or angel, however. There was still strife in the country. Public hangings occurred as a result of stringent laws against terrorism. Political violence was seen as such. This, however, is not uncommon in a highly religious society. It doesn't make it right, but if it is called out on principle in one location, it should be called out in all. We have a massive divide in our own country, the fact that some of the population does not like the leader is not a legitimate reason for regime change to be forced on

---

[46] Reuters, "Libyan Congresses delay Gaddafi's oil share-out plan" March 2009

[47] Luxner Larry "Libya's eighth wonder of the world."

[48] Notice how every single policy mentioned here is Productive Labour. When plans are decided upon democratically, they serve to make the lives of the citizens easier. When your life is more accessible, you have more time to devote to new challenges and improve in new areas.

us by an external power. Why then should we think it is ok to do it elsewhere? Are these American values?

I ask because it was primarily America who was the voice against Gathafi and his "human rights" violations. Yet we had willfully turned/continue to turn a blind eye to our allies in Saudi Arabia committing similar, more frequent, and often far worse actions. Like the genocide that is happening in Yemen right now, more than 70,000 people have died so far.[49] In the past, we turned a blind eye to the apartheid in Africa until world opinion forced us to change. At present, we are still turning a blind eye to what is happening in Palestine committed by our ally Israel.[50]

What actions did Gathafi take that led to his eventual ousting, besides the unsubstantiated claims of killing his own people? Well first was the nationalist stance and preventing outside powers from exerting influence over Libya. Fortunately for him, there was no multinational corporation who had their teeth in Libyan oil. However, into the 80's he became a thorn in the side of many powerful nations, primarily America and the Reagan administration. His people established forums for revolutionary leaders to meet and discuss ways forward, share experiences learned, and hardships faced. These forums hosted such figures as Fidel Castro, Hugo Chavez, and Nelson Mandela. Libya would provide support for such movements around the world. This led the Reagan Administration to try and overthrow Gathafi. Reagan failed. They tried to justify the overthrow by claiming Libya was supporting terrorism. Gathafi responded by saying:

"There is a clear difference between supporting the just cause of nations struggling for their liberation and freedom, between that and terrorism, and it is one of our fundamental principles to help those nations struggling for the sake of their freedom to support those exploited and oppressed. Be they in the southern Philippines or in Northern Ireland. To support them morally at least." -Muammar Al Gathafi

---

[49] It should be noted that since before September 11th we had planned on ousting Gathafi from Libya. 4-star United States Army Gen. Wesley Clark discussed a Pentagon memo under Donald Rumsfeld that, in his words, "describes how we're going to take out seven countries in five years, starting with Iraq, and then Syria, Lebanon, Libya, Somalia, Sudan and, finishing off, Iran."

[50] When a tagline for war is used, and you can look around and see the hypocrisy of such a line, more likely than not, it's a lie. The real reason for our propaganda is to hide the economic exploitation through undemocratic means.

This viewpoint highlights the difference between a socialist government and a Capitalist one. The semantics of the term terrorist lie with your perspective. To the Capitalist, historically at least, a terrorist seems to mean any individual/group harming the Profit rate of an existing company or undermining the nation's economic interests. The actual definition of terrorism in how it is used lends itself to upholding the status quo. It does so by labelling political violence aimed at overthrowing the system as evil, yet it ignores the structural violence, which leads to the rebellion.[51] This term was used again against Libya by labelling their support of freedom movements in the form of money and weapons as terrorism. This is only one side of the story; you must also understand the opposite side. To the socialist Libyan government and to those freedom movements. They saw terrorism in the form of oppressing people's freedom and silencing their voices of dissent through murder. They saw that when they attempted political change, their heroes were overthrown and more often than not killed.[52] What options do you have then? Do you continue to let yourself be exploited, or do you fight back? Libyan principles said you fight back. Hell, even American principles say you fight back. That's what we did when we were being exploited by the British. Are our founding fathers' terrorists? Perspective is important.

America and the West tried throughout the Reagan administration several assassination attempts and trade restrictions.[53] But without the full support of

---

[51] The Indians and all the farmers who live along the river you're damming hate you. Even people in the cities, who aren't directly affected, sympathize with the guerrillas who've been attacking your construction camp. Your government calls these people Communists, terrorists, and narcotics traffickers, but the truth is they're just people with families who live on lands your company is destroying - How locals viewed John Perkins company, from the book Confessions of an Economic Hitman.

[52] "Demonstrating outside the offices of an oil company— Occidental, I think. He was protesting drilling on indigenous lands, in the forests of a tribe facing extinction— him and a couple dozen of his friends. They were attacked by the army, beaten, and thrown into prison — for doing nothing illegal, mind you, just standing outside that building waving placards and singing." She glanced out a nearby window. "They kept him in jail for nearly six months. He never did tell us what happened there, but when he came out, he was a different person." -Personal story of how a brother became a "terrorist" told in the book Confessions of an Economic Hitman.

[53] Operation El Dorado Canyon if you wish to look it up in depth. Funny how assassinations and sanctions don't fall under our term for terrorism even though it is violence committed with a political ideology. We purposefully harm the citizenry and is

other powers, Libya was able to survive. It wasn't until 1992 when the bulk of Capitalist countries banded together at the UN to place an embargo on Libyan oil, which their economy was wholly dependent on did they achieve any success. They cited Libyan support for Palestinian independence, its support for revolutionary Iran in its 1980 and 1988 war with Iraq, it's backing for liberation movements in the developing world, as well as a bomb which it was claimed, was directed by Gathafi to be planted and that led to the death of 200 individuals.

In order to end the Embargo, Libya was forced to pay 10 billion in payment to the victim's families of the bomb.[54] Gathafi was adamant that they were not guilty and did not play a role, but the strain of the embargo was too much. The Libyan people voted to pay it for entry back into the world community. This characterization of influential figures as things they are not is a common theme. For your populous to believe you are righteous and the people you are attacking, or sanctioning, are evil, you must portray them as such. As we have seen, this is not always an accurate description.

"In the darkest moments of our struggle, when our backs were to the wall. Muammar Gathafi stood with us." - Nelson Mandela

In 1997 Nelson Mandela ignored the United Nations and flew to see Gathafi. At an earlier point, Nelson Mandela, too, was viewed as a terrorist.[55] Mandela was trying to end the Apartheid in South Africa and was included on the terrorist watch list. He went against Capitalist corporations who relied on that exploitative structure there to make a Profit. Only after the truth is forced down the throat of history are Capitalist nations forced to recognize these anti-imperialist figures as true heroes of human rights. At which point, they become those heroes' largest celebrators. All the while refusing to talk about the fact it was they who were the perpetrators of human rights violations attempting to portray the heroic individuals as monsters.

---

doing so to change their government's policy.

[54] Professor Robert Black, a lawyer in Scotland, claims the verdict and trial was unreliable. In fact, many of the families of the victims are calling for a full public inquiry. They feel the real perpetrator is still at large and justice has not been administered.

[55] Mandela remained on the United States Terrorist Watch List until 2008. This was a result of Americas paranoia over communism once again. They saw the freedom movement as communist influenced. The DoD even listed the group Mandela was with the ANC, as one of the key regional terrorist groups.

So how did Libya eventually fall, what was the economic reason for it? Oil played a role of course, but that wasn't all. Gathafi started pressing buttons starting in 2008 with his address to world leaders. Posing the questions "why Iraq?", "Is Osama Bin Laden in Iraq?" "are WMDs in Iraq?", "Did Iraqis attack you on September 11th?". He was ultimately out of the crosshairs the previous 8 years, mainly because Iraq had taken the attention of the world away from him. So why would a "terrorist" go out of his way to call the spotlight back on himself? The answer is simple, he believed what he preached. You don't risk your neck if you're a maniacal dictator, you do everything you can to hold onto that power. That was not Gathafi. In 2009 he gave a long speech questioning the power structure of the UN, questioning its function, it's very principles. He demanded equality. He critiqued that it isn't right the general council must listen to the security council, which is monopolized by the 5 superpowers. He stated this was inherently wrong and needed to change.

"this is the united nations, 192 states, it is not the security council, which is only 15!...how can we be happy and believe in the global security of the world when it is controlled by 5 states?.... If we need the security council and it goes against the interest of any of the 5 superpowers, they veto it, however, if they wish to violate the charter of the UN, they ignore it...It shouldn't be called the security council, but the terror council." -Muammar Al Gathafi

It was this pushing of buttons that led to his overthrow.[56] He was challenging the status quo, which means he was challenging the interests of the United States. Not just one multinational corporation, but every single one of them at once. The implications of his statements at the UN are vast. Everywhere that the US is propping up a corporation by destroying democracy or financially supporting an oppressive government his comments would apply to. Opponents to these situations will raise objections in the general assembly. These are then voted on in the council which the US being

---

[56] This and the fact that he was sitting on large sums of oil the countries would like to get their hands on. There was also speculation that the pricing of the oil was a reason for the invasion. Saddam Hussein priced his oil in euros instead of dollars in 2002. This was obviously detrimental to the US. It came as no surprise that immediately after invading, the oil fields were the first things captured and their sale was converted back into dollars. Libya was speculated to be plotting the same thing, but with Gold. Libya wanted a United States of Africa and wished for the currency utilized to be gold. This would have undermined the entire economic structure of the western world, seeing as how they all left the gold standard back in 1971 in favor of floating currencies. If Africa achieved a gold-based currency, it's value and purchasing power it was feared would destroy the floating currencies in the long run. This is because inflation of non-diluted physical currency is significantly more challenging to do, given that it is limited in quantity.

a superpower has veto authority over. This means that if any objection comes up that a violation of the United Nations Charter is occurring, the US will simply veto it, and the international community must drop it. Gathafi challenged this structure. Without it, Israel wouldn't be able to subjugate Palestine. The backing of Colombian paramilitary units by foreign powers to challenge the rebel fighters would have been stopped, and the list goes on and on.

The impact of Gathafi's sound and reasonable suggestions would destroy the Profit margin of many multinational companies. That is simply something that could never happen. Thus, we saw the same playbook that was used against Iran and Guatemala get used against Libya. Import fighters into the country you want to overthrow (we used Al Qaeda)[57] and have them insight violence. You then manipulate the media in your state to only show the portions that will obtain public sympathy, and finally, tell outright lies to justify an invasion.[58] This propaganda campaign was enough to fuel the fire of Americans who were lied to and had little way of discovering the truth. This led to Executive Order 13566, which was the authority to remove Gathafi by any means necessary.

What happened after Gathafi was overthrown? We claimed it was for "human rights", but after Gathafi's death the terrorist armed forces which overthrew it split up into multiple militarized factions. These factions terrorized the people of Libya. To the point where today there are open slave trades in its streets. Where is our anger? Where is our call for "violations of human rights now?" They are non-existent. We gained the oil of Libya. We eliminated a revolutionary voice who was challenging the very structure by which multinational corporations protect their Profits, by which America protects its advantage. He was demonized as a villain. When in reality the moment he was gone, everything we claimed he did to justify his overthrow, we then allowed to happen as we turned our backs. This is the true nature of Capitalism, the need to protect Profit, to preserve power, and to violently

---

[57] "President Obama signed a secret finding authorizing the CIA to provide arms and other support to Libyan rebels." New York Times, "U.S.-Approved Arms for Libya Rebels Fell into Jihadis' Hands," December 5, 2012; New York Times, "CIA Agents in Libya Aid Airstrikes and Meet Rebels," March 30, 2011.

[58] An example of a lie, warplanes were firing on opposition supporters from the air. Independent reporters went to Libya, and the populace in huge mass confirmed that it was all lies being told. That no such thing had happened. There was no shooting of protesters, there were no 6000 people killed. Many of the footage shown was from Egypt, not Libya.

silence dissenting voices. The need to lie to maintain control of the bottom line, and the need to deceive the people to accomplish all that.

Libya was a prime example of how an impoverished country which lacked water, food, and shelter was able to use its one asset, oil to achieve prosperity. To turn itself around into a socialist nation, ruled by the people, with the ability to provide every citizen with electricity, food, water, shelter, education, and even healthcare. Regardless of its imperfections, the claims of its human rights abuses were false or at the very least greatly exaggerated. Regime change is the tool used by Capitalists to secure their interests when they have lost the economic and social battle. It is not something forgotten in the past, but one that is consistently applied, even today.

Overthrow alone we have toppled governments we don't like either by invasion or government-sponsored coups. We have done so in: Cuba, Iran, Guatemala, Chile, Korea, Vietnam, the Philippines, Nicaragua, Panama, Libya and Iraq, and that doesn't even come close to listing them all. Perhaps you are of the mindset that these countries are better off after our intervention. Maybe you will point to Chile and remark on their economic growth under a brutal dictator who killed thousands and attempts to justify it by saying "well they are better off for it".[59] Or another argument I have heard is "if we didn't do it, someone else would." I find it disappointing that individuals whom I have met in my life and who are extremely smart differ in this fundamental way. Differ in this concept of identity. They see themselves as Americans, whereas I see myself as merely human. Somehow the status of "American" is enough for them to justify all the above. Enough to justify international exploitation, wars for Profit, the overthrow of governments who oppose us. Enough to justify the propping up of dictators who help us, and the death of innocent life so that we may obtain an economic benefit. All the while, not finding any contradiction in the principles of what it is to be American. Our beliefs which are supposed to be life, liberty, and the pursuit of happiness mean nothing unless we uphold them. Right now, we are profoundly failing at that.

---

[59] Ignoring the fact, the only thing that kept the Pinochet regime economy up was Allende's nationalized copper industry.

CHAPTER 6
HOW WE SUPPORT AND PROPAGATE OUR INTERNATIONAL EXPLOITATION

International exploitation is indeed a series of saddening chapters when you begin to include the real-world examples of how it is accomplished. I would like to take a step halfway back into the Capitalist structure for a second to see what objectives need to be met to propagate the system and what policies we have implemented to meet them.

If we were to imagine an entirely free market, one that goes beyond the creation of Adam Smith. The logical process, as outlined in the first chapter, dictates the perpetual accumulation of Capital. This being forcibly driven by a constant threat from competition. If you do not innovate someone else will, that will lead to a loss of market share, and your bottom line will suffer. This causes productivity to increase, but it also causes the rate of Profit to fall. The only way to counteract the falling rate of Profit is to increase the mass of Profit, which is to capture a more substantial portion of the market share. This inevitably leads the Capitalists to cannibalize their own class. This tendency creates a monopoly. This obviously results in massive inequality, and it eliminates any notion that the market is then "free" since the sole provider of a good or service has all the power and innovation available to them to crush any competition that might arise and after can set whatever price they see fit. The market, in other words, is enslaved to the monopoly. This is the reason a "free" market is a silly idea and exactly why Adam Smith and David Riccardo, the two fathers of Capitalism, utterly dismissed it.

"Envy, malice, or resentment, are the only passions which can prompt one man to injure another in his person or reputation. But the greater part of men are not frequently under the influence of those passions; the very worst men are so only occasionally. As their gratification too, how agreeable so ever it may be to certain characters, is not attended with any real or permanent advantage, it is in the greater part of men commonly restrained by prudential considerations. Men may live together in society with some degree of security, though there is no civil magistrate to protect them from the injustice of those passions. But avarice and ambition in the rich, in the poor the hatred of Labor and the love of present ease and enjoyment, are the passions which prompt and invade property, passions much more steady in their operation, and much more universal in their influence. Wherever there is a great property, there is great inequality. For one very rich man, there must be five hundred poor, and the influence of the few supposes the indigence of the many. The affluence of the rich excites the indignation of the poor, who are often driven by want, and prompted by envy, to invade his possessions. It is only under the shelter of the civil magistrate that the owner of valuable property, which is acquired by the Labor of many years, or perhaps of many generations, can sleep a single night in security. He is all the time surrounded by unknown enemies, whom, though he never provoked, he can never appease, and from the whose injustice he can be protected only by the powerful arm of the civil magistrate continually held up to chastise it. The acquisition of valuable and extensive property, therefore, necessarily requires the establishment of civil government." -Adam Smith

Given the first chapter of this text, we can see some fallacies spoken by Smith in this passage. Which is that the rich man gathered his wealth through many years of Labour, this is true, but it ignores that he exploited the five hundred poor to achieve the level of property he owns. The poor know this, and their hatred of the inequality and injustice perpetrated by this system builds up over time until it erupts. If there were only the free market, the rich man's head would be lost once the injustice became too much. For this reason, the government is necessary in a Capitalist system. It is required precisely because of the inequalities that are inherent in the system, the government, therefore, serves to protect the rich.[60]

It is for this very reason that the government itself is but an arm of the economic elite. They are intertwined. This is why the study from the birth of Capitalism up until the 1900s was called Political Economy; We see that certain functions of the economy are best left to the state. The state holds extraordinary power in the eyes of the world as it represents a far more considerable amount of people than a company ever could. This gives the world confidence in any policies passed by the state, confidence in the money printed by the state, and since the state can tax its inhabitants, it can give more

---

[60] Re-read our constitution, it was written by the rich for the rich. Who else could take months off in the heat of summer to sit in a room and write up the constitution, certainly not the poor! When you re-read it look how it talks about landowners and the protection of property. Look at some history and read the transcripts of James Madison during the convention. You will find that many of the authors of the constitution did not want a bill of rights. It was George Mason and Thomas Jefferson whose adamant call for the Bill and the states refusal to ratify the constitution without the Bill of Rights that gave the majority of this country any rights whatsoever.

substantial amounts of money to execute large scale programs. Far more so than a company would be comfortable doing, due to the amount of risk involved. For example, providing loans to a third world country. If a company undergoes that adventure and it fails, the company loses out. If a State power does it, it has many options on the method of collection available to it, and even if that should fail the state has an advantage over the company since somehow, it is always fine even if the loan is never paid back.

The way this is possible, at least for America, can be understood in a 3-part system. Those three parts are the Bretton Woods system, the fiat currency system, and the petrodollar system. Those three systems work in the United States favor to provide us with unrivalled financial power. After explaining these systems, we will then explore the structure of financial Capital, and how its role is relevant in the maintenance and propagation of the domestic and international exploitation already talked about.

Bretton Woods System

The Bretton Woods system was established after World War II, and the purpose of it was to create a system that allowed the world to rebuild from the devastation, to avoid a World War III, and to avoid a second Great Depression. The system established the creation of the World Bank and the International Monetary Fund in July of 1944 and was ratified by 44 allied countries.

This system served to replace the international Gold Standard with an international Dollar/Gold standard. The reason for this was that after the war, the United States had accumulated most of the world's gold. They sold weapons, ammunition, supplies, and infrastructure to countries during the war, and at the time, these products were paid for in gold. This left the world in a massive imbalance in terms of each country's purchasing power relative to the United States. As a result, it was agreed that the dollar would be fixed to gold at $35/ounce.

This conversion rate was the responsibility of the United States to maintain. There was no structure set up to monitor whether or not the United States had enough gold in its reserves to honor the conversion rate. As a result, over the next 27 years, the United States utilized its privileged position of being the world's reserve currency to overprint its dollars. When the world community found out about this, they attempted to convert all their dollars back into gold.[61] Which led Richard Nixon on August 15th, 1971, known as

---

[61] All throughout history, there have been runs on banks. This is essentially the cause of

the Nixon Shock, to declare to the world the separation of the dollar from its convertibility into gold. This ended the dollar's status as being a gold backed currency and turned it into what is known as a Fiat Currency.

Fiat Currency System

A fiat currency is a currency in which there is no backing. It is a floating currency. It is money for the sake of money, and it costs next to nothing to produce. The thing that allows for the existence of a fiat currency is the power of the state. The trust that the state will constrict the money supply in such a way that inflation and the like will not occur.

In the United States, we have the Federal Reserve to serve the task of controlling the money supply.[62]

This task in itself is a much easier one when your currency holds the status of the world reserve currency, and there is a global economy. This is because without a global economy if you are having to print for the whole world, you run the risk of having those very same dollars flood back into your economy, which might cause inflation.[63] Unless your economy can supply all the necessary goods your population will then demand, a bidding war will occur

---

every economic depression throughout the 1800s. Banks were privately owned and would give certificates of deposit to individuals storing their money in the banks. It is easier to trade certificates of deposit than it is to go to the bank to withdraw your money to spend it then. As a result, the banks noticed only a certain number of their funds were being withdrawn at any given time. This led to the idea that we can issue the money in our vaults out as loans and we can make interest off those loans. The problem was that when people get an inkling that the bank no longer has their money stored in it, they get scared and go try to withdraw their money. When a whole lot of people do this, it is called a run on the bank. Since the bank has made some loans, it cannot honor all the certificates of deposit. This destroys the credibility of the bank and causes it to go under. This process is precisely what was happening to the United States in the early 1970s.

[62] The Federal Reserve itself is a rather precarious institution. To learn more "The Creature from Jekyll Island" by Edward Griffin is a great book to check out.

[63] This risk isn't really a concern. Inflation results primarily from a lack of commodities of necessity. If you have massive amounts of money but not enough products of necessity (food, water, etc.), then those items get bid up massively in price, and the confidence in the purchasing power of the currency plummets. In a global economy, this is rather hard to do. Unless you have a powerhouse country such as America placing sanctions on your country such as what we are currently doing to Venezuela resulting in the restrictions and availability of necessary goods causing inflation to occur in that country due to a lack of supply.

on scarce essential items and inflation will result. So long as a global economy exists and supply is not an issue, there is no risk of hyperinflation.

What becomes important then is the relative power of the dollar itself. If we are printing for the whole world, then the global purchasing power of the dollar becomes necessary to maintain. If we overprint relative to another currency such as the Euro, the Euro gains in purchasing power. This purchasing power is determined by the amount and the demand for dollars. Since our money supply continues to grow, in other words, we continue to print, we must maintain the demand for dollars throughout the world. Either by making it so that our currency is trusted or that our money is needed. [64] After August 15th 1971, with Nixon's removal of the dollar from the gold standard, there wasn't much need for dollars around the world. In other words, demand for dollars was dropping, and as a result, the trust in the dollar was also declining.

Petrodollar System & Saudi Arabia

This brings us to the Petrodollar system. Which is the system by which the United States maintains the need of the dollar globally, and by extension maintains the public's trust in its purchasing power. To begin our journey, we will start with a bit of history about our relation to the Kingdom of Saudi Arabia.

It all started with President Franklin Delano Roosevelt's (FDR) meeting with the King of Saudi Arabia after the Yalta conference.[65] FDR understood that oil was going to begin to play a huge role in the coming years. This was made abundantly clear during WWII. This led to an agreement between the Saudi King and Roosevelt. That agreement was that we would protect Saudi

---

[64] The reason for this is that if the purchasing power of the dollar falls, the relative price of goods and services we can buy becomes more expensive. The dollars purchasing power will change far more drastically than wages ever could.

[65] In meeting the Saudi King, there were a couple of funny stories that came out of their encounter. The first was that the King insisted on bringing sheep to the U.S. Naval vessel, the USS Quincy, which Roosevelt was to meet him on. This led to perhaps the only time sheep would be ritually sacrificed on a military ship. The second interesting story was how Roosevelt and the Saudi King bonded. They bonded by talking about their ailments. Both of the men being quite old and Roosevelt being a wheelchair user always carried a second with him. He offered it as a gift to the Saudi King. While the King was too big ever to put the wheelchair to use, he was tickled pink at the gift. Saying it was one of the best symbols of American friendship he ever received.

Arabia with our military⁶⁶ And the King would allow the U.S. to export oil from Saudi Arabia. He wasn't going to give it to the British, wasn't going to give it to the French. Later, when asked why Saudi Arabia chose the U.S., his answer was simple "You are very far away." To achieve this there were some conditions. Roosevelt had to promise that the U.S. would never intervene, invade, or comment on the actions of Saudi Arabia, the second was that anything regarding a Jewish state in the region, the United States would consult with the Saudis first. Well, Franklin died shortly after, so that last one obviously was never held up and actually led to tensions in the 1970s which we will touch on later, but the first condition has been kept quiet amazingly.

This handshake deal led to an interesting relationship between the U.S. and Saudi Arabia. You see Saudi Arabia is comprised of a large Wahhabism clergy which was in direct ideological conflict with the lifestyle of the Saudi Royal Family and most important their new relationship with America. The Wahhabi clergy being a very militant and fundamentalist group had devoted itself to overthrowing whenever possible regimes like the U.S. and the Saudi Royal Family. This made the internal conflicts within Saudi Arabia fascinating indeed. The deal to keep the peace within the country went like this: do not criticize us, the royal family for our lifestyles, do not criticize us for our relationships with the United States, and do not incite any opposition to us. In exchange for this, we will give you unlimited sums of money, which we will earn from our oil sales to the United States, to build mosques wherever you want.⁶⁷ To go out anywhere in the world to spread your teachings, and to rebel against other Muslim regimes which you don't agree with(such as Iran, Yemen, etc.) so long as you don't do it here.⁶⁸

This was good for America at the time, but we realized that our deal with Saudi Arabia needed to be amended. When we failed to uphold the Jewish state side of the FDR bargain, Saudi Arabia and the other nations of OPEC (Organization of Petroleum Exporting Countries) joined together to place an oil Embargo on the United States which led to the 1973 Oil Crisis.⁶⁹

---

⁶⁶. This was appealing because they were bombed heavily by Italy in 1943 and didn't have a sufficient army of their own to protect themselves. 1951 we establish our first military base in Saudi Arabia.

⁶⁷ Paraphrased from Stephen Kintzler

⁶⁸ 15 of the 19 Hijackers on September 11th were Saudi Arabian. That fact mixed with the scientifically suspect way in which the towers fell (especially tower 7), the kneecapping of the investigation into the event, the lackluster conclusion of the investigation and our subsequent invasion of Iraq and Afghanistan and our complete avoidance of Saudi Arabia has led to many conspiracy theories surrounding that event.

Structure

In 1974 to end the oil embargo, the United States entered into another deal with the Saudi Arabians. The terms of the agreement were as follows:

1.) The U.S. was to transfer Aramco to Saudi Arabia, creating Saudi Aramco gradually.

2.) The U.S. pledges further military protection and weapons to Saudi Arabia.

3.) Saudi Arabia agrees to only sell oil for U.S. dollars and gets OPEC to do the same.[70]

4.) Saudi Arabia pledges to lower oil prices and stop the embargo.

What this served to do is fix the demand for the dollar. It was now necessary to have dollars to purchase oil. This allowed our system to have a fiat currency whose need was required by the entire world. This makes the circulation of Capital far more natural to perform, and so long as its status is validated by the world community, it makes devaluation of the dollar due to loss of trust significantly more difficult. As a result, the motion of money becomes almost instantaneous, and it no longer serves as a limiting factor in the accumulation of Capital.[71]

---

[69] Yom Kippur war was the catalyst. The United States supported Israel, and Saudi Arabia supported the Palestinians.

[70] This stipulation is the birth of the Petrodollar System.

[71] Consider what money is, it is merely the representation of Value. It has no actual value beyond the exchange it can facilitate. Therefore, holding money contains a risk. If society decides that money no longer has the exchange value it claims, then the holder of the money loses the Value it used to represent. Since Capitalists work off of the MCM principle, they are always in possession of money and therefore are most vulnerable to this outcome. Should money suddenly lose its Value, the mass of people is least affected as their wealth is primarily held in commodities due to their value metamorphosis circuit being CMC. It is for this reason in periods of boom money is King, while in periods of bust commodities are the only true containers of Value.

[75]

CHAPTER 7:
EXPLORING THE CIRCULATION OF CAPITAL

With international exploitation over with. It is time to relook at Capital; what it consists of and how it moves. There was a big commotion in Marx and Smith and Riccardo on what exactly constitutes Capital. Some thought it was a thing, some thought it was Value in motion. I'd like to explore the same concept as its exploration generates understanding. I personally like how all three approach Value as Labour itself. One of the interesting questions that arise out of this comes from the fact that machines can also do work; so, can machines also create Value? It is this question that leads to a difference in opinion by the three and led to different perspectives of what Capital is. Smith and Riccardo see machines as producing Value, but Marx is explicit that this is not the full case. The distinction occurs in what kind of Value do they create. Smith sees machinery as Labour saving, which leads to the advancement in production and the accumulation of Capital. Whereas Marx hints at this observation in volume 2 of Capital when he is trying to break down the Value of commodity-Capital[72] and declares that this quality is based on its Use Value. Both definitions say basically the same thing but with different perspectives. As we already looked at in chapter 1, Use Value is utilized as a method of distorting price from Exchange Value, by having the Use Value of a machine be Labour saving would fit this relation. It is, for this reason, we declared that Use Value's only purpose was that it served as the activation energy for an exchange to occur and its presence in the pricing of a good served to re-monetize Labour. But Marx didn't follow that line of thinking, he started to apply money Values to the Use Value similar to how other political economists had, which I believe acted as a limiting factor in his analysis, and as a contradiction to his earlier observations.

Here then is what I would like to introduce. That commodity Capital is simply an item whose purpose is to re-monetize Labour when it has removed more Exchange Value from the market than went into its creation.[73] The

---

[72] Marx calls this fixed Capital

[73] This re-monetization is done through the changing of spending habits; you have less

reason for this is that while commodity Capital does, in fact, perform Labour (or save on Labour), it does not enter into the market of exchange as a consumer. This means that the living Labour this commodity Capital displaced has reduced the Exchange Value mass available in the market by transferring that displaced Value to the Capitalist in the form of Profit. This is because every producer is a consumer and every consumer a producer. To gain money, the consumer must first perform their own Labour. That Labour is the production of some other commodity. In this sense, Exchange is the summation of consumers and producers. Capitalists thus utilize Commodity-Capital to distort this exchange as we explored in chapter 1 to steal Value for themselves.

Therefore, the Value of Commodity-Capital is the Social Average of the Labour Value it displaced. That is to say the amount of Labour Power it freed up. The Value of Commodity-Capital should have nothing to do with its price. Its Use value is to save on Labour time and Free up Labour and its Exchange Value is the Labour it took to produce that commodity. If it is priced in terms of its Use Value all that does is re-monetize Labour since it distorts price from the Exchange Value of Labour.[74]

Let's look at an example.

- You have a machine that you bought for $1,000, and it generates $100 a month over its maintenance costs.
- That means in 10 months it has paid for itself.
- However, if it continues to run for 10 more months, that's an extra $1000 of "Value" you have obtained.

---

consumption power than before, so now you must prioritize and sacrifice a part of your consumption. This means the same amount of work is being done, and the same amount of Value is being created. But the consumers can't purchase the same amount of Value as before. Their purchasing power to Labour ratio has been decreased. This is a result of the social relation between productivity increases and Profit.

[74] What this means is that its Value is what it took to create the commodity, just because it can perform Labour doesn't mean anything to its Exchange Value, that is a part of its Use Value. Use Values of commodities in an exchange are non-equivalent, only their Exchange Value, aka the socially necessary amount of Labour it took to create them is. This is the reason why exchange is based on the Exchange Value and not the Use Value. If it takes 10 hours to produce a machine and that machine can generate 100 hours' worth of Labour is its price 100? No, of course not, you will only pay 10. But the market still ends up paying that 100 by charging the market for the products it produces as if it was worth that 100. We again see this in detail later.

This, however, is not the actual Value in the sense of the whole organism of the market. This is what we termed super Profit. It will not last because the market will eventually equilibrate and the price of the commodities it produces must drop to the Socially Average Labour Time that goes into the product. That is to say that while the fixed Capital does indeed generate a Profit, and does indeed perform Labour, the Value contained within it is not Exchange Value precisely because the Labour it performs is Free Labour whose income does not serve to perpetuate market exchange. As a result, the "Free Labour" it performed only served to re-monetize Real Labour... Now there needs to be a caveat here.

For a short time, it is possible that the Labour performed by the machine is the same as the Labour performed by a person in that if a person were to be paid for their Labour they would go out and facilitate exchange with their earnings. If a machine performs the same Labour as a worker, and if the money that would have gone to the worker now goes to the Capitalist who owns that machine. The question then becomes "does the Capitalist have the same rate of consumption as the Labourer?". If so, then the innovation is technically still generating Exchange Value until the market catches up and competition forces a price reduction. If the Capitalist is unable to maintain the same rate of consumption as the Labourer[75] Then the Exchange Value generated by the machine is reduced. That is, the Value present in the system as a whole for exchange has fallen, and therefore, Labour has been re-monetized by the exact amount of Socially Necessary Labour Time the machine has displaced.

We can further flesh this concept out by taking a look at the circuits of Capital. We can trace the complete flow of Capital from a bank to return and divide it up into individualistic Capitalist circuits all of which operate on the same principles regardless if they are in the realm of production, transportation, or fictitious. There is no need to justify **HOW** Surplus Value (Profit in this case) is created in each circuit. We already know the mechanism; the original exploitation of the worker and the divorcing of Price from Exchange Value.

Said another way: Whether it is the bank who loans money out expecting to get more in return, a merchant who buys a product to sell at a higher price, the employer that pays for Labour to produce a commodity and sells that commodity at a higher price. These all revolve around M-C-M'. Regardless if

---

[75]. Which is most certainly always the case since the Capitalist does not spend all his money on consumption as the Labourer does.

there is only one cycle of it, many cycles of it, or what form it might take we need only concern ourselves with the circuit itself.

Consider the following:

Farm → transportation → grocery store

The wage for farmers → production of food

The wage for drivers → Transport food

The wage for grocery personnel → sell food

At the end of the day that whole process is an MCM, the farm industry pays the farmers a wage and extracts a Profit. It doesn't matter that they have to pay a transportation company who pay drivers a wage while also extracting a Profit, and also it doesn't matter that the grocery store has to pay a wage and then sell for Profit. That Profit all comes from the exploitation of the value added by the workers. The end price of the commodity encompasses the entirety of that Profit and divides it amongst Capitalists of those three industries while none of those workers realizes their share of the Value created in the form of money and only receive their wages.

All can be summed together in their distinct categories. The givers and the takers. One group provides the other receives.

It is, therefore, the social relation of the system that truly defines the impact of the system. Not Capital itself. In a sense "Capital" has always existed in every system. This is because every exploitative system's end result is the exact same; Capital is but the exploitation of Value in motion, rather than the direct exploitation of Value as was done in slavery.

What exactly is Capital than? We know society has Necessary Labour it must do for it to even exist. We know that there is a bottom limit where if you drop below that Necessary Labour you die. And if you go above that Necessary Labour spectrum, you begin to waste.[76] We also know that for a society to grow Productive Labour must be performed. We can define Productive Labour as anything that reduces the Socially Necessary Labour Time in the creation of anything that has a Use Value.

---

[76] You can't live off a spoon-full of rice, but a bag of rice a day is too much to eat, it would be wasted on you

Since Capital must, by the very structure of our system, continue to grow or else it will die, we can surmise that Capital, in so far as we have explored it, requires the utilization of Value to reduce the Socially Necessary Labour Time of anything that has a Use Value, while returning as much of the difference as possible back to the owner of the Capital. This explains the actions and tendencies of Capital; however, it does not serve as a sufficient definition since it doesn't encompass every case of Capital. The all-encompassing definition, therefore, is what its circuit tells us it is, M-C-M'. A Value which is utilized to accumulate more Value.[77]

It is, however, not the definition I would like to focus on but rather the implications of this definition. This is because it is this implication that leads many to advocate for Capitalism. That being it leads to advancement; It leads to constant growth. But I would like to challenge these notions and point out that there is an inherent flaw in the system that needs to be addressed. This flaw is Crisis.

We talked in the first chapter about the Theory of Crisis but haven't really given a detailed example of how it actually occurs. To illustrate the effect by which this begins to happen we will perform a thought experiment. On in which we will have a firm who does not attempt to grow and two that do, and we will utilize the lessons learned to expand upon it, thereby illuminating the sections of motion where Capital extracts Value from the system and thus becomes no different than any other system of exploitation. We will then look at removing the structure of this exploitation to achieve the same end goals of advancement and growth.

Initial Setup

- Firm A, B, and C all start out with 33% of a market, and all have equivalent Socially Necessary Labour Times
- All have 10 employees ($10/hour, 40hr/week → $4000/week)
- All have the same rates of Profit, that is they are selling a product for $10, and it costs them $8 to make it.

---

[77] The problem with this definition is that it is broad enough to encompass then systems like slavery and the feudal system where the direct exploitation of the slaves and surfs are explained as human Capital and people thus become objects….which Capitalists will assert is not Capitalism. However, I would argue differently. Any system based on the premise of exploitation falls under the umbrella of Capitalism. Its form changes, its circulation changes, but the underlying social relation remains the same.

- o This means that in a week where 3,000 products are sold in the market, each company gains a Profit of $2000.
- We will break up the operating expenses half and half between Labour and production cost.
  - o That means with 10 employees, each are working for $4000 a week. And the expenses of the company are also $4000 a week or $0.4 per product.
  - o We will assume a crash and burn point to occur the moment no profit is made.
- We are assuming a constant market mass in this example as well as the constant purchasing power of the market.
- We will also assume maximum accumulation by dispossession.[78] This doesn't change the analysis it only speeds it up, so we need only go through a few iterations.

Question: What will happen if we decide firm A will not utilize its Capital to reduce its Socially Necessary Labour Time? Instead, firm A will utilize its money to pay for the means of production and to pay its Labour Wages and simply sit on its Profit.

Unequal Competition

Let's assume Firm B and C both make an innovation that lets them increase productivity.
1. They can reduce the Socially Necessary Labour Time by 10%.
   a. This means that Firm A now has 10 employees, and the other two firms have 9.
      i. Firm B and C fired an employee because they did not need them to maintain their level of supply any longer.
   b. At $0.40/employee per product, Firm B and C can now reduce the price of their good to $9.60
   c. Just because the price of the product could be reduced to $9.60 based on Labour saved doesn't mean it will go that low but doesn't mean that it can't go lower.
      i. The price will be reduced to whatever it can be while maintaining the current Profit of $2000 per market cycle (whatever their share of the 3,000

---

[78] This to the accumulation of something by taking it from another. In this example, it serves as the lowering of price by one competitor to maximize the competition's Profit loss, without cutting into the Profit mass of the company lowering the price.

products sold is). The purpose of this is to eliminate competition while not hurting yourself.[79]
1. This is the implication of the maximum accumulation by dispossession assumption made. To find out the lowest price we can set we must first discover the market share our initial price change generated.
2. We don't exactly know how the market share will change but let's assume for simplicity the market share gets distributed to 30%, 35%, and 35%.
    a. At a 35% of 3000 products they sell 1,050 products. The price to maintain $2000 Profit is ([$4000+$3600+$2000]/1050)
    b. Therefore, we get a new price of $9.14
    c. At 30% firm A only sells 900. Which means only $1400 in Profit for them, [900*$10 − (900*$0.4 + $4000) = $1400]
3. That 10% innovation in Firms B and C served to reduce the market share of Firm A by only 3% which reduced their Profit to 70% of what it had been.
    a. This shows how innovation deals a heavy blow to non-innovating competition
4. Let us see what happens if firm B and C innovate again by another 10%, eliminate another employee, and get that same 2% boost in their market share.
    a. At 26%, 37%, and 37% we see firm B and C to maintain their Profit would price their product at ([$4000 + $3200 + 2000]/1110)=$8.29
    b. A's total sales going down to 7,800 which nets them only $680 in profit. We can see how one more iteration of this process will cause them to go negative. As a result, unequal competition has a squeezing effect on the market. For brevity let's assume Firm A quits before the next round of innovation does them in.
5. This then leads to a B and C, both capturing half the market share due to a loss of competition.
    a. $8.29*1500-($7200)=$5235 in Profit for both companies.
    b. They also have no incentive to change the price as they are making more than they were before. Both can sit happily in this range. The rule we have applied is that they will not

---

[79] By making this assumption, we simply speed up the example of what will eventually happen. The only hard fast rule is that the companies don't want to take a loss in Profit.

willingly accept less. Since they have the same technology, they could both bid the price down to the $2000 Profit and have a product of much lower price but that is disadvantageous for both companies since they can't maintain the increased market share from a price drop for very long due to having the same technology.[80]

Constant Competition

1. Let's explore some iterations of this innovation in a constant competition environment. This is to illustrate the effect productivity increases have in situations where competition remains constant.
    a. If Firm B innovates and removes a worker. They can sell their product for $8.00. Let's assume this price reduction affords them a 10% market share bump (60% vs 40%)
    b. 1800*$8 -$6800 = $7600 in Profit and it hurts the competitor by reducing their Profit to only $2748.
    c. Since this is constant competition, the competitor (firm C) discovers the method after a while and mimics it returning market share back to 50/50.
    d. With the lower price, each firm's total Profit is now at $5200.[81]
2. This creates the rule of competition, which is "grow or die". You can see just how big of a hit Firm C took to Firm B's innovation. Firm B got a significant short-term gain from that innovation. Both will continue to innovate out of fear of the competition stealing market share by doing so, and out of a drive to achieve short term super Profits. If neither innovates, then that opens the door for a competitor to enter the market with newer technology in which case they drastically lose market share and experience an even greater hurt than if they remained in competition with each other.

---

[80] By sitting and not innovating however they run the risk of a new competitor entering the market while they stagnate and that would drastically cut into their market share and hurt their Profit line. Instead they will enter into constant competition with this new profit rate becoming the baseline. It is now the expected profit rate.

[81] We are working on the assumption they want to maintain this Profit as their baseline. Really, they could get into a bidding war and reduce this Profit down to near 0 if they so wished. But for the purposes of this examination we will attempt to maintain some semblance of this bottom line.

3. It is for those reasons we will see what happens after 5 more iterations.
    a. The price is now $6*1500 - $4800 = $4200 in Profit.

We can see how the Profit rate falls with the reduction of Human Labour, we can also see that if the cost of means of production is also severely reduced to where the machinery replaces all humans and runs efficiently and cheaply we can get the price down to nearly $3 without altering these two companies bottom lines by much. You could further follow this logic and see that if the cost of new means of production drops to near zero, then new competitors will enter the market. So even with a $3 price, the Profit drops to $2800 with 3 competitors. To $2100 with 4, to $1400 with 6 and so on and so forth. This is the essence behind Marx's Falling Rate of Profit and the Theory of Crisis. Without human Labour to extort, the Profit relies on the means of production for its Value[82], which is replicable, once it is replicated the Profit then depends solely on the market share you have. This means that so long as a Profit can be made, the competition will increase.

The execution of the above situation in how it has been described. Relies on the fact that the displaced workers are removed from the consuming class, and that their removal did not affect the purchasing power. We have operated on the assumption that the Capitalist can make up for their loss in Exchange Value by increasing their own consumption to offset the loss. We worked off this assumption to simplify the mechanism so that we could see why growth is necessary for a Capitalist system, and how one of the methods of accumulation by dispossession occurs.

Understanding the implications of this assumption is the key to understand why Marx doesn't include machinery in his generation of Value (because it doesn't generate Exchange Value). This is because Marx makes a distinction in what exactly Value is.

He consistently defines Value as Labour itself. But not just as Labour, it is Labour which contains a social relation. Indeed, a machine can perform Labour, but that machine has no social relationship. That is, as we have said before it receives no wage and does not contribute to consumption. In effect, we can visualize productive improvements as commodities that have the same properties of nature.[83]

---

[82] Here we are making the assumption that the Capitalist will maintain the purchasing power of the displaced workers so that our consumption class is not affected by the loss of Exchange Value adders.

Consider the following. If we apply arbitrary figures to the example explored above, we discover something about this relation.

Round 1
- The Value created by production= 10
- The Value available for use by consuming class = 8
- The Value available for use by the Capitalist class = 10
- The Value that ends up with workers in the form of commodities= 8
- Extra consumption Capitalist must engage in to prevent Labour re-monetization= 2
- Accumulation of wealth the Capitalist achieves = 8 (really 10 since all money flows up to the Capitalist class anyway)[84]

All workers performed Labour, and as such created Value, they received a wage and spent that wage on commodities, since all commodity production is the result of Capital in this example the Capital class ends up with the circulating money that bought those commodities. They then pay the Labourer to repeat the process ending up with a Profit, which is the difference in the Exchange Value created by the Labourer and the wages paid by the Capitalist.

Round 2 (innovation occurs and replaces a worker)
- The Value created by production= 10
- The Value available for use by consuming class = 7
- The Value available for use by the Capitalist class = 10
- The Value that ends up with workers in the form of commodities= 7
- Consumption Capitalist must engage in to prevent Labour re-monetization= 3

---

[83] This is because nature is inherently free, yet it provides. A hill of berries provides a Use Value, and its product, the berries, is free to you in a state of nature. A productive process encompasses that same relation. That once it has paid for itself, it generates a free Use Value.

[84] The disparity here between 8 and 10 simply serves to show that capitalists as a class gain 10. The individual capitalist in round I gains 8 and another capitalist ended up with this capitalist's expenditure of 2. This is the very reason that capitalists end up cannibalizing each other in crisis.

- Accumulation of wealth the Capitalist achieves = 7 (really 10 since all money flows up to the Capitalist class anyway)

We see how Labour re-monetization can start to occur: When there are more products than Exchange Value entering the market. This is why Marx harps on Exchange Value over Use Value. Productivity increase can be viewed as a commodity in that it provides the Use Value of saving Labour Time. However, it does not contain the social relation of Exchange. Workers operate off of the C-M-C principle. While the productivity increase is merely the C-M portion of the M-C-M Capitalist circuit. The question revealed above then arises on whether or not the Capitalist has the same purchasing power as the workers.

Workers:
C-M-C
Capitalist:
M-C-M'-C+m

The above circuit is to illustrate that the worker's consumption is equivalent to that of their production. While Capitalist consumption is not equivalent to their accumulation.

If $M' = M+\Delta M$ than to avoid a re-monetization of Labour and maintain equilibrium, the Capitalist must be able to convert all of the ΔM into C. If they do not, then Labour re-monetization occurs. This can also be mitigated by lowering the price to make sure demand meets supply. However, by doing so, the Capitalist would lose their Profit obtained through innovation. Since It becomes an unreasonable demand upon the Capitalists to expect them to maintain the consumption rate of the masses, and the reduction of price to the point of eliminating Profit won't occur, one might ask about a worker entering back into the market after being displaced. So then let's explore what happens when displaced workers find a new industry.

New industry means more Exchange Value is added to the market. This means the total Value of the market increases, but the consumption power is the same as it was before. It is for this reason that Labour re-monetization will occur and market share will still be affected. Let's cement this idea. In the example, we had 1000 consumers. But with there now being more Value available in the market but less Exchange Value this will cause some of the market share of those 1000 consumers to make a choice about how to spend their money. If we say that all industries experience an equilibration shift, we can see how this plays out.

Numbers help us visualize.

- 9000 consumers
- 9 industries
- 1000 consumers per industry.

Add in a new industry, and we get

- 900 consumers per industry.

If you have an increasing number of products, which is what productivity increases lead to, but you do not have a growing number of consumers, then either the consumer's total Exchange Value must increase, or product's Exchange Value must decrease to stay in equilibrium with each other.

Commodity Exchange Value = Consumer Exchange Value.

If they do not, we have a few situations we must think through and see what questions might arise to help us better understand the relations.[85]

Situation 1: productivity increases, a worker loses their job, and cannot find a new job.

The Exchange Value available to the consuming class has decreased. That is to say, the consuming class can't consume as much as they did before since they have one less contributor. This will re-monetize Labour in the long run as the market discovers that the consuming class has less purchasing power than it did before.

This then brings up the question about the price. If the price drops by the wage of the Labourer, then shouldn't that balance be maintained? Actually, it should, but then why in our thought example did we clearly end up with a situation where there was an off balance. The answer comes in the form of the means of production. The equipment used to increase productivity is a commodity. That means when it is purchased, it has a definite Exchange Value which it can pass on to the things it produces. The Capitalist wants to get his money back as soon as possible. He chooses a rate of return and production starts. Once the Value of the commodity has been returned to the Capitalist, its Exchange Value has been offset, the price of the commodity should drop to just the Exchange Value of Labour doing the work at this point. But that doesn't happen.

---

[85] I apologize for hitting this from multiple different angles. The hope is that each perspective illuminates a new cog in the machine and by the end, we can view the entire motion for what it is.

If we consider the Capitalist as outside the consuming class. That is to say, they have more Value than they need for consumption, therefore obtaining even more Value won't change their consumption habits. We can then observe that their primary influence on the money pool is investment; If they purchase a means of production, they are adding in more Value to the exchange pool than would typically exist. Let's say that the Value added is 10. The Capitalist then utilizes that means of production to get rid of a worker, a Value of 2, they then lower the price by 1, and utilize the extra Value of 1 to begin paying back his investment spent on the means of production.

If we imagine a consumption pool of Exchange Value to be 100 before the investment, and 110 after the investment. We see that with the firing of the worker (who in this situation will not find another job) the consumption pool of Exchange Value in the first iteration drops to 108. 2 is lost due to the worker no longer being able to contribute Exchange Value due to not having a job, a Value of 1 is returned due to the price drop, and a Value of 1 is removed due to it going to the Capitalist which removes it from the realm of consumption.[86] The next iteration we see it go down to 107. Go through 9 more repetitions, and we are at 98, and the machine has paid itself off. But we see what has happened as a result of that worker losing their job, that the cost of consumption is at 99, but the consumption pool is at 98. Once the dead Labour Exchange Value of the means of production is removed from the market, the total power of the consumption class has been reduced. If at this point, the Capitalist drops the price of the item by 1, it would decrease the cost of consumption down to 98 and return the purchasing power back to equilibrium. However, that means the Capitalist is in the same situation as he was before, and he took a risk to increase productivity for no reason. His machine is still good even though it has now been paid off, therefore he has no reason to reduce the price. But what this then does is it siphons Exchange Value out of the market. The Exchange Value of the consumption pool, in this case, will not drop below 98. This is due to each round having a new addition of Labour Value added.

Consumption pool= (Exchange Value added by Labour + what was added by the Capitalist- what is removed by Capitalist)

Value removed or added to consumption pool = (Consumption pool - consumption cost)

---

[86] Again, the Capitalist's rate of consumption is constant. It is less than their total wealth and as a result, giving them more money does not increase their consumption.

1st round: 10 = (100+10-0) - 100 (the purchasing of the means of production)

2nd round: 8= (98+10-1) - 99 (the worker is fired and does not find work, repayments begin)

3rd round: 7= (98 +9 -1) - 99

...

10th round: -2 = (98 +0 -1) – 99

...

12th round: -2= (98 +0 -1) – 99

13th round: -2= (98+0 -1) -99

We see that this gives us an idea of how Capitalists re-monetize Labour. Through the use of productivity increases that do not translate to a reduction in prices which offset the loss of Exchange Value added by Labour, we see precisely how Capitalist siphon Exchange Value. This will eventually lead to a re-monetization of Labour. This re-monetization is done through the changing of spending habits; you have less consumption power than before, so now you must prioritize and sacrifice a part of your consumption. This means the same amount of Value is being created by the workers, but they cannot purchase the same amount of Value that they could before. Their purchasing power to Labour ratio has decreased. This is a result of the social relation between productivity increases and Profit.

This has the effect of reducing the Capitalist's Profits back down to where they were before or possibly lower.[87,88] This then becomes another driver of

---

[87] This is dependent upon which sector the Capitalist enterprise is in. Are they in an essentials sector such as food, water, medicine, etc.? Things that are necessary to survive? If so, then their market share is unlikely to decrease as its consumption is prioritized first. This is precisely why pharmaceutical companies can raise the price of medication by 700% over a couple months and not experience a significant loss of market share beyond the individuals they killed as a result.

[88] We have so far explored the rate of Profit and how that can be offset by increasing the mass of Profit, which is done by increasing market share. Now we introduce market mass. If you gain new consumers through the reduction of price or through the increase of wages, this can offset the falling rate of Profit, and even falling market share if the mass of the market is increasing at a faster rate. 1000 consumers in a market you have 35% market share that's, 350 customers, if your market share is reduced by 5% but your market mass increases by 200, then you now have 500 customers. Despite falling rates of Profit and reduced market share, you still end up with more Profit due to more market mass.

innovation as a means to return Profits back to the levels that they were before the re-monetization occurred.

We can look at another situation and see the same effect happens even when the worker goes out and finds another job.

Situation 2: Productivity increases, a worker loses their job, and that worker finds a new job.

The Exchange Value available to the consuming class has remained the same. But with the productivity increase and the acquisition of a new worker creating Value in the market, we have the Exchange Value of the commodity sphere being increased. This too has the effect of re-monetizing Labour in the exact same way.

1st round: 10 = (100+10) - 100 (the purchasing of the means of production)

2nd round: 10= (100+10-1) - 101 (worker fired but finds a new job)

3rd round: 8= (100 +9 -1) - 101
...
10th round: -1 = (100 +1 -1) - 101
...
12th round: -2= (100 +0 -1) – 101

13th round: -2= (100+0 -1) -101 (it is at the point in round 10-11 the Capitalist can make some choices[89])

The root cause is again the treatment of Labour performed by the productivity increases as Exchange Value, that is the Use Value is influencing the Price. It has the effect of adding a ghost worker to the market, one that works, one that gets paid an Exchange Value but one that does not consume and whose Exchange Value doesn't enter back into the market.

It is by this method of circulation that Capital steals Value. The assertion that socialism makes is that this social relation does not need to be present in

---

However, you can only get more market mass if the consumers purchasing power is increasing, not decreasing.

[89] The Capitalist can re-invest which would inject Value into the economy and stave off re-monetization of Labour, but if this is continued for too long then the market comes to believe there is more Value than there actually is which exacerbates the problem when purchasing power is finally reduced.

the system. That by returning that Value of Profit (even Profit made by machines) back to the Labourer, aka the consuming class, you not only increase the productivity of production to the same degree as you do with Capitalism, but you do so without disrupting the relation between the commodity Exchange Value and the consuming Exchange Value. [90]

Let's do the same thought experiment with that in mind.

Consumption pool= (Wages of Labour + what was added by the purchase of means of production from the cooperative fund- what is removed by cooperative fund)

Increase or decrease in consumption pool = Consumption pool Value (CPV) - consumption cost

1st round: 10 =(100+10) - 100 (the purchasing of the means of production)

2nd round: 10= (100+10-2) - 98 (worker not fired, but redirects realized Profits back into the cooperative fund.)

3rd round: 8= (100 +8 -2) - 98
...
7th round option one is: 0 = (100 +0 -0) - 100 (workers redirect realized Profits back to themselves and Profits enter back into the circulation)
Or...
7th round option two is: 0= (98+0-0) - 98 (where workers choose to lower their required hours of work, notice here the supply of materials is still technically at the "100" mark since the machine is doing the work for near free cost)
Or...
7th round option three is: 0= (100+0-2) - 98 (where workers continue to increase the cooperative fund)

Same structure but the social relation that made it exploitative has been removed. In Capitalism, as it is today, the social relation is used to accumulate Exchange Value into the hands of the Capitalist. In Socialism, the social

---

[90] This is also why Keynesian economics of government intervention makes sense as a control of the Capitalist system. Because when this trend continues, the consumption power of the mass is lost and needs to be primed to keep running. That middle variable the consumption pool Value, Keynesian economics fills that up. The glass still has a leak in it, but you just need to fill it back up before it goes dry and you are fine.

relation of Capital is utilized to accumulate Use Value into the hands of society. With this understanding of motion in mind, we can now tackle Crisis in depth.

CHAPTER 8
THE STRUCTURE OF CRISIS

Let's start by redefining some variables introduced in chapter 1. The reason for the choice of variables in chapter 1 was to enforce the **M-C-M** and **C-M-C** circuit notation. Now I would like to analyze Value, Money, and Consumption. I am altering Value from C as it was in chapter 1 to V so that I can use C for consumption. I believe this aids in the thought process and makes the math easier to digest.[91] Variables are just placeholders, after all, we can put whatever we want there as long as the meaning is understood.

- $M^P = V^C - M^{I+W}$ [Profit = Price - Cost of Production(investment + wages)]

- $M_C = M^I + V^L$ [Price = Initial investment + Labour Value]

- $M^P = (M^I + V^L) - (M^I + M^W)$ [substitute in Values]

- $M^P = V^L - M^W$ [Profit = Labour Value - Wages paid to Labourer]

Consumption Money= (consumers wages + gross investment- return)

- $M_C = M^W + M^I - M^R$
- $M^R = M^{Fi} + M^{FP} + M^P$ [Return =Finance principle +Finance Interest + Production profit] [92]
- $M^{Fi} = M^I$ (once paid off completely)

Gross investment + Capitalist consumption + worker consumption = Gross national product

- $M^I + C^C + C^W = C_{GNP}$

---

[91] C was used in chapter one to enforce the commodity and the money relation. In this Chapter I would like to enforce the value and money relation.
[92] You can throw in taxes here too if you break out M^I into private and public investment as well.

Gross Profits + Wages and Salaries = Gross national income

- $M_{GP} + M^W = M_{GNI}$

We can then make the assumption that gross national income is equal to gross national products in a closed system.

- $C_{GNP} = M_{GNI}$ (Gross national product = Gross national income)

We do this by assuming that wages and salaries = worker consumption

- $M^W = C^W$ *this is assuming workers spend what they earn*

This reveals the relation that

Gross Profits = Capitalist consumption + Gross Investment

- $M_{GP} = C^C + M^I$

This informs us of a couple intricacies. That Capitalists as a class make what they spend. Since all receivers of Profit are Capitalists all money spent in the system makes its way back to the Capitalist. If a Capitalist of a landscaping company spends money on a haircut, that money goes to the Capitalist who owns the barbershop. The money has remained within the Capitalist class as a whole.

This is where Kaleski in 1933 came to this conclusion.

"The conclusion that the increase in Capitalist consumption increases, in turn, their Profits contradicts the common conviction that the more is consumed, the less is saved. This approach, which is correct in regard to a single Capitalist, does not apply to the Capitalist class as a whole. If some Capitalists spend money, either on investment or consumer goods, their money passes to other Capitalists in the form of Profits. Investment or consumption of some Capitalists creates Profits for others. Capitalists as a class gain exactly as much as they spend or consume, and if in a closed system, they ceased to construct and consume, they could not make any money at all." - Kaleski 1933

This serves to help us explain the origin of Crisis when combined with the understanding of the previous section of how Capitalists steal Value through the motion of Capital.

We see that Capitalist Profits as a class come from what they spend and invest as a class. But there is a hidden relation to the worker here. Since the exchange is essential for this to occur and since Capitalist can only consume so much, we can assume their consumption is constant. It is, therefore, only their investment that varies. We can thus analyze the rate of change to discover the true relation.

- $M_{GP}^{Final - initial} = C^C_{Final - Initial} + M^I_{Final - Initial}$

This leaves us with the change in gross Profit is dependent upon the change in investment.

- $\Delta M_{GP} = \Delta M^I$

This reveals the reason as to why investment has a positive reinforcement in the market. It also explains why there is a negative reinforcement in the market during a crisis.[93] But what drives the investment? What drives the Profit? It's a nice relation, but it is divorced from the things in the market that matter, i.e. production and consumption. Which is where the workers come in since workers are the ones that perform Labour, they are the creators of commodities, and they are the drivers of consumption. This means we need to look at the rate of change in consumption. To do this, we must analyze purchasing power.

Purchasing power % change = [Consumption money - consumption cost]/ Consumption money*100%

$$PP = \frac{M_C - C^P}{M_C} * 100\%$$

If we use the example of the previous chapter:

---

[93] Similarly, it explains government interventions such as quantitative easing. Because investment in its simplicity is just an injection of money into the market that previously had been removed, be it removed by profit or by taxes, the only thing that matters is that it is currently not circulating. This reveals the reason why bailing out the banks was so diabolical, if you inject money to protect profit but not to increase productivity you have done absolutely nothing for growth, you have simply subsidized private risk with no public benefit.

Consumption pool= (Exchange Value added by Labour + what was added by the Capitalist- what is removed by Capitalist)

6= (98 +8 -2) - 98

Where 6 is the Value given by the Capitalist to consumption money. 98 is wages to Labour, 8 is investment, 2 is repayment and 98 is the consumption cost. We can use this to discover the purchasing power.

(106 - 98)/ 106 *100%= +7%

If our unit of money is $1, then this means that $1 will be able to purchase $1.07 worth of goods. We see that this follows the principles of price inflation that when there is more money in the economy, prices will rise to meet that amount of money. This is due to the equilibrium that purchasing power likes to maintain due to intuitive understanding of Abstract Labour; equivalent exchange in other words. This is also termed re-monetization of Labour.

We also see this relation in that continued repayment to the Capitalist is the culprit for reducing the purchasing power.

-2 = (98 +0 -2) - 98

Where -2 is the Value taken by the Capitalist from the consumption money, 98 is wages to Labour, 0 is investment, -2 is continued repayment, and 98 is the consumption cost.

Plug that into the Purchasing Power Equation

$$\frac{(96 - 98)}{96} * 100\% = -2\%$$

So, $1 = $0.98

In this case, you are only able to purchase 98 cents worth of goods for every dollar. Which creates an interesting dilemma. Since this motion of Capital forms a Profit, this taking of Profit is what causes purchasing power to drop, which in turn should cause prices to drop.[94]

---

[94] This in turn causes profits to fall, which makes investment less attractive which then causes smaller capitalists to fail. This leads to people losing their jobs which further reduces consumptive power and a domino effect ensues.

With this relation, it becomes easy to see how Profits and investment are related. Increasing investment for an extended period drives up the purchasing power of the money precisely because there is more circulating Exchange Value in the economy now. To maintain equivalent exchange, prices must rise, or wages must fall to maintain the purchasing power of 1 for 1. This portion of the cycle has a downside for the Capitalist class in that they are unable to realize Profits. This is because their repayments have not yet equaled what they have invested. Conversely the opposite is true, once repayments overcome the investment, that is to say, once the Capitalist class begins taking Profit, this causes the purchasing power to be diminished.

The long-term result of this is that all Capitalists wish to realize these Profits; otherwise, there would be no point to the investment in the first place.[95] Thus the overall repayment must always be larger than that of the investment. This results in a more extended period of lower purchasing power than higher purchasing power for the majority of society. This causes the re-monetization of Labour to occur. Prices may or may not drop as a result though. What happens instead is purchasing habits are prioritized, and this results in changes to both market share and market mass of different industries. This results in less Profit either through lower prices, higher wages, or merely a reduction in sales. A.k.a This occurs through the re-monetization of Labour.

Since this reduction of market mass and market share of the Capitalist class results in a loss of their Profits as a whole. This then signals the downturn as gross Profits fall even further as the Capitalist class begins to halt on investment ($\Delta M_{GP} = \Delta M^I$). This results in the rate of repayments being even higher than the rate of investment. The differences in rates lead to an ever-higher mass of repayment to mass of investment, leading to a further reduction in purchasing power, therefore leading to even less Profit, which leads to even less investment. This is the structure behind Crisis.

Crisis then leads to price stabilization as the Profits taken by the Capitalist are forced to be bid down due to competition between competitors fighting for the remaining market share and mass. Once Profit is reduced as a whole for the class, the consumption cost and the money available for consumption begin to approach each other. Purchasing power returns and the rate of investment overtakes the rate of repayment.

---

[95] Under a Capitalist system structure at least.

We now see how consumption plays into this rate of investment and return. Can we break it down further? Can we give a relational visualization of this?

To do this, we must look at money in the economy circulating (M_C) then we must look at money outside the economy as well (M_A); which we can define as the accumulation of Capitalist money. We can write this as:

Capitalist Accumulation = Sum of Profits – Investment

- $M_A = M^{\Sigma P} - M^I$

Where at any given moment the M_T which is the total money:

- $M^T = M_C + M_A$ (total = consumption money + accumulation)

We can confirm this by saying that since Labour is Value itself then the M^T, which is the representation of that Value should be equal to the Labour Value. If we look at our first definition of Labour Value, it was the wages paid to Labour + Profit taken by the Capitalist. Looking at these relations we can show how Labour becomes re-monetized.

- $V^L = M^P + M^W$

Round 1: $M^T = M^W$ (assuming start of the market, circulating money is total money)
Round 2: $M^T = (M^W - M^{P1}) + (M^{P1})$
  - Simplify and we find that $M^T = M^W$ still (workers were able to use 100% of their value added to the market to consume and their consumption was worth their Labour Value added.
Round 3: $M^T = (M^W + M^I - M^{P2}) + (M^{P1+P2} - M^I)$
  - Simplify and we find that $M^T = M^W + M^{P1}$. The total money has been increased by the amount of the profit taken. This occurs precisely because profit is taken out of circulation and only enters back in in the form of investment. This investment under capitalism however only serves to increase the profit which reduces the workers percentage of total Labour Value. This is how inequality begins, how the seeds for crisis are planted.

You cannot change the value of value itself. As a result, the money is only able to account for the work that has been done. The entirety of the money is and always will be the equivalent of what has been paid for the work, I.E the wages of the workers. This means the first round of value created by the workers is what pays for the wages and profits of the second round:

- $M^W_1 = M^W_2 + M^{P2}$

This is the siphon effect that must be understood to understand crisis. And the culprit of that crisis resides in the introduction of the variable M^R.

This rate of return (M^R) is an interesting variable when added to the equations above. So far we have only dealt with Straight profit. Investment is limited in the above to being no more than the sum of the profits made.

- $M^I < M^{\Sigma P}$

This means that wages paid cannot be less than profits anticipated or else crisis will occur.

- $M^{Pn} < M^W$
- $M^T = M^W - M^{Pn} + M^{\Sigma Pn-1}$

If the capitalist class has made an investment and their expected profit is greater than the wages of the consuming class this means that some capitalist out there will not be able to make back what they need to pay for their investment. Circulating money can't go to zero.

To overcome this limitation Capitalism created an interesting cycle. This is continual investment. M^I siphons profit out of accumulation and places it back into circulation. This means that crisis can be averted temporarily and the market can continue functioning once $M^{Pn} = M^W$. This is because as Kaleski noted, capitalists earn what they spend. The new limit of the market becomes the total money available in the market.

- $M^{Pn} < M^W + M^I$

This can be achieved through perpetual re-investments of money. But we know that money is only invested if it is going to lead to a greater return, aka more profit. Once this limit is reached, no more profit <u>can</u> be made. When no more profit can be made, investment ceases. Because investment ceases that lowers the amount of profit that <u>will</u> be made. This initiates crisis because the limit is now violated. It forces the Capitalist class as a whole to begin cannibalizing each other until an equilibrium is reached. This crisis is far worse than the previous crisis because it takes longer for that equilibrium to happen. One would think Capitalism would learn its lesson but no.

The name of the game is accumulation and each individual Capitalist will work to prolong their accumulation for as long as possible.[96] It comes as no surprise then that Capitalism has found yet another way to prolong accumulation. That is through the introduction of Credit. This is where M^R gets added to our equations because now its not just profits being taken out of circulation but also principle payments as well.

While the underlying relations are the same even with the introduction of Credit, that being that accumulation occurs when investments outpace repayments for a prolonged period and Crisis occurs when repayments outpace investments for an extended period. The credit system is said to introduce two things, one is an astounding capacity for growth in allowing for massive investment[97], the second is a drastically increased effect on the repayment variable brought about by the introduction of interest. This brings us into one of Capitalism's greatly applauded strengths and worst structural weaknesses.

The Credit System

I would like to show the effect credit has, followed by the method by which it obtains that effect.

First, let's define growth again: Growth is the change in Value of a society. Specifically, Productive Value as we have iterated before. ($G = \Delta V$)

Thus, we see that growth is the accumulation of Exchange Value and Use Value. That is the accumulation of productive commodities produced and the amount of Labour Time they save.

So how does Credit fit into this? It does so by bastardizing the Use Value. In production, Use Value takes the form of the machines or processes that

---

[96] Once the game is up the capitalist will simply declare bankruptcy, take their personal payday letting the business fail and with it all the workers. The true Capitalists shoulders no burden while the petty capitalists (small business) and the workers take the brunt of the crisis. Once crisis is over guess who has all the money to them come back around and buy everything back up for cheap.

[97] Really credits ability to allow for such growth shows the inadequacies of the Capitalist system. Credit simply allows you to purchase unsold commodities. The reason these commodities were unsold in the first place was because the consuming class's purchasing power was reduced so that the Capitalists could obtain Profit.

save on Labour Time in exchange for profit. Credit doesn't do this. Credit serves to loan out Capital in exchange for an interest rate (profit). This means that when Credit enters the system, contained within the investment variable (M^I), the Capitalists who take the Credit must now funnel a portion of their return variable (M^R) to the creditor to satisfy paying off the interest and paying down the principle while simultaneously trying to make a Profit.[98]

With the increasing rate of growth introduced by Credit, we must also recognize that productivity is increasing as a result. The economy is gaining productive Use Value, which is essentially Free Labour once its Exchange Value has been returned. This leads to a reduction in turnover time. Turnover time is the period it takes to go through the Capitalist circuit from raw materials to the sale of the commodity.

This introduces a puzzle for the Capitalist class. Reducing turnover time increases your Profits, which means your market share and mass are also increased, but this creates a dependency upon Credit. Since one Capitalist takes out Credit to increase productivity, they can get ahead of the competition. This forces the other Capitalists to do the same. This leads to a situation where the pool of Capital is continuously being depleted. In a credit-less system, you would build up the pool to then invest it back into the economy to increase your productivity. However, this method limits the rate of growth by the length of time it takes to accumulate the necessary investment Capital.

With Credit, we see we do not have that problem. Instead, we end up with a situation where speculation arises. Speculation is the investment of Capital in the hopes of acquiring a higher rate of return than the repayment that will be owed.

Since we now have two classes of Capitalist we see why M^R is split up into two separate forms of Profit: Finance and Production. We can break up the commodity price to investigate the motion further.

$$PP = \frac{M_C - C^P}{M_C} * 100\%$$

---

[98] This also has the detriment that not all of the M^I is utilized to invest in Productive Labour. In fact, much of it instead goes into the creation of non-Necessary Labour. Things that have a demand and satisfy a use value but don't increase productivity. Fidget Spinner for example. Credit chases Profit, not productivity. Sometimes the two align, but usually not.

$$C^P = M^P + M^I + M^W$$

$$PP = [(M^W+M^I-M^R) - (M^W + M^P + M^I)] / (M^W+M^I-M^R)$$
$$PP = (-M^R - M^P) / (M^W+M^I-M^R)$$
Multiple both sides by -1
$$-PP = (M^R + M^P) / (M^W+M^I-M^R)$$
$$-PP = [M^R/(M^W+M^I-M^R)] + [M^P/(M^W+M^I-M^R)]$$

We see that Purchasing Power is inversely related to production Profit (M^P), has an even stronger inverse relationship with repayment (M^R), and is positively correlated with wages (M^W) and investment (M^I). With this we can explain two things and warn about a third.

First is the reason why periods of accumulation are longer than periods of crisis. M^R and M^P's effect on PP is far more drastic than that of investments is. When investment stops the rate of fall is greater than the rate of rise.

Second, it explains why purchasing power does not increase when Credit is present, but also how the economy grows despite that. What I mean here is that while purchasing power does not rise, the Productive Labour of the economy still grows, and this is due to the accumulation/utilization of Productive Use Value that was already produced but had not yet been purchased. [99]

This creates a warning for that society. Capital seeks the rate of highest return. Should you combine the above-circulating principle with the previous chapter on foreign exploitation, you begin to see a worrying trend. That productive commodity Capital leaves the society in pursuit of Profit for the Capitalist. As a result, Productive Labour within society is reduced. The society then subsists on Necessary and Luxury Labour to generate their Exchange Value. Should a crisis occur, it is then possible for the productive commodity Capital to be lost entirely, and its Use Value no longer apart of the society which created it.[100]

---

[99] In regards to the accumulation of productive Use Value, we must be conscious of what that is. Simply accumulating commodities does not constitute to accumulation of productive Use Value merely the accumulation of general Use Value. A game system falls within the realm of Luxury Labour in that it produces a commodity that does not have a productive Use Value, i.e. it does not save more Labour time that went into its creation. The danger with Credit, therefore, is the utilization of Capital in society to pursue money itself, instead of the accumulation of productive Use Value. I.e. commodities which save on Labour Time.

Credit is, therefore, a double-edged sword. It creates massive growth potential, but also creates the potential to end the society itself. Should Capital chase credit, and the economy become built upon Credit alone, that is to say, the countries primary source of income be financial Capital itself, that country is guaranteed a very harsh wake up call. This is because Crisis is inevitable, and the financial wealth accumulated is but temporary.

Let's reason through the growth and decline of the credit system. Its sole existence resides upon the promise of future Labour Value. If you have financial Capitalists, they will, by the necessity of the Capitalist circuit, charge an interest rate, doesn't matter what it is, the only thing that matters is that money can evolve into more money. They make loans to other Capitalists who then invest those loans to get a rate of return higher than the interest they have to pay. The only condition is that M^P must be higher than M^{Fp+Fi} so that the production Capitalist too may engage in the turning of money into more money. But as investment grows, so too do Profits. This can lead to an increase in interest rates but doesn't necessarily have to. What it does do is lead to the creation of more Capitalists. Entrepreneurs can form due to the increased mass of money in the market coming from the Capitalist pool. These entrepreneurs go into both production and finance. This leads to several conditions.

- One is that more competition means lower interest rates as well as lower Profit rates.
- Two is that more financial Capitalists mean more money for investment and a need to invest more to stay ahead of the competition.
- Three, as Labour is re-monetized over time, there is guaranteed to be a loser.[101]

---

[100] We see this in the United States. Productive Labour has moved overseas. The commodities they produce are shipped back here. Americans obtain their Exchange Value through a small amount of Productive Labour, a small amount of Necessary Labour, but mostly engage in Luxury Labour. Since the good is produced overseas and sent back here, we as a society can still purchase whatever we want, but since Credit has the trend of reducing the purchasing power, this results in necessary commodities maintaining their market mass while wasteful commodities experience a reduction in mass. This is the start of a crisis. Reduced market mass to Luxury Labour will result in fewer Profits, which results in fewer investments, which results in even lower purchasing power. Once a reset has occurred, which can only result in the equilibration of purchasing power, many firms will have already gone out of business. If those firms that went under contain the productive commodities which are housed in a different country and was not repurchased by an American, then America's Use Value will have fallen.

This is because every loan and investment made are speculation. Speculation that the investment will generate enough Profit to pay back the principle and the interest. But when Labour is continuously re-monetized, there has to be an end. At that endpoint production Capitalists who are not able to make enough Profit to cover their repayments must default, and should those financial Capitalists have put themselves in a position where they lent out all their money and were living off the interest, all of a sudden that interest is dried up and that money resides in the form of the commodities it was invested as.

The limit of this system is that the rate of return must be less than the total money in the system.

$$M^R < M^T$$

The violation of this limit results in the transition from accumulation to Crisis. Forcing the Capitalist class as a whole to cannibalize each other. Financial Capitalist either find their money completely lost or end up with commodities they are unable to use, while the productive Capitalist loses everything they have as do the workers underneath them.

This is a peculiar aspect of Capitalism, after all, every bit of the infrastructure is still there, the workers are still there, the money is still there, the only thing that is no longer there is the promise of Profit. As a result, a crisis occurs, and people die. Crisis will continue until it becomes Profitable to reinvest again. This structure is inherent to Capitalism regardless of the presence of credit or not. Credit merely prolongs the accumulation and increases the dreadful effects of Crisis. Only a Social setup to the market can eliminate the structural inevitability of crisis.

---

[101] In other words, who can find a chair when the music stops? Each consecutive series of these rounds leads to further accumulation in the hands of fewer and fewer Capitalists. This is why we have several small recessions before we experience a large recession. The large recession is when there are no chairs left and people are pissed off that they haven't been allowed to be a part of the game.

CHAPTER 9:
RELATING THE EXPLOITATIVE SYSTEMS

To expand upon the ideas laid out in the previous chapters, we shall look at a moral argument against Capitalism. We have shown that exploitation exists and highlighted the structural flaws. Yet we will still encounter resistance toward change. The purpose of this chapter is to explore and compare the exploitation of each system. To look at what aspects of each was considered exploitative. And to analyze what their advocates had to say in defense of each system. Each system resisted change, yet each of them once changed were considered to be outdated and wrong. My argument is that the same will eventually happen to Capitalism, and we have the power and moral obligation to facilitate that change.

Slavery

The method of exploitation of this system was straight forward. You would own another human being, and they would work for you without pay. They were your property.

Social Relation:
- Master-Slave

Method of Exploitation:
- People are personal property
- All Labour performed by the slave belonged to the master.

Arguments for perpetuating the system:
- It's Natural some people are made to be slaves
    - The natural order and "God's Will" were common defenses
- Inferior Beings
    - They are seen as animal or savage's incapable of being civilized, slavery makes them more human.
- Slavery is good for slaves
    - Slaves are incapable of running their own lives, so they are better off in a system where the decisions are made for them.

- Slavery is too challenging to abolish
- Slaves are essential to industry
    - Without slaves, specific industries would fail, and it would be an economic disaster.
- Abolishing slavery would threaten the structure of society
    - Similar to the above argument where culture is dependent upon the exploitation of another, without that exploitation, there would be a hardship, and society would collapse.

As you can see the attempts to justify slavery in those societies where it existed were many. In fact, these arguments were generally accepted. Today we can see how ludicrous this concept is and how these justifications are morally repugnant. Let's do another.

Feudalism

Social Relation:
- Lord - Serf

Method of Exploitation:
- Debt Bondage, your bondage is the Lord's personal property
- Half of your Labour goes toward the Lord the other toward subsistence

Arguments for perpetuating the system:
- Serfs receive protection for their work
    - The exploitation of the serf is justified by the protection they receive
- It is the natural order
- They are essential to the order of society
- Having Lords is good for the Serfs
    - Serfs wouldn't be able to manage by themselves; they need direction.

You can see a few themes cropping up between the justifications of the two systems. Natural order, compensation for their exploitation, structural necessity in that society would collapse without the current system, and finally, the guidance argument that they don't know how to lead, care for or manage themselves.

Politically we can see these same themes as justification for Monarchy.
- The king is chosen by God (natural order)
- The king provides protection and leadership (compensation)
- The society would collapse without a king (Structural necessity)
- The people need a king to lead them, they can't rule themselves (Guidance)

In fact, we can see parallels between these systems and our own. For example, in the feudal and monarchical systems, we had the Magna Carta and the Charter of the Forests. The Magna Carta provided mostly barons, but the peasantry as well, with certain civil liberties. Along with protection of rights from the encroachment of the aristocracy who had been continually abusing those rights. The charter of the forest, served to protect peasantry access to the land and affirmed that the "forest" was that of the commons. It belonged to all and guaranteed the usage of it by the masses.

We can see that the economic and political interests of the masses vs the few hardly vary from today. This is because the social relations that exist are the exact same. All that changes are the stories that surround them. In evaluating the Aristocracy and the Monarch so far as the political sphere is concerned, we have tossed every single one of those concepts aside. Guess what, society is doing just fine. As a result, the mass of people no longer believe they need a king, nor do they want one. They want self-governance, and they got it. Unfortunately, the economic interests of the elites still stand, so let's look at Capitalism and see the relations it lays out. See if we can do in the economic what we achieved in the political. [102]

Capitalism

Social Relation:
- Employer-Employee

Method of Exploitation:
- Employees share of the Profit is taken by the Capitalist
- Productivity increases are utilized to siphon Value from the consuming class

Arguments for perpetuating the system:
- Compensation
    - Employees receive a wage they agree to so it's just
    - There is less poverty with Capitalism

---

[102] Achieved at least in the ideological sense

- Natural order
    - Hierarchy is the natural order
    - Alpha male and lobster argument
- Structural Necessity
    - Without Profit, there is no incentive and society would fall
- Guidance
    - Employees wouldn't be able to manage by themselves; they need direction.
    - It is the Entrepreneur that creates innovation.

Again, we see those same categories, the natural order argument, the compensation argument, the structural necessity argument, and the guidance argument. All four are played out in multiple different ways.

The employees receiving a wage is used as a justification. We already explored in chapter 1 that the Use Values of the employer and the employee are in direct competition. The employer has more power since the employee needs the job just so they can survive. They agree to the exploitation so that they can live. This is no different than the social relation of the slave working, to avoid death, or how the surf was agreeing to work on the Lord's land, so they could also survive. All parties have technically agreed to the exploitation of their system, but that doesn't make it right. The social relation is still Exploiter and Exploited.

The compensation argument of poverty is a pointless argument. Of course, it is less, because innovation continues to happen. Poverty at the end of feudalism was less than at the beginning. This therefore is not a justification for exploitation. It is the natural result of increased productivity, which is not unique to Capitalism. Nor is Capitalism even the best at it.[103] We can look at the Soviet Union and say the same thing that poverty was less than it was at the beginning.

The natural order argument is as absurd as it was with slavery and with the Monarchy. Indeed, you can make the hierarchical argument based on a

---

[103] Communist East vs Capitalist West Germany in terms of growth (900% growth in East Germany vs 500% growth in West Germany). There's a fact you don't ever hear about. West Germany was just always better since it historically had more production centers and therefore started out much farther ahead than East Germany did. But then you get into the argument about "reality of figures" they simply dismiss those figures as not being real. Which in turn completely shuts down any possibility of further discussion since they are adhering to ideology over numbers without ever trying to dispute the figures simply claiming that they are wrong.

meritocracy where those who put in more work deserve to have more, but that argument as a justification of Capitalism ignores the exploitative nature of the system. True meritocracy is giving everyone the Value which they have created, not stealing it from those below you. Capitalism by it's structure is the opposite of a meritocracy.

The Structural necessity argument is a little more nuanced than it was in the previous systems. It relies on the concept of incentive. This is a true statement, but it suggests that Profit is necessary for motivation to exist, that exploitation is the incentive that sparks growth. This is false. While Profit is an incentive for the Capitalist, it's also a barrier to the incentive of the masses. The masses have the incentive to increase productivity so that they can work less. Innovation provides them with the Use Value of time which can be spent doing other things. In Capitalism, innovation provides the Capitalist with a means to obtain more Exchange Value. Incentive exists in both systems, and it is, for this reason, that it is not a reasonable justification for the existence of Capitalism. The opposite can and should be argued in fact. Innovation in Capitalism provides an incentive for the minority of society, while innovation in socialism offers an incentive for the majority of society.

The final argument is the guidance argument. That employers are needed to structure and run a business. That is to say, leaving business decisions up to the employees will result in mass chaos and mismanagement. This is as ludicrous a justification as it was for Monarchy. The ones operating the business know the ins and outs better than any one person can. The old adage two heads are better than one applies here. The reality is that more often than not, desirable qualities are magnified in cooperation, not bad ones.

These arguments and justification at the end of the day are pointless. The system itself is exploitative, attempting to justify that instead of working on fixing the problem falls into one of two camps. Apathy or Obstruction. Either a person is apathetic to the exploitation and doesn't have the activation energy needed to do anything about it, and so they go with the flow, or they are benefitting from the current system, or believe they are and work on obstructing any notion that a problem exists.

One final argument that is often made is that we are a democracy and have chosen this system, that it is the will of the people that keeps us in a Capitalist system. This needs some more unpacking than the previous arguments did. Let's explore this notion by exploring our political system.

CHAPTER 10: POLITICAL CHANGE WITHOUT ECONOMIC CHANGE

This chapter's purpose to help us understand the reason why political change does not translate to economic reform. In fact, in many ways, political change without economic change is utterly pointless. To understand why let's analyze our system's structure. We shall break it up into three sections. Party, Class, and the Plebiscite.

Party

The problem with the Party is that functionally it is just another form of authoritarianism. Structurally it is the rule of a part over a whole. It is composed of only those people who share common interests, a common perception, or a shared culture; or those who belong to the same religion or share the same beliefs. They form a party to achieve their ends, impose their will, or extend the dominion of their beliefs, values, and interests to the society as a whole. A Party aims to achieve power under the pretext of carrying out its program. Fundamentally a party is formed as an instrument to rule over non-members of the Party.

Therefore, the Party presupposes that its accession to power is a way to attain its ends. It also assumes that its objectives are also those of the people. This is of vital importance to understand. Because when you have multiple parties, each Party aims to obtain power. Therefore, if you are not the Party in control, you work to remove the Party that is. This creates the root problem of our current political system; the opposition must minimize the government's achievements and cast doubt on its plans, even if those plans are of benefit to society. To not do so would go against the purpose of the opposition party because it allows the ruling Party to gain validity and thus hurt the opposition party's goal of obtaining power. As a result, the interests and programs of society become victims of the party's struggle for power. This doesn't even get into the corruption that parties undergo or how smooth and natural a transition it is since it is built directly into the system's structure.

Class

Originally a party is formed to represent a whole group of people. Subsequently, the party leadership becomes representative of the entire membership, and that leadership becomes the elite. Here is how Class comes into the picture. Classes form the same way parties due but are not meant to represent anyone, instead, they create an ideology. That ideology arises naturally within society from people who share common interests, and those interests arise out of blood-relations, belief, culture, locality, economic interest, social rank, and standard of living.[104] The existence of these shared interests and by extension ideologies, create social structures which then become political entities directed toward the realization of the goals of that group. Class exists across society and across party lines. As a result, the existence of a party leadership naturally tends toward Class. Class is naturally already existent in our society due to the economic system that perpetuates difference as a critical feature of its function. This creates a political system whose party elite (democrat and republican) are of a single class. That our goal is Democracy, yet the design of our system perpetuates the authoritarian rule of a part over the whole, that part being the Party, with the effect being, regardless of which Party, the same Class still holds power. Our representative Democracy therefore is but authoritarian rule of the rich over the poor.

To summarize thus far. The function of the parties is to obtain power. This is done by limiting the achievements of the ruling Party by the opposition party, sacrificing societal benefit in the process. This occurs because while in power it is of interest for both the opposition party and the ruling Party to advocate for goals which serve their Class, since their Class is the minority and the opposing Party can still utilize the rhetoric that the ruling Party is not ruling in a way that is beneficial to the majority of society.[105] It can

---

[104] In our system, the elite are those who hold influence, and who are the owners of the economy. This is because the social relations that exist within the economy are uneven, and as a result, produce economic classes. This then serves to create the Political Class of the parties.

[105] Tax cuts to the rich, for example. Republicans scream about the national debt and use it as a way to mobilize the support of their Party as a whole. But while in power, they cut taxes, which only serves to increase the national debt and increase the income inequality their base is against, but their ruling Class is for. The democrats can utilize tax cuts as a means of re-obtaining power since it is a policy that is harmful to the majority of society. They also serve as an accomplice in letting it happen since the elite Class of the Democratic Party also benefits. In this way, the Democrats are both able to obtain benefits for the Class of their Party which make up the party leadership while simultaneously utilizing it as rhetoric that the Republicans are damaging society as a whole. Any action by either Party to

also be spun in a less malicious framework where the party leadership aims to obtain the goals of the Party. However, since they are the representatives of the members of the Party, they attempt to achieve their own goals, assuming it is good for the whole. This arises due to ideology and is false in the sense that it is beneficial for the whole Party since it is only advantageous for their Class. This leads us to the ultimate problem of attempting to call representative governments "democratic", and that is what creates the existence of the Plebiscite.[106]

Plebiscites

These are individuals who are only permitted to vote "yes" or "no", but are denied real Democracy because that is all they are ever allowed to say is "yes" or "no". Real Democracy is when the population can put forward policy and have a real discussion about a topic. Discover why other real people are advocates or opponents, and a consensus is drawn. Only then can the solution to the problem be found by discovering common ground. The Party does not allow for that to happen. They control the dialogue. The worst part of this representative Democracy is that the Party is doomed to self-destruct in the long term due to the very nature of its structure. Since the Party represents the rule of a part over the whole. And the Class leadership of the parties dictates the rule that is imposed. It becomes a rule of the minority over the majority, with the majority never being able to say anything more than "yes" or "no", and never having any say in the questions which are asked. Since the Class of both parties is similar, rule by both parties become identical. This creates discontent with the party system by the majority Class, which is not being represented. The meaningfulness of their "yes" and "no" is lost, and when voice is lost action results.

> **"Those who make peaceful revolution impossible, make violent revolution inevitable."** -John F Kennedy

Though their parties differ, they see the system is not functioning to represent their interests and what little choice they originally had, no longer matters.[107] The illusion of Democracy is shattered, and the system is shown to

---

perform well for the entirety of the population is actively repressed by the opposing Party so as not to give validity to the ruling Party, i.e. universal healthcare. This particular issue is also actively suppressed within the ruling Party because it goes against the interests of the ruling Class within the Party, which we see being done by the Democratic Party.

[106] You can think of a Plebiscite as a voter who has no say.

[107] We can see this in our history. That when the mass of people took political power back

be nothing more than an authoritarian rule of one class over another. This then leads to revolt. However, this revolt is pointless if Representative Democracy is maintained. As it merely leads to the destruction of the previous parties and classes, creates a new party of representation, thereby creating a new party elite which seems always to mimic the economic elite, and thus the eventual formation of a new ruling class. The process then repeats. It is for this reason; representative Democracy is but the modern instrument of authoritarianism.

There are two ways in which the party is able to maintain itself, both intentionally and naturally and therefore protect its structural authoritarian rule. Intentionally it does this through the use of the lesser of two evils argument in the general election and the electability argument in the primary. Naturally it does this through a process called Duverger's Law.

Duverger's law

This law states that plurality vote systems will always tend toward a two-party system. When there are multiple positions being voted upon the populous will vote for its interests. These interests, however, are not fulfilled when their chosen candidate doesn't win. In a system of multiple candidates, the majority of people's preferences will not win. As a result, they tend to the more popular candidates whose positions are kind of like theirs thus creating a two-party system naturally.

Electability

This law of the tending of individuals to a single party is how electability is intentionally brought in. The primary serves as the weeding down of candidates to represent the party. The party's interests are that of its elite, and so it will elect whatever candidate best represents the party elites' interests. This is done by pushing certain candidates and dismissing others through the concept of electability. A candidate can have the most popular positions, have the most name recognition and still be considered unelectable. This hasn't been decided by anyone other than the party elite who utilize this narrative to control the party representation. This is because the policies that serve the masses and which are popular go against the interests of the party elite as

---

in the 1930s, the platforms of candidates represented those of the people. But as time goes on, class forms within parties, the parties attempt to obstruct one another fighting for power. We see a conjoining of policies by those two parties. In America, we say that we are moving farther and farther right each year. The mechanism behind this is the Class and Party system.

already discussed. As a result, they must be stamped out before they have a chance to harm the status quo. The absurdity of the electability argument can then be seen in the immediate 180^0 that then becomes present in the general election.

Lesser of Two Evils

Once the electability is utilized to dismiss all popular candidates whose policies support the people, the party elite switches focus away from those policies immediately to the lesser of two evils. It's no longer about what the party will do for you, it's how bad the other party is or will be. The party openly acknowledges that the majority of people do not like the policies of the chosen candidate and preferred the policies talked about in the primaries but justify it by claiming they are the lesser of two evils and must be voted for to prevent the worse candidate and party from taking power.

All this serves to do is create a ratchet effect where the policies that would benefit the masses are continuously depressed while the policies of the elite are continuously promoted.

The Lesser of Two Evils is the moral thing to do, and to not vote makes you an immoral person, or so the argument goes. However, this is simply fear mongering and attempted peer pressure through unjustified shaming. You can and in some cases should abstain from voting. The party has to earn your vote, and if they do not put forth a candidate who represents your vote you are under no obligation to accept that candidate. Voting for a candidate means that you are endorsing their rule over you. To not vote is the same as the statement you do not approve of either candidate. The cultural backlash that comes with this decision is just another tool put forward by the party to legitimize their rule. Under this dialogue to vote for them is to legitimize them and to not vote for them is to vote for the other party. This cultural norm has rooted itself so deeply in our voting populations psyche that there are individuals who will become violently emotional toward those whom they perceive as allies but will feel betrayed by this non-vote. People who will literally cut off the social ties they have with people because that person decided to exercise their right to not vote.

This notion of not voting for one part is a vote for the other, however, is a fallacy. To not vote for the lesser of two evils has a rebound effect not acknowledged by the party because it hurts their narrative. This rebound effect is that it informs the masses of people who vote in the primary as to what "electable" is.[108]

This means that to not vote for the elite's candidate serves to inform the masses that the party's definition of "electable" is wrong. This signals the population to begin picking candidates in the primary whose policies more reflect the people's wishes. The more and more the electability argument is pushed and the more and more the lesser of two evils candidate is chosen the more likely this rebound effect will take place and a candidate who the people connect with will be chosen.[109]

The kicker of this whole argument of electability is that in the end, the elite's concept of electability doesn't matter. The mass of people who will show up to vote for the establishment candidates are the cheerleaders for the party. They will vote the party line regardless of who it is because that chosen candidate will always be the lesser of two evils. The real electability is who excites the mass of people the most and whose policies benefit the mass of people the most. By pushing forward that candidate in the primary you increase the people's voice and you bring to the general the individuals who will withhold their vote in protest. True electability comes from the policies that benefit the largest number of people because they will bring the largest number of people to the ballot boxes. It is for this reason that representative democracy fails in many regards and direct democracy is far better.

Direct Democracy is often called "mob rule", or rule by the majority over the minority. However, the representative government is just the opposite, control by the minority over the majority. Direct Democracy at least operates in a way which is most beneficial to society as a whole. If it ever falters in that respect, the opinion of the community as a whole alters, and self corrects because everyone has a voice and their voice is more than that of "yes" or "no".[110]

---

[108] To continuously push for a candidate whose policies favor the party elite means that as time progresses the inequality between the commoners and the elite will increase. This divide occurs in both parties until the candidates of both parties are more similar to each other than to the masses they supposedly represent.

[109] Look at the Republican party from 2008-2016. The populist choice was Ron Paul, he had the larger crowds, the more popular positions, however each time the elite candidate was chosen, one which served the party interests. In both general elections, the disenfranchised voters who supported Ron Paul did not show up to vote in the General. This changed what "electable" was in the republican party. It created an anti-establishment fever which is how Trump came to be. After having John McCain and Mitt Romney shoved down their throats the people wanted someone they felt represented them, and someone who would win.

[110] The founding fathers feared direct Democracy because they saw the futility of it in the current economic system. That being if you maintain a system that thrives off of exploitation, discontent arises, and the people will utilize their numbers to "steal" the

Once you understand the structure of the political system and how it works hand in hand with perpetuating the economic system it is natural to see why socialist thought was stamped out so viciously, and why countries who attempted to socialize were, and still are demonized. Socialism aims to remove the Class within the representative structure, in favor of a society whose sole focus is the benefit of the community as a whole, not the individual. The representative structure fails in that its aim is not the betterment of society. Instead, it favors a single class through the formation of the Party elite. This is done by obtaining power which is only achieved by limiting the effectiveness of government of the ruling Party which results in the active repression of what is beneficial for the majority of society by the opposing Party so that they may then obtain power.[111]

---

wealth of the wealthy for themselves. This view, however, ignores that the structure of the system is what originally stole the wealth from the majority. That they were exploited, realized their exploitation, and now they revolt.

[111] This is why we saw Democrats pushing so hard against Romney care, only to falter to the interests of the Class once in power to adopt that very same plan and call it ACA. This is also why we see those very same republicans who were backing Romney care turn around and villainize their own plan because their goal is not the betterment of America but the acquisition of power. We have a dual problem, the problem of Party and Class.

CHAPTER 11: MANUFACTURING THE RED SCARE

Let's take a look at how Socialism was stamped out in the United States. We had a long hard fought Labour struggle throughout the early 20th century which culminated in the great depression. This led to the uniting of the majority over the class of the minority and created radical social reforms. However, these reforms maintained the same economic system and the same political structure as before. As a result, the class system was never abolished, parties remained in place, and the people while they forcefully won many benefits were reduced back to being plebiscites, back to the "yes" "no" subservience. The class and parties remained and gave the majority what they wanted. These short-term wins for the majority created validity for the party, the Democrats, who maintained the structure while quelling the social unrest and over time eventually returned the power back to the ruling class.

Passing all these social reforms shows what power the mass of the population has on policy when they cast off their shackles and demand revolution. The elite class had lost its validity with the great depression, and with it, its power. The majority banded together and forced the government to bend to their will. It was the will of the majority which created the greatest age of prosperity our country has ever seen, not an individual man, and certainly not a party. The passing of these social reforms annoyed the establishment and scared many of the elite class.[112] This is because, at the same time, communism was sweeping the world. Workers were rising up against their oppressors. And it was working, the communist system was so successful that it was marketing itself as meaningful change within a single generation. To prove this, just look at the Soviet Union. 3rd world to world power in 25 years. Increasing the quality of life for its people drastically, all while being sanctioned, and going through two civil wars, as well as two world wars. That is impressive no matter who you are or how you view the Soviet Union...say what you want about their political sphere, but their economic sphere was damn successful.

---

[112] Henry A Wallace is a perfect example. The democratic party stole his VP nomination in an attempt to seize power from the majority back into the hands of the elite class.... And they succeeded. https://truthout.org/articles/henry-wallace-americas-forgotten-visionary/

This success is what led to the demonization of communism by the Capitalists to maintain their interests. This led to the political representation of our country to concede economically to the majority temporarily to save the ruling classes preferred system from total revolution. Meanwhile planning an attack at the foundation of that social movement; an attack that exposed the ruling class's political ideology. This attack was the Red Scare and McCarthyism. The foundation being attacked was the communist party and the assertion that socialists were no different from communists.

This was achieved by misrepresenting the Communist Manifesto. They cherry-picked passages and eliminated context while portraying social revolutions around the world as acts of the evil Communists. One such passage utilized is this:

"The Communists disdain to conceal their views and aims. They openly declare that their ends can be attained only by the forcible overthrow of all existing social conditions. Let the ruling classes tremble at a Communistic revolution. The proletarians have nothing to lose but their chains. They have a world to win."

The propaganda declares that the forcible overthrow is violence. And that the social revolutions around the world are not for the people but for the violent communists aiming for world domination. This is absolutely ridiculous, but it needs to be addressed. First is the misconception which is that "violence" is how the communist wants to overthrow things.

Let's look at the communist manifesto itself:

Violence is not found a single time in the manifesto, the word violent is found 7 times. 5/7 times the violence is perpetrated by the Capitalist. The remaining 2/7 times is an analysis that if the Capitalist class continues to deny the wants of the society and continues to oppress the society forcibly, then that society will be forced into violent revolution. Nowhere does the communist manifesto call for violent revolution, it merely warns of it.

What of force? After all, the quote utilized contains the word "force", not violence. Well, we find the word forcibly 3 times, once as seen above in a warning, and twice about the ruling class forcibly oppressing society. What of the word "overthrow" how is it utilized? It appears 9 times in the manifesto. Only twice is it used historically to talk about the overthrow of systems. The remaining 7 times it talks about the overthrow of social conditions. Of standards. To change, to transform, or to recreate would be synonyms that serve the same purpose.

Let's give a little more context to the quote that was chosen to attack communists as world dominators. It was taken from the chapter on "Communist Relations with Other Political Parties" not exactly a world domination sort of a chapter. In fact, this chapter starts off with what communists in each country are doing to SUPPORT the political parties who share their views.[113]

"In short, the Communists everywhere support every revolutionary movement against the existing social and political order of things. In all these movements, they bring to the front, as the leading question in each, the question of Property, no matter what its degree of development at the time. Finally, they Labour everywhere for the union and agreement of the democratic parties of all countries. The Communists disdain to conceal their views and aims. They openly declare that their ends can be attained only by the forcible overthrow of all existing social conditions. Let the ruling classes tremble at a Communistic revolution. The proletarians have nothing to lose but their chains. They have a world to win."

Should the forcible overthrow still be misunderstood as violence, it is easy to explore the rest of the manifesto to reject the propaganda of the red scare. We find this next section in the "Communist Confessions of Faith". Which is a series of questions and answers to help the reader understand what a communist actually is. And what it is that they believe?

"Question 6: How do you wish to prepare the way for your community of Property?

Answer: By enlightening and uniting the proletariat."

"Question 14: Let me go back to the sixth question. As you wish to prepare for a community of Property by the enlightening and uniting of the proletariat, then you reject revolution?

Answer: We are convinced not only of the uselessness but even of the harmfulness of all conspiracies. We are also aware that revolutions are not made deliberately and arbitrarily but that everywhere and at all times they are the necessary consequence of circumstances which are not in any way whatever dependent either on the will or on the leadership of individual parties or of whole classes. But we also see that the development of the proletariat in almost all countries of the world is

---

[113] https://www.marxists.org/archive/marx/works/download/pdf/Manifesto.pdf

forcibly repressed by the possessing classes and that thus a revolution is being forcibly worked for by the opponents of communism. If, in the end, the oppressed proletariat is thus driven into a revolution, then we will defend the cause of the proletariat just as well by our deeds as now by our words."

"Question 15: Do you intend to replace the existing social order by a community of Property at one stroke?

Answer: We have no such intention. The development of the masses cannot be ordered by decree. It is determined by the development of the conditions in which these masses live, and therefore proceeds gradually."

"Question 16: How do you think the transition from the present situation to the community of Property is to be affected?

Answer: The first, fundamental condition for the introduction of community of Property is the political liberation of the proletariat through a democratic constitution. "

As you can plainly see the advocation of "violence" and "world domination" is nowhere in here, and "revolution" is not advocated for unless it is forced upon them and becomes necessary due to their continued and increasingly harmful repression. To drive this even further we can go but two chapters later on the "principles of communism" to see how Marx and Engels saw communism coming about in each country.

-25-

"What is the attitude of the communists to the other political parties of our time?

This attitude is different in different countries. In England, France, and Belgium, where the bourgeoisie rules, the communists still have a common interest with the various democratic parties, an interest which is all the greater, the more closely the socialistic measures they champion, approach the aims of the communists – that is, the more clearly and definitely they represent the interests of the proletariat and the more they depend on the proletariat for support.

In England, for example, the working-class Chartists are infinitely closer to the communists than the democratic petty bourgeoisie or the so-called Radicals.

In America, where a democratic constitution has already been established, the communists must make the common cause with the party which will turn this constitution against the bourgeoisie and use it in the interests of the proletariat – that is, with the agrarian National Reformers."

I hope it has become painfully clear how these attacks on communism were nothing more than propaganda for McCarthyistic brainwashing. It undermined the foundation of the social movements that followed the great depression and led to a taboo of the communist and socialist party in the United States. We are finally overcoming all that propaganda and misinformation and fear mongering. But it still exists, so to combat that here are some examples of such propaganda.

This example can be found immediately after the great depression. It is one of the most propagandized sections of USSR history: the Holmondor famine. This was used to claim that the USSR was starving its people and communism was the cause. It is also the foundation for the assertion that making everyone equal means making everyone poor, and that communism and Socialism only lead to a lower standard of living for everyone. Another widespread and related attack is that communism and Socialism create dictators, this is justified by claiming that Stalin was an evil human being who purposely starved his people, or that he hated the Ukrainian people and deliberately starved them.[114] There were many outright lies which came out of this attack on the foundation of the social revolution. Every one of them follows the trends we have already witnessed back in Chapter 5. That when it comes to the class agenda, demonization is a handy tool for achieving your ends.

The truth is that the Soviet Union by no means purposely starved its people and even did a decent job at dealing with the disaster. One old lie that likes to be propagated is that Stalin continued to export grain while his people

---

[114] Personally, I find this laughable as there are a plethora of Capitalist examples where this exact thing has happened. Ireland during the potato famine, for example. The government continued to export potatoes because there was Profit to be made. The penniless peasants would not help the bottom line, so let them starve. This is the same attack used against the USSR. Only difference. The USSR was doing what it could to feed its people for free, gambling on a better upcoming harvest, dealing with unreasonable sanctions, and focusing on industrialization to better its people as a whole in the future, whereas the Capitalist countries simply refused to feed their people because they could not pay, and exported food for self-serving Profit(~1 million people died). The same thing happened in British India (12-29 million people died as a result). This argument itself is hypocritical and invalid precisely because it applies more to Capitalism than it does to Socialism.

were starving. When you actually look at the numbers and the history, you can see how unjust the insinuation this accusation makes really is. The Soviet Union had a problem in its infancy. That was that they were the first country ever to attempt communism, and they were starting out from the bottom as a third world country.[115] The Soviets only option to survive was to innovate as fast as possible. Increase productivity so they could supply for all their people. There was a decision to be made regarding the circumstances of the time: you have a vast country, a national plan, and one part of that country suddenly began experiencing a famine. What is best for the whole? What decision do you make? Those are the questions that the USSR had to deal with. Let's take a look at the decisions that were made and see if they justify the Capitalist assertion that the USSR was demonic.

The facts: In 1930 and 1931, the two years before the famine, 4.5 million tons and 4.8 million tons of grain were exported. During the year of famine, which is 1932 and 1933, the Soviet Union exported only 1.8 million tons of grain.[116] That's a 65% reduction in the amount of grain exported and diverted to feeding its people. Not only that but when it was noticed that there were still food shortages, they imported in those same years 700k tons of grain. Meanwhile still providing it to its people for free. In fact, during the same

---

[115] Read a Road to Life by Anton Makarenko to see what life was like in the 1920-30s in Russia. It was hard, no heat, but one horse to a farm, having to use hand tools for nearly everything. Electricity and Plumbing indeed weren't the norm.

[116] Figure 4 - Commerce and demolition in Tsarist and Soviet Russia: Lessons for theories of trade politics and the philosophy of social science.
https://www.researchgate.net/figure/Soviet-Grain-Exports_fig4_30523454

[117] In November 1927, Joseph Stalin launched his "revolution from above" by setting two extraordinary goals for Soviet domestic policy: rapid industrialization and collectivization of agriculture. He aimed to erase all traces of the Capitalism that had entered under the New Economic Policy. And to transform the Soviet Union as quickly as possible, without regard to cost, into an industrialized and completely socialist state.

Stalin's First Five-Year Plan, adopted by the party in 1928, called for rapid industrialization of the economy, with an emphasis on heavy industry. It set unrealistic goals—a 250% increase in overall industrial development and a 330% expansion in manufacturing alone. All manufacturing and services were nationalized, managers were given predetermined output quotas by central planners, and trade unions were converted into mechanisms for increasing worker productivity. But because Stalin insisted on unrealistic production targets, serious problems soon arose. With the highest share of investment put into heavy industry, widespread shortages of consumer goods occurred.

time in many Capitalist countries, people were dying from hunger because they couldn't pay for food during the great depression. [117]

Is the attack that the USSR went about their industrialization demonically by ignoring its people valid? I would argue no. Their gamble had short term pain, but the pain was not anticipated to be as bad as it was. The intent, therefore, was excellent, its execution less so.

Just to provide even further proof, as to the type of person Joseph Stalin was and to break some of the propaganda that surrounds him, as well as describe the kind of people the USSR had. Let's look at a direct correspondence to prove they were not the monsters we tried to make them out to be. But rather human beings, dealing with typical social problems, trying to cope with mistakes as best they could.

"The political Bureau believes that shortage of seed and grain in Ukraine is many times worse than what was described in comrade Kosior's telegram; therefore, the Political Bureau recommends the central committee of the communist party of Ukraine to take all measures within its reach to prevent the threat of failing to sow field crops in Ukraine. Signed: Secretary of the Central Committee- J. Stalin"

The context of the " prevent the threat" is that the creation of kolkhozes or collectivized farms was met with opposition from the individuals who once owned them. They actively repressed the sowing of fields. As a result, much of the land did not have crops planted on them, which led to famine. The reply to this message was:

"There are isolated cases of starvation, and even whole villages that are starving; however, this is only the result of bungling on the local level, deviations from the party line, especially in regard of kolkhozes. All rumors about "famine" in Ukraine must be unconditionally rejected. The crucial help that was provided for Ukraine will give us the opportunity to eradicate all such outbreaks of starvation. - Joseph Kosior"[118]

---

[118] Kolkhozes were collectivized farms. This was a rough transition period from privately owned kulak land to collectivized farming. The enforcement of farms being collectives was left to the OGPU, which is the regulatory/enforcement agency set to make sure the 5-year plan was carried out. The two options available to the Soviets was gradual collectivization or forced collectivization. Given the speed at which things were changing, it was the policy choice of the Soviet government to rip off the proverbial band aid and force collectivization to eliminate privately owned farms and steamroll the country into industrialization. This

To which Stalin replied that same day with

"Comrade Kosior! You must read attached summaries. Judging by this information, it looks like the Soviet authority has ceased to exist in some areas of the Ukrainian Soviet Socialist Republic. Can this be true? Is the situation in villages in Ukraine this bad? Where are the operatives of the OGPU, what are they doing? Could you verify this information and inform the Central Committee of the All-Union Communist party about taken measures? Sincerely J. Stalin"

Obviously reading the above correspondence it is an outright lie to try and paint Joseph Stalin as a maniac who enjoyed watching his people suffer. It is also incorrect to attribute the starvation to a failure of the socialist model since in the end, it became such a resounding success. It could be said that the implementation of that model contributed to the famine[119], but to blame it solely on one man or the government as purposeful is reaching, and to then blame that on the system itself is outright wrong. Private Property was abolished, the individuals who had owned that land weren't happy. But it was the decision of those individuals who prevented the sowing of that land which caused the famine, not the fault of the Soviet government who abolished Private Property since that is what the people wanted, that is what they had fought for. The model, if followed, would have worked, and eventually did.

It must also not be forgotten that the USSR was a third world country attempting to become self-sufficient and industrialize all while trying the first ever country-wide experiment of achieving this thing called communism. This famine was, therefore, a result of the transition period. A fight between the old way of life and the new. It had nothing to do with whether the socialist model worked, it was a result of not wanting to leave the old system behind. I am not saying that the policies put forth by the USSR were right, not saying that the Ukrainian people brought it upon themselves or that they were wrong, but what I am saying is that the intent was not evil. That the governmental policies it chose to pursue to achieve the transition to Socialism were their own and should be separate from the system itself. That the

---

turned out to be beneficial in the long run but painful in short. In Ukraine many of the kulaks resisted this transition, even going so far as to slaughter their livestock before having it taken away and turned over to society as the whole. There was no way around the moral dilemma the Soviet Union faced. They had a massive uprising, they won a civil war, the will of the majority of the country was communism. To the Soviet government that required the abandonment of Personal Property because that is what the people willed and what they fought two civil wars to achieve. This is what truly scared the Capitalists.

[119] "The agrarian strike of 1932-33" -D'Anne Penner

government policies should be viewed through the lens of historical fact and not propaganda.

Propaganda, unfortunately, is not quite so easily debunked, it is often hidden in truth, and preys upon deep-seated ideologies. Let's address the propaganda quickly. One such example is of a newspaper clipping in the Chicago American "Six Million Perish in Soviet Famine" which was continuously cited in the press and used as a backbone of validity.[120] This was written by Mr. Thomas Walker. Who was he and how did he get this story? Well records show that he visited the USSR via a transit visa. In September 1934, he was in Moscow on the 13th and remained in Moscow until the 18th, where his whereabouts remain unknown until he boarded a Trans-Siberian train which brought him to the Manchurian border on October 25th 1934, his last day in the USSR. A total of 26 days. In the article, the lies start immediately claiming Mr. Walker spent years in Russia. False, it was 26 days, and it is unlikely that even a single day of it was in Ukraine as his travel there would have been documented.

So how then did he get pictures from Ukraine?[121] The more obvious question is how did he get pictures of the famine in Ukraine when it occurred in 1932 and 1933, when he only visited in 1934, a year after the famine was over. This is propaganda, plain and simple. This is the same strategy employed in international exploitation. While the headline may be right, the story itself is made inflammatory to demonize something that goes against our Capitalist society. You can bet 99 times out of 100 that when this occurs, it is because something is threatening a Profit line, threatening the structure of a system, and that the owners of that system will do everything in their power to stop it. They don't care about lives, about integrity, about human rights, or even about their own country, not when all those things are compared to Profit. And that is what Capitalism is, the unfettered ideology of Profit above all else.

Even if you do not personally hold the belief of Profit over people. The structure of the system does, that is what matters. To defend Capitalism in light of the analysis presented to you over its structural exploitation becomes morally questionable the minute you attempt to demonize and judge another system through the use of propaganda while ignoring your own systems faults.

---

[120] This particular article was printed in media run by William Randolph Hearst, you can do your own digging to learn about the kind of integrity his newspapers held.

[121] He actually utilized stock photographs from the 1921 famine in Ukraine.

For one to defend Capitalism as moral and that it is but the few rotten eggs that make it so, requires the defender to throw out anything that comes from a population who is exploited past their comfort level...but for the defender to do this is nearly impossible. They assert their morality but are unable to comply because their survival and quality of life depend on it. They have already become conditioned to accept the exploitation, accept that their quality of life justifies the death and suffering of others. They accept this by not thinking about it, by saying it is out of their control. They reject the moral trespasses of Capitalism and go along with the system by telling themselves it is the best we can do. They do their best not to question, not to think because it is uncomfortable. The knowledge that they are complicit in perpetuating the exploitation of others makes them squirm makes them feel things they prefer never to feel. But we need to begin to question, we need to feel that filth, that guilt, as we push forward into a brighter future, a future where Profit isn't king and loss of human dignity and life actually matters. Where exploitation is removed.

CHAPTER 12:
IS GROWTH WITHOUT EXPLOITATION POSSIBLE?

Of Course, it is! You can produce Growth by yourself, can't you! Adam Smith's rude and early state was able to deliver Growth without exploitation. The trick is to define where exploitation comes from and why, which we have already identified and now understand. All that is left to do is show that structurally, Growth without exploitation is indeed possible, and that the rate of Growth achieved by Capitalism is also possible.

We will start with Growth which is
$G = \Delta V^L$
$V^L = V^E V^U$ (Value is made up of Exchange Value and Use Value)

When Purchasing power is constant wages paid to Labour are equivalent to the value added.
$V^E = M^W$ (When Purchasing Power is constant, wages equal the Exchange Value)

Use Value in Capitalism served to re-monetize Labour. But in a non-exploitative system, it takes on the definition that Adam Smith gave it, that it saves Labour Time.

*Productive Use Value is merely a percentage which Labour value is multiplied by. It is not known until after production has occurred. Once production has occurred, it can be calculated. *

This is because the purpose of productive Use Value is to free up Labour to pursue other activities, and should those other activities go into production as well, then the change in production represents the amount of Labour being added back into the system. Therefore, the change in production is equal to the change in Labour value which is the Exchange Value (Labour Time) multiplied by the Use Value (Labour Time saved as a percentage of productivity increase).

$G = \Delta V^L$

$G = \Delta C^M$ (growth is equal to the Change in productive output)
$V^L = C^M$ (Productive Labour value is equal to productive output)
$C^M = V^E V^U$ (Productive Exchange Value and the productive Use Value)
$V^U = (C^M_{Final}/V^E_{Final}) / (C^M_{Initial}/V^E_{Initial})$

Example

- Let's consider a typical day's work as collection 10 bundles of firewood for 10 hours.
    - This is not productive Labour, it is Necessary Labour. It is needed for survival but doesn't help one achieve Growth.
- If one day the worker decides to be productive and go and collect firewood for 10 hours, and spend 6 hours making an axe. That first day's Labour yielded a day worth of firewood and an axe for 16 Labour hours.
    - $C^M = V^E V^U$
    - 10 bundles Firewood + 1 Axe = 16 hours Labour*1.
    - Its 1 because (16 Labour hours of commodities/16 Labour hours)/(10/10) = 1
    - The worker has done extra Labour, it is unknown at this point if it was or was not Productive Labour. It can only become productive if it saves on Labour time.
- The next day it only takes the worker 3 hours to collect firewood thanks to the axe.
    - 10 bundles Firewood now only takes 3 hours Labour
    - This means the Use Value the axe provides is (10/3)/(16/16) = 333% increase in productivity.
    - The production of the axe in the previous round was, therefore, productive Labour.
- The worker now has extra hours of Labour Time to invest in more production.
    - Whatever they produce is a change in the total commodities for the day.
    - This is all thanks to the axe. But it is not the axe which does the new work, it is the Labourer. The axe merely resets the baseline of necessary Labour Time.
- If they were to work 10 hours the next day and produce more wood. Would we see a productivity increase?
    - 33.33 bundles of Firewood = 10 * 1
    - Why is it 1? Well (33.33/10)/(10/3) = 1

- o There was no productivity increase. There was a production increase, but that resulted from more Labour Power being added in, not an increase in productivity from the previous round.
- The axe still has an effect of increasing productivity by 333% compared to hand Labour. BUT there was no productive Use Value produced between those cycles. Therefore, productive growth has not occurred.
  - o Productive Labour only occurs when human Labour is used to create it. Just as the axe was created.
  - o The productive Use Value of the axe simple serves to free up the Labour Power of the worker to spend time performing other productive Labour.
  - o Why is this important?
    - Growth is measured in the commodities produced. This means we must be careful in how it is done.
    - Measuring Growth as commodities themselves is fine but gets tedious when you have many different kinds of commodities.
    - I produced 10 shirts, 4 apples, 2 tables, and 1 saw this year. That would be ridiculous.
    - It's much easier to say we grew $X this year. But that is only an accurate assessment of the economy's growth if Labour wasn't re-monetized.
  - o To base "growth" off of production increase instead of productivity increase leads to a re-monetization of Labour. This is why we must distinguish between what kinds of growth we are talking about.
    - Consider an economy who increases productivity by 2%. They are able to work two percent less and still meet the demand of the market. If we keep the prices and the pay the same then their Labour has not been re-monetized since output is the same.

With that understanding of the difference between growth and productive growth out of the way, and how it is you achieve it, we can see that the only requirement for it is Labour itself. Moving forward we will only consider productive growth as it is the most important kind because it allows for advancement.

From our understanding above we can also surmise that the maximum amount of Growth can be determined by the total amount of Labour Power present in society. The extreme case would be that overnight all of our Labour is automated, and somehow, all of our society's members find Productive Labour to perform the very next day. That would be the maximum amount of Growth possible.[122]

How Growth is possible in a non-exploitative system:

We know that credit is essential in the Capitalist system in enhancing growth. We must start there.

We know that the rate of return must be less than the sum of wages and Profits.

$M^R < M^W + M^P$ and since we are getting rid of exploitation Profit gets rolled into wages.

$M^R < M^W$

That is to say

$M^R < V^E$, which is the supply of the Exchange Value of the economy.

This means so long as your rate of return toward paying off the investments is less than the supply of the economy, you are golden.

There is a full breakdown of these relations available via the website

(https://andrewplotner.com/growth/)

Following is a small excel economy to test the relations put forth so far to analyze their effects if only a little.
(Interactive Section text, visit and download the excel document to see what this section refers to)

In creating the setup of this thought experiment the necessity sector proved to be the most difficult to maintain workers in. This was controlled for by manipulating the "guaranteed" wage paid to those working in the sector. [123]

---

[122] Again, this is different from an increase in commodity output.

Other sectors are more forgiving as you can maintain a low wage, and utilize the divvying out of "Profits" to workers as the driver of worker mobility into new markets balancing out supply and demand.

To see the impact credit has on the system, it was supposed that for every X number of commodities purchased in the productivity sector, a small percentage of productivity would be added to the economy. This was calculated by saying a worker could create a certain number of products in a given round. The methodology then multiplies that amount by the number of workers that have moved into the sector and then adds that product onto itself multiplied by the increase in productivity.

$$\#Workers * Output + \#Workers * Output * \%Productivity\ Increase$$

In total there are 42 independent variables to which you can manipulate, those variables get placed within a 30-column consumption cycle which then feeds into a 10-column payment cycle. This repeats for 15 cycles. What it shows is that when comparing a credit vs a credit-less system, the non-exploitative exchange cycle productivity increases hardly change.

Income → Pays Wages → Pays Back Investment → Splits Profits Evenly Among Everyone

It was seen that credit version of the non-exploitative system led to a greater gain in productivity than did the non-credit version of the economy. [124]

---

[123] The guaranteed wage is hourly wage, the variable wage is the workers share of Profits once the market realizes the value of the commodity and divvies it out to all the workers.

[124] This occurred as a result of being able to purchase the commodities which remained in the market after the previous cycle. However, an appropriate distribution of workers allows one to perfect the economic balance. This removes worker mobility but enables one to place just enough individuals in the necessities sector to provide for the well-being of everyone and divert that excess Labour value into the productivity sector. Since all workers are getting the Exchange Value that they put in, what the market produces is also what it consumes, which eliminates the need for credit. However, in a world economy, credit still has its place since you cannot control the whole world in such a fashion. The goal of the system is to optimize the economy for export. To receive a beneficial Exchange Value or an equivalent Exchange Value with better Use Value. Those exports then become the basis for trust in your economy and therefore your currency, and you can utilize credit to bring in even more productive Use Value.

It must be noted that while it appears the credit did, in fact, generate more productivity based on the equation utilized. Aka the productivity derived itself from the variable input for productivity increase. The actual consumption between the credit and the creditless system hardly differed at all. In fact, the creditless system actually had more consumption at the end despite the productivity increase of the credit system.

This raises an interesting observation which is that even though the credit system had higher productivity gains, its overall consumption was less and its prices were higher. The reason for this is quite interesting

When credit is added to the system, it creates massive demand. The mechanism by which this occurs is that money floods the system to purchase the excess supply of the commodities. The price the workers get paid for the commodities is based on the previous round of supply. Therefore, there are always leftover commodities in the current round due to the increase in productivity from the last round. This increased consumption however, drains the supply to extremely low levels when credit enters the system, which drives the price of those commodities up to extreme levels since it forces the commodities to become scarce in the market.[125] The workers, therefore, can buy less than what they should be able to due to credit increasing the demand and therefore, the price. This explains why even though credit was flooding into the non-exploitative system, it only allowed for a small increase in total consumption.

This increase in the total consumption was not enough to overcome the migration of workers into the banking sector to chase after the repayments required from taking out credit. So even though we had a productivity increase in the sectors we had worker flight into a sector of Wasteful Labour. As a result, more of the economy became consumers than producers. This had a cumulative effect over the 15 rounds to where the creditless system was able to obtain more production and consumption as well as achieve lower prices because it was able to utilize a higher percentage of its population's Labour Power toward meaningful production.

To rephrase that:

---

[125] This would have the effect of one group of individuals being able to purchase a ton of some commodity reducing its supply and driving the price up for everyone else. If this were to continue it would be a way for inequality to creep into the system. This is only possible however when credit is present. Given the small differences in growth from a credit to a creditless system, this risk might not be one that has to be taken.

In the non-exploitative structure, this difference between rounds and the productivity increases are what lead to excess supply. In the credit less version, the excess of supply stays constant, prices drop at a steady rate and workers productivity, and consumption increase at a regular rate and the money supply hardly changes. Meanwhile in the non-exploitative structure with credit, the productivity increases caused by the influx of credit resulted in massive price swings as supplies dwindled to near zero. Additionally, the loans lead to a very mobile market as workers flooded in and out of the productivity and banking sector chasing the investment and repayment profits. This resulted in less overall workers participating in meaningful production in the long term and therefore a less productive economy overall in terms of production, consumption, and the price of commodities.

As a result of this observation, I believe It would be wise to remove the Profit distribution mechanism for the bank sector to reduce its volatility. Instead, the compensation for that sector should be job security in that their pay goal is the average of the economy, whatever that is. Since either luxury or necessity (they seem to seesaw) have the highest wage in periods without investment, and productivity has the highest wages in periods of investment, it would be beneficial for this class to price interest rates at a level to achieve their wages. Should interest payments exceed the average wage, the excess in interest that is paid back to the bank should be treated as a payment on the principle of the loan.

This method of cooperative banking would reduce the length of the payback period which would, in turn, increases the amount of lending that can occur in the economy more than the present Capitalist system allows and therefore more Growth can be achieved. After all, the only benefit that credit gives us is the ability to purchase excess supply.[126]

(Interactive Section over)

We have explored the concept of Growth both theoretically as well as by generating a model to test the relations.

We discovered that:

- The only benefit of credit is the ability to purchase excess supply.

---

[126] One other interesting application of this could be the utilization of the interest rate to balance the amount of money present in the system. *This note becomes relevant in chapter 15.

Is Growth Without Exploitation Possible?

- That revealed to us that in a Capitalist system, the re-monetization of worker's Labour is first done by pricing their Labour with the productivity increase.

  - Meaning that they get paid less than they produce, and when they go to market the prices are more than their pay.

- This results in a continually growing excess of supply, which leads to the conclusion in the Capitalist system that credit allows for growth when really all it allows for is the full utilization of what has been produced.

- Since credit is a Capitalist circuit, it requires repayment which only exacerbates the problem as Capitalists try to make the M^R payment without hurting their Profits.

- This, in turn, hurts the consuming class, which in turn hurts the Profits, and thus we have Kaleski's business cycle.

It is for this reason that the long-term growth is actually better in a socialist structure than a Capitalist one. Especially since the socialist structure lends itself to fuller utilization of societies production without the need for credit, and without the siphoning effect it generates. That isn't to say credit is useless in a socialist system, it can be utilized strategically to direct societal production goals.

In the Capitalist system, the rate of return cannot be less than the Exchange Value of the commodities. But in a Socialist one, the limit of credit is the supply itself. That is to say production itself. The distinction is that in Capitalism, it is the living Exchange Value that is the limit. In socialism, it is both the living and the dead Exchange Value that is the limit.

We have also seen that the division of Profits helps to maintain the percent purchasing power of the economy and keep inequality out of the system, unlike Capitalism. Capitalists will attempt to boast that they increase purchasing power through productivity gains, but this is a misnomer.

Percent Purchasing Power = %of total economy goods you can purchase

Total Purchasing Power= # commodities your money can purchase.

It is the percent purchasing power that is extremely important as its maintenance ensures that massive inequality does not enter into the system. Indeed, one can argue the purchasing power increases in Capitalism but to make that argument would be to ignore that under a socialist one, those same productive increases are in existence as well if not magnified.

CHAPTER 13: HURDLES TO TRANSITION

Transition always involves friction. This is something that the Soviet Union came to realize. They took a rather hard-lined stance to some of these hurdles. However, those hard-lined stances came at the expense of freedoms and choice. The Kulaks who owned the land had their personal Property ripped away from them in favor of turning them into communal farms. This led to the backlash of kulaks slaughtering their animals, destroying their land, and working to undermine the collective. Their response while childish and selfish was in fact understandable.

To understand why they resorted to the stances they did, you must not only understand the structural reasons but also the cultural ones. We have thus far explored the structural reasons, but that is not enough to initiate change, it only informs us why change is needed. We must also understand the cultural aspects that surround the structure. Changing the structure is easy, but changing the culture that surrounds the structure is hard. Any fast implementation of these structural changes will be met with widespread cultural resistance. That resistance must be managed and managed delicately.

These cultural points of resistance are the hurdles to transition. They utilize concepts of democracy to make Capitalisms claims seem valid. As a result, the path to overcoming these hurdles is to identify the core belief that surrounds each, and then dismantle it through the narrative of democracy. Once we have discovered the talking points needed to break down the cultural resistance, we must implement a gradual policy change that alters the structure of power away from the Capitalist to the Labourer. During this transition of power, we must work to change the fundamental understandings surrounding the hurdles so that further change can be pursued.

Hurdles to Transition
-concept of Profit
-concept of Growth
-concept of Incentive
-concept of Compensation/Ownership
   Subcategory: the concept of Risk

Profit

We have already tackled this one in depth. Throughout the book, we have seen that Profit is the difference in the value the market has deemed a commodity to have, and the cost of its production. The hurdle of Profit comes in changing the understanding of who deserves to have it.

This is done by emphasizing that the individual skills of the Labourers and managers is what wages pay for. But the existence of the commodity would not be possible without the cooperation from everyone involved. As such, the Profit belongs to all those involved.

Any assertions of difference. A difference in skill, in marketing capability, in raw material procurement, any and all of those differences must be relegated to the difference of wages. Profit, however, is something that belongs to everyone involved equally. Altering this understanding of Profit eliminates the primary means of exploitation.

Growth

The concept of growth must also be changed. We cannot continue to measure growth merely in dollars. This method of measurement distorts reality and allows for the living conditions of the masses to stagnate or get worse, while those in power declare that "growth" is occurring.

To combat this, we must define growth in terms of the people. If the purchasing power of the people grows, that is growth. If our productive capacity grows, that is growth. If poverty declines and people's access to healthcare increases, those are growth. Growth is, therefore, an increase in the standard of living for the mass of the population.

Accurately accounting for that growth allows the population to inform its policies. Their votes and the policies surrounding those votes become more appropriate.[127] Understanding that growth and Profit combined lead to productivity gains focused on the well-being of the people as a whole rather than the few individuals in the ruling class.

---

[127] The tax cuts from Donald Trump did not lead to an increase in jobs, it did not lead to a rise in the people purchasing power, what it did do is lead to a decrease in public funding and an increase in the Capitalist's private wealth. The economy will "grow" by the standards we have set because we will see more investment and the bidding up of stocks, but meanwhile, the stats that actually matter have not gone anywhere. People are waking up and seeing these lies for what they are. Slowly understanding in this area is growing.

Incentive

We will never convince anyone that incentive is not essential or that Profit is not an incentive. It is, and it is a powerful incentive. The focus of the conversation regarding this hurdle is to focus on the fact that Profit is not the **most** powerful incentive. That in many cases, in fact, Profit becomes a barrier to innovation and growth.

We need to focus on the fact that the incentive of the masses is far greater than incentive for the few. That an increase in productivity instead of it generating an increase in Profits reduces the necessary working hours without affecting the pay. The incentive to work less than becomes a massive incentive for everyone to push for innovation. This is because the benefit of innovation is felt by everyone now and not just a few.

We need to focus on situations where Profit actually hinders growth. Because growth would lead to a decrease in Profits. This focus can be found in industries that are monopolized and whose Profit depends on artificial scarcity or patent rights. The health care and pharmaceutical industry is huge on this. Their Profit is in direct competition with how the field should operate. Why invest in a life-saving drug if you have drugs which manage the symptoms already? Creating a new drug won't bring you any more Profit. It is in cases like this that Profit becomes a barrier to innovation.

Energy is another one. Why invest in an unknown technology when it might not turn out to be Profitable, if it might go bust. Your current model is Profitable why rock the boat. If someone else does go out and creates an innovation, you can just be second and steal it. No need to take the risk of being the first mover. In effect, no one wants to be the first mover precisely because it is risky, they don't know if it is Profitable.

Focusing the conversation on the benefit to society, on the interest of the masses. That is a far better driver for innovation. Why invest in new drugs and research when you already have some that can manage the symptoms? So that people don't die, so they aren't forced to live their life out taking pills every day. Why invest in new forms of energy? Because we are killing the planet with our carbon emissions and if we don't alter our behavior, we will suffer in the long run. Focus the arguments on the fact that innovations serve the needs of society and as such, letting society be the driving factor for innovation is a far better source of motivation than Profit.

Also remind them that money is not the deciding factor, but Labour is. If society deems it essential, they will do the work for it.

Compensation and Ownership

This one has more to do with the very concept of ownership. The ownership of Profit, the ownership of intellectual rights etc. The most significant hurdle within this concept is the entitlement and greed that is associated with it. The belief that taking a risk entitles you to perpetual returns. That because you went out and did this one thing that you forever own the rewards from that thing. That this reward system is necessary for innovation. As you can see, the Profit and the growth all tie into this. But it's that belief that because you have done something you own it forever. This belief neglects the fact others have also done stuff too, they have contributed to the success, so where is their ownership?

Let's take a patent, for example. You go perform chemistry, and you create a new drug. You put in the work; you own the rights to the formula. But you used the tools provided to you by society, the literature of all those scientists papers whose previous work you relied upon. Is it right that only you receive the benefit at the cost of the community? Yes, you should be rewarded, but perpetually? Should finite work guarantee perpetual returns? Should your intellectual Property on something natural that might have been discovered by someone else entitle you to prevent someone else from ever creating that something? You found the drug, but you get to charge whatever you want for it? You get to prevent others from utilizing that chemical composition? That's absurd.

The best way to combat this is to focus on the fact that nature should not be able to be monopolized. That innovation serves to benefit society, not one individual. That it is a society that allowed the individual to discover it, but that the reward of perpetual ownership was not necessary to the discovery. That yes reward is a powerful incentive, but that continuous ownership should not be in the cards for that reward. This is actually very anti-Capitalist in terms of ideology. It is the utilization of the state by one Capitalist to limit competition, to protect the Profits of the few. This is but another way Capitalism utilizes the state for its own benefit, to reduce its competition.

Focusing on the fact that this type of ownership is detrimental to society as the whole is how we need to proceed. That yes you made it, but that doesn't entitle you to the perpetual ownership of the idea. Doing so stifles competition and innovation by locking away advancements behind an imaginary door of Property. You should not be able to own an idea. Ideas themselves should reside in the public domain. If you create something and it gets reverse engineered, that's perfectly fine. Why? Because it allows for innovation to occur, it is better for society as a whole. If you apply the concept of Profit, growth, and incentive to this understanding, you see how Capitalism is actually impeding innovation not spurring it on.

But what about ownership of the Profit. Why should that belong to the workers when I am the one who took the risk with my money?

Risk

Let's start this one with a story. I have a friend whose daughter just graduated from college. She has gotten in with a startup beverage company. They pay her a wage, and she does all the coordination with label makers, flavor testers, market researchers, etc. Having put in all that work, she thought it only natural to receive a stake in the company. After all, it was her Labour that even allowed this company to come into existence, she was essential to its creation, she's basically the one who has built it. Without the workers, herself coordinating, the scientists testing the flavor, the artists making the label designs, and the analysts doing the market analysis, this company could not exist. Low and behold, it is the owner of cash who took everything in the end. All the work that went into the creation of this company. All those who did the work to stand it up. Simply paid and forgotten. No stock, no ownership, no say.

Our society deems this right, Capitalism deems this right. It says those individuals took the risk with their money. Without that risk, none of those workers would have done the Labour to create the company. We won't even touch on the question of how they got the money in the first place. We have seen through this book how primitive accumulation occurs. If they worked for and gradually earned the money that they are investing that is absolutely a real risk. But that is not how Capitalists work. They work off of M-C-M'. Those owners paid others to build a business, doing very little to no work and then take everything for themselves. The idea being, well if it fails and the workers are out of a job, they can always go find other work, they are no worse off.

One could then argue that, well, the same is true for the Capitalist. To which you then get the rebuttal of, but they lost all that money. To which you reply, well they are no worse off. The idea that you should have perpetual ownership of a project that you have worked with other people to create simply because you supply the materials is the conceptual root of validating inequality in this system. If you buy ingredients for a meal and your friend cooks that meal, and you both eat it. Afterwards, when the meal is over, they want a share of the leftovers. Do you say, no? Does it feel right to say no? You see, we recognize the moral violation in other areas of our lives, but we refuse to acknowledge it in the economic sector due to the conditioning of being brought up in such a system.

The risk argument is perhaps the most frustrating one to combat. We recognize the inequality, we realize the exploitation that is occurring, we may even understand the detriments such a structure has on the system as a whole. Yet we still find ourselves having this little voice saying the Capitalists deserve ownership due to the risk. Let's break down the flaws with this mode of thinking.

First, we can submit and say sure, the investor deserves an increased rate of the return initially, however once that Capital has been returned, the risk is gone. This leads us to the first flaw in this argument. That risk is temporary, while exploitation is perpetual.

Second, is the concept that the worker did not take a risk. This is an absurd argument as workers generally get paid at the end of the month for the work that they did during the month. This means that Capitalists obtain the money to pay the workers before they actually pay them. If the company goes under then so too do those wages that were meant for the worker. More importantly, the worker is more reliant on income than a Capitalist is, their consumption, and therefore, survival depends on having that job. Losing a job and "being no worse off" neglects the fact that the pain inflicted on the aftermath for the worker is at a much harsher degree than it is for the Capitalist. The only time this second argument does not apply is as is the case for the above situation where Capitalists pay up front. But this brings us to #3.

Third, how big is the risk actually? Capitalists have more wealth than they need to consume, and they utilize that wealth to invest in things to make them more money. How significant then is the risk to justify the perpetual exploitation. For my friend's daughter's case, let's analyze that situation. She, the scientists, artists, and analyst's Labour combined with the Capitalist's money have created a Profitable beverage company. Those workers have sacrificed months to years of their lives, creating this while the Capitalist has risked what? 1/36th of their wealth perhaps.[128] Is that really a risk? Does that

---

[128] This becomes even more apparent when you consider the fact that "market research" can give you a general probability of how Profitable something will be. If the research suggests, something has a decent chance of being Profitable, like the analysts in the example. And if you apply a smaller amount of your wealth toward that investment then the odds of success, is that really a risk? If you have a 1/10 chance of a company being Profitable and you invest 1/20th of your wealth. You are bound to find 2 Profitable companies given

really justify sole ownership over the combined product? Do you really think that permits you to say no to sharing the leftovers of the meal?

Fourth, is combating the argument that if the risk were low, then the workers would take it themselves. So let's utilize a casino example to dismiss this argument. You work for a casino. You get paid a wage, but your salary is smaller than the cost of a minimum chip needed to be able to play in the casino. You get told all the time about some lucky bastard who saved up, got a chip and won big. But you realize that the game is rigged against you. That your saving up to play in the casino will most likely result in the loss of your money. It is only those with money who can gamble with it so freely.

If the economy were non-exploitative, the very structure would encourage the cooperation of individuals since their combined success yields more substantial Profits for all involved in that company. Being a part of a company gives you the incentive to help that company succeed so you can get a more massive payout, and then utilize those savings to build your own company. This risk argument, while conditioned into our very beings, is simply an absurd attempt to justify perpetual exploitation in the current system.

I will end this section with a long quote from Professor Richard Wolff in regards to Risk.

"Why are we in the position of doing all the work here, having to beg to get more of what we produce? There is something wrong here. Why are we not a part of the apparatus that decides what to do with what we have produced? Don't we have some claim on the output that our brains and muscles helped to produce?... You know if you grow up in the United States you hear often from employers or people who have been bamboozled by them, that gee the employer takes the risk. He deserves some extra, some Profit because he took some risk. I always found this extraordinary. He did take a risk...but so did everybody else... What?! The worker who moved into this state to get that job, took a *Risk*. That the job would be there, that the job would be bearable, that the job would pay enough. Took a *Risk!* He takes a risk everyday he comes in. He doesn't know whether at the end of the day he'll be told not to show up tomorrow. He bought a house based on the *Risk* that, that income would be coming. *Risk*, everybody takes. The difference between the employer and the employee is the employee takes a risk and then somebody else makes the decisions. The employer takes the

those odds. That's not risk, that's a guarantee.

[142]

risk but he's got all the power, to shape whether that *risk* works out. And whenever he has trouble you know where he shifts the burden? *Hmm mmh*, he fires the workers. Because he doesn't want to bear the cost of the *Risk*, he took that didn't work out. If you want to reward risk, *all the workers get a piece of that...* Stop it, in fact your risk is less, because you're rich. You take a part of your money, if you lose that part, it doesn't shake you, but the worker, he has no wealth to fall back on, has no savings account. The risk he takes is if he gets fired, he's lost, **you're not!**" -Professor Richard Wolfe, Economist

At the end of the day, it is the combination of Labour and money that created the company. Thus, the ownership of the company (the commodity) should be shared between all involved. They all took the risk.

CHAPTER 14: POLICIES TO STRUCTURALLY OVERCOME THE HURDLES

Those hurdles being:
Profit, Growth, Incentive, and Ownership.

The goals of the policies need to focus on altering the power relationship between the Capitalist and the Labourer. They need to work at making structural changes that enforce the culture change we desire around those four hurdles:

Profit
- Policies need to increase Labour's voice in decisions involving Profit
- Policies need to increase Labour's ownership of the Profits
- Policies need to undermine the M-C-M' circuit or remove it completely if possible

Growth
- Policies need to enforce proper measurement of growth
- Policies need to implement real growth
    - Doing so creates a positive feedback to the people giving the policies validity
- Policies need to create positive examples outside of the United States as well.
    - By allowing socialism to spread in the third world through advocating democracy in both the political sphere as well as the economic sphere, we bolster the validity of the system.

Incentive
- Policies should enforce to the people what non-Profit incentive is.
- Policies should focus on rewarding non-Profit incentives
- The incentive of the policy should always be the betterment of the people

Ownership
- Policies should focus on societal ownership of necessities
- They should not initially ban, but should first limit perpetual ownership.
  - They should gradually transfer ownership from individuals to the society where patents are involved.
  - They should outline a reasonable timeline and a reasonable reward for ownership
- Policies should work to increase communal ownership of the means of production.

Some Policy ideas that serve these intents

Each policy will have a difficulty rating associated with it (1,2, or 3, 3 being the hardest). This comes from the level of "freedoms" that will claim to be attacked based on the hurdles we have analyzed. **1** means that no freedoms are being violated and should not meet much cultural opposition. **2** means that some liberties may be perceived to be violated and the hurdles will offer friction to the implementation. **3** implies that the "freedoms" of the old system will be breached and thus, firmly opposed.

1. Bernie Sanders proposed Law mandating at least 50% of a company's board of directors be Labour. (**2**)
    a. This policy idea enforces the cultural change in Profit and incentive.
        i. It provides a step toward the Profit cultural change by increasing Labour's voice in the say of how Profits are spent.
        ii. It provides a step toward an incentive cultural change by increasing Labour's voice in where the company is heading.
2. Jeremy Corbin's "Right to Own" cooperative solution which gives workers first rights on buying out a company that is being dissolved, sold, or floated on the stock exchange. (**1**)
    a. This can even be furthered by providing government assistance toward the purchasing of these companies by the workers
    b. Promoted even more by providing training in the managing and running of a cooperative

              i. This provides a step forward in the ownership category of cultural change, which in turn offers a cultural change to all the hurdles at once.
3. Setting up a national cooperative bank. Where any cooperative that is set up via government action is automatically a member. **(1)**
    a. This provides cooperatives with a community of support from which they can draw from. It also allows for the creation of interest-free credit within the cooperatives. This would make them more competitive against Capitalist corporations.
    b. Corporate taxes could be reduced for cooperatives, or instead of reduced have them funneled into the bank to serve as the reserves for the interest-free credit. This would then incentivize the loaning out of those reserves to improve the productivity of the cooperatives.
         i. This policy focuses on the growth portion of the hurdles. By making cooperatives more competitive with Capitalist companies, we also get to witness the different kinds of incentives that arise out of a democratized economy.
4. Cooperative resource sharing program. Extra materials are put into a communal pool, and the transportation cost is taken care of by the government. **(1)**
    a. This is a recycling program that allows for complete usage of extra resources. And sharing of resources between cooperatives.
5. Allow Latin American countries to pursue democracy. Simply make a public statement to all of Latin America that the United States will no longer impose sanctions on countries who try to democratize their workplaces and governments. Announce that we will provide aid and expertise in building up a cooperative economy. **(2)**[129]
    a. That we will incentivize cooperatives within the Latin American economy (or any 3rd world economy) by trading with them at cost. That means our Labour value equivalent to theirs.
    b. This will make their cooperatives far more competitive than their Capitalist enterprises and create a democratized economy in the third world.

---

[129] This will receive massive pushback from corporations who are benefiting off of those countries. Name calling of communist will be common.

    c.   This while detrimental to us in the short term is of long-term benefit to us. Latin America has resources which we need. Up until now, we have been taking them by force and deceit. The people know this and resent us. By helping to give the people a voice, by making the economy theirs we do two things.
        i.   First, we win their admiration. We right the wrongs of the policies of the past.
        ii. Two, we give them an economy where their productivity increases become our gain as well. By building them up, we, in turn, build ourselves up even more.
        iii. This satisfies the ownership principle and more than that, it provides the entirety of the third world with examples of how democracy in both the political and economic sphere can create prosperity. This serves as an essential step into transitioning not just us, but the world out of Capitalist stagnation and into socialist prosperity.

6. Altering the rules surrounding patents, eliminating sole ownership and instead implementing a royalty system. (**2**)
    a.   This ensures that the current incentive structure is still in place and that guarantees buy-in from the masses, while at the same time, it serves to reduce the Capitalist ownership opening these areas up to competition and innovation.
    b. Something as simple as 1% of Profits for 10 years, or 0.1% of Profits depending on what it is.
        i.   For example, if a company utilizes your patent, all the Profit associated with the utilization of the patent you get a small chunk of.
        ii. This serves to reduce Capitalist ownership and promote Profit sharing.

7. The breaking up of natural monopolies such as electricity and internet. (**2**)
    a.   Instead of forcefully taking away someone's company or property, you divert enough resources to either buy them out keeping all the employees in place, or you build up your own state enterprise to compete with the company.
        i.   The issue here becomes the infrastructure. Grids and cables are already in place.
        ii. But those grids and infrastructures are ageing and in need of desperate upgrades.

iii. Building up of new infrastructure gives the government the benefit of then owning said infrastructure. Making their services of higher quality and able to be offered without the Profit incentive, thereby making them the better cheaper option to the consumer.
   b. The entirety of the work should not be contracted out. Specialists can be purchased, but we must implement the Chinese policy. Have our own engineers standing by learning the process during the first couple projects and then taking over afterwards.
      i. China can build an entire 20 story building in 90 hours. They have a very efficient building structure in place already. We can contract out to one of their companies for the first couple projects with the same rules they applied to us.
         1. That we have someone standing over their shoulder, learning the process from them.
      ii. This is how the government becomes the best in these areas. This is how we grow our knowledge of production and management. [130]

8. Nationalize our natural resources. The earth belongs to everyone, it belongs to society as a whole, not just a single individual. Also nationalizing them gets rid of many of the lobbyists who influence public policy to protect the Profit of those companies. **(3)**
   a. Through nationalization, we ensure that control of the country's resources belong to the people.
   b. The Profits from the land of the United States should go to the people of the United States.
9. Pursue Roosevelt's and Bernie Sanders Economic Bill of Rights and get those added into the Constitution. **(2)**
   a. The right to work
   b. The right to a living wage
   c. The right to a decent home
   d. The right to adequate medical care

---

[130] Private vs Public is a silly debate. At the end of the day, it is people who do the work. What their skills are and how they are managed. In the current system, private simply pays more than public and as such pulls better people. The government can do the same thing, pay for expertise and the training of individuals in specific sectors, making them SMEs.

- e. The right of sufficient protection from economic fears of old age, sickness, accident, and unemployment
- f. The right to a good education
- g. The right to sound banking and financial services
- h. The right to a safe and clean environment
    - i. We will touch on many of these in coming chapters, but these serve to disrupt the power balance of the class system. It gives the worker protection from accepting low wages out of necessity for survival.

10. Breaking up of the banks. Having the government be the provider of credit. (3)
    - a. Control of the money should be in government and not private hands in the first place
    - b. By having it in control of the government, policies of old like debt jubilees can be performed
        - i. Remember, credit simply allows you to purchase the excess Labour that has already been created.
        - ii. Once spent the paying back of credit can actually be halted at any time with zero consequence to the general economy except for increasing the amount of circulating money.
        - iii. This frees up the consumers class's wallets to spend on items of value instead of paying down debt. Paying down debt is only good for:
            1. Increasing the Profits of the banks
            2. Removing money from circulation
    - c. This means that once in control, the government can wipe the slate clean with a positive effect on the economy as it would free up spending power for consumption, which then raises demand and gives us a kickstart for growth.
        - i. This policy tackles the ownership aspect of an essential service, and it serves to disrupt the Profit hurdle as well by attacking a core sector that relies on the M-C-M' circuit.
        - ii. Breaking down these pillars changes them into the minority, and as a result, makes the dialogue on discussing how morally wrong their exploitation was much easier to have. The same process applied for slavery and serfdom. [131]

11. Changing the structure of the media, removing its Profit incentive. **(3)**
    a. A free press is absolutely essential to a functioning democracy, but that means a press that is free of control from any form of authoritarian control; Government or economic.
        i. If the Capitalist class owns the media, the media will naturally not report on events that go against their interests. (coverage of Pol Pot genocide but absolute silence on the U.S backed East Timor genocide for example)
        ii. The media should serve the masses, not the elite.
    b. One idea on how to overcome this is by government funding of a non-biased media whose workers are voted for by the people.
    c. Another way is through subsidizing cooperative media outlets. Ones where the reporters themselves are the owners.
        i. Hard to say how this idea would turn out. There are conflicting interests. The interest of money which the reporters can all cash in on by selling out to the wills of the advertisers, and the interest of honest reporting.
        ii. I am reluctant to say, but even with a cooperative structure here, the necessity for the elite to control the narrative through the media is far too high for it to stave off corruption.
12. The implementation of a maximum wage **(3)**
    a. A maximum wage does one main thing
        i. It stops companies, both private and cooperative, from sitting on an effective model and hoarding the benefits of that model solely for themselves. Jeff Bezos with Amazon for example.
            1. This provides the incentive to either increase worker pay, or hire more

---

[131] When you are a part of a system, you want to get ahead, and when the way to get ahead is through exploitation, it is against your interest to criticize it. Because to criticize it means that your desire to get ahead makes that criticism now apply to yourself. No one likes to criticize themselves or think themselves morally in the wrong. So, they justify the system as a way to avoid the hard truth that they are indeed perpetuating exploitation by engaging in it.

individuals at the same pay and reduce everyone's hours.
   2. Re-invest in the productivity of the company allowing for the reduction of everyone's hours, or the increase in everyone's pay.
b. This can be done through the use of taxation brackets as it is now. The rate of taxation simply climbs up to 100%. Capping off at some maximum wage determined by the populous.
   i. My personal recommendation would be not to exceed the ratio that is present within current governmental structures.
      1. That's a ratio of roughly 1/13 between the bottom pay and the top pay. E1= $1,700/month, and O-10 = $21,500/month
   ii. Whatever is implemented as the living wage can be multiplied by 13 to achieve the maximum wage. If it is $50,000 then a wage of $650,000 would be the max.
   iii. The question that needs to be asked in determining this ratio is: is the Labour Power these individuals are performing X times greater than the Labour done by an average person. In the example we ask, arc they really doing 13 times the amount of work? 13 times more input in time, intensity, skill, monotony, and stress?
      1. No, this will not stop someone from being motivated. Motivated individuals don't do it for the money, Tesla and Westinghouse certainly didn't.
      2. Edison maybe, but if you do the patent law right then royalties on new patents are not included in this maximum wage. Individuals who are then motivated by money will have to continuously chase productivity if they want to make more than the max.

CHAPTER 15:
STRUCTURAL POLICY GOALS:
SOCIAL SECURITY & TAXATION

We see the hurdles; we have some strategies and even some transitional policies. Now we need a direction, we need goals to reach toward. This chapter will start with social security as a tool into understanding the government's role in providing services and its utilization of taxation. With this understanding, we will see that the idea of "cost" is illusionary when it comes to government expenditure and that the only thing that matters is the society's capacity to work and the proportionality of the money utilized in the exchange of that work. Let's begin with what Social Security is.

Social Security is the recognition that to survive, one must work, but that there comes a point where working is no longer possible. As such, that person is given an amount of money to allow for continued survival, and this is termed, Social Security. If we are to abolish the M-C-M' principle, methods by which people save for retirement will also become obsolete. So how then do we address the social security question? Quite simple, actually. You provide it to them for free. Just give them money that is of a living wage. Here is why.

When they were working, they were increasing the productivity of the economy. That productivity increase is what allows for the supply to meet the demand in the current economy. This means that social security is paid for by the extra hours of work needed to create the supply. Without that generation's contribution to the productivity of society, those hours would have had to be worked anyway. In all likelihood, the productivity increase was greater than the extra hours needed to work to supply for the retired populations increase on demand. In other words, no one is giving them anything for free, they have already earned it, and are merely taking back what they have already contributed.

In effect we pay for it by the same mechanism in which Capitalists currently take Profit. By continuing to charge for the productivity increases as if Labour was still doing the work. This will not lead to Crisis in this situation because by giving it as Social Security means that it will enter back into circulation. Remember that a Crisis forms when productivity is treated as Free

Labour and Capitalists remove that siphoned value out of circulation. We therefore, do not see a reduction in the purchasing power of the consuming class with Social Security like we do when Capitalists take the Profit.

This method of paying for social security is the right way to do things. However, this structure is decentralized away from the government. It utilizes the circuit of production and pricing to pay for social security. But that needn't be the case, that is merely a way of understanding why we can pay for it without influencing purchasing power. The source of the social security doesn't have to originate from company or cooperative. We simply provide from the government to the retired citizens a living wage. The main economic effect of this is the addition of demand to the market. We don't need to worry about it from there, as the companies will produce to the demand automatically. It is as simple as that.

The only other economic effect that we need to concern ourselves with is the increase to the amount of circulating money. This is where taxes come in. As a way of reducing the amount of circulating money. In fact, the only role for taxes should be as an instrument to control the amount of circulating money.[132] You can view it as a way to pay for social security, but that is flawed. Work is what allows the economy to continue. As long as demand doesn't outstrip the ability to supply there is no detriment to the economy, everything beyond that is secondary.[133] All social security does is increase demand. Taxes, serve in this case, to balance out the money supply to keep prices from elevating as a result of more money in circulation. Taxes therefore serve to prevent Labour Re-monetization.

In the non-exploitative system of *Profits to all* advocated throughout this book, that "*all*" would include society, and having a portion of the Profits go toward taxes as a means of regulating the currency supply is only natural.[134]

---

[132] Government prints money, it provides that money to the people as a means of exchanging Labour value. It doesn't need to be paid back anything since it can print it. Thus, putting money into the economy is a way to direct social production, and taking money out is a way to balance circulating currency to prevent Labour re-monetization.

[133] We can prove this to ourselves through the national debt. That is the government's influx of money into the economy that hasn't been taken out in taxes. But the reason we don't have massive inflation is that the Capitalist class continually siphons that money out of circulation away from consumption. Government spending is the only reason the economy is still functioning at the moment. Without its influxes of money, the purchasing power of the consuming class would have fallen to drastically low levels by now, and revolution would have occurred.

Let's do a thought experiment to understand why taxation is only a means of controlling the currency supply and nothing more.

Setup
- You have a functioning economy of 10 workers.
- Those 10 workers each produce $1 worth of Labour value.
- One of them retires and is unable to work.
- Because he is unable to contribute Labour value, he is also unable to consume.
- This means that the economy is now at 9 workers each producing $1 worth of value.
- We provide that retired individual with $1 Social Security so he can survive.
- We now have $10 in the economy for $9 of Labour which means that Labour is now re-monetized to $0.90 unless we remove that extra dollar by taxation.
    - The taxation's only role is to maintain the purchasing power of the workers, and prevent Labour re-monetization

Let's utilize a Capitalist system for a second. To provide a similar perspective on how taxation works.
- 9 workers, 1 retiree, 1 Capitalist.
- Workers each spend their $1 in wages in this first round and the retiree gets $1 in social security.
- Capitalist makes $10 and takes 10% out for himself. This divvies up the $9 to the workers.
    - Each worker makes $1, and the Capitalist still makes $1
    - We see that by taxing here in order to "pay" for social security what would happen is that we would be reducing the purchasing power of the workers.
    - Taxation in this particular example is not needed because the Capitalist removed the Social Security from circulation through the actions of their Profit taking and money hoarding.
    - It is for this reason the sole purpose of taxation is the maintenance of the proportionality of money to the Labour performed. That is the maintenance of the population's purchasing power. Taxation has no other role than that.[135]

---

[134] This could be done through several measures, a sales tax would perhaps be the best way once a non-exploitative system is in place, until then, however, taxation of wages and Profits is the way to go.

Structure

We have so far tackled the money portion of why we can provide Social Security, now for the analysis that really matters. That is the actual ability for the society to accommodate the demand that the retired population will bring to the market. We say that this isn't an issue because: *The increases to societal productivity produced during the lifetime of work the retired population performed has added more to supply than their future demand could possibly remove.*

We can think through this in yet another thought experiment. Let's imagine a single retired worker in a population of 10 people.
- When a worker starts, let's say everyone worked 10 hours.
    - That is 100 total hours with 10 workers
- If during her working years she provided more productivity increase than her percentage of the working class, then there is absolutely nothing to worry about.
    - That is, she makes up 10% of the working class, so her productivity contribution needs to be more than that.
- Let's say the worker provided 11% production increase throughout her working life.
- This means that at the start of her working life, 100 hours of work was needed to meet demand. In the end, only 89 hours of work was needed to meet the demand.
- This woman's living wage then is 8.9 hours' worth of Exchange Value
    - That is the living wage provided to her by the government.
- Society has still prospered even with taking care of the retired because the total amount of work hours needed to satisfy demand is now only 97.9.

If we split generations up every 20 years. 20-40 is a generation, and 40-60 is a generation. 60-80 is a generation, and the 80-100 is where most people tend to die off, and their consumption drops significantly, so they will only be counted as half of a generation. This means that throughout a generation's life, they simply need to make an economy that can increase its production capacity to take care of them. This has certainly happened over the last several

---

[135] We can also see that in Capitalism when Profit is moving money out of the economy it is hurting the purchasing power of the workers. This leads to the interesting observation that this can be counterbalanced by government spending to maintain the purchasing power. So, the more Profit that is taken the more government spending can occur to counterbalance this. The downside of pursuing this observation is this basically leads to a perpetual increase in the wealth of the Capitalist facilitated by the government.

generations. Our production capabilities have skyrocketed. Therefore, there is no physical limitation to the system in being able to provide for the social security of the retired generations. The only limitation is our will.

Taxation

Let's look into other examples of taxation to enforce that it is but the mechanism by which the government can control the currency supply.

Military expenditures, for example:

Paying a soldier to manage the payroll for other soldiers who manage a network for other soldiers who monitor the world. Effectively nothing is getting produced.[136] As Non-Productive Labour, they are an expense of the government.

In today's understanding, we say that tax dollars pay for the budget. This is, in fact, false, as government services and taxation are merely two sides of the same coin. Injection of money into the economy and removal of money from the economy. For example, Military expenditure is a massive injection of money into the economy. This injection will lead to the re-monetization of Labour if it is not removed from circulation. To avoid this outcome, taxation is utilized. It removes currency from circulation to maintain the balance between Labour value and money. [137]

---

[136] It could easily be argued that this pays for the security of trade, and is a necessary expense for the perpetuation of peaceful relations and that historically military adventures such as GPS and Nuclear energy have been productive. That really isn't a concern for this argument. We will simply assume that they are not Productive Labour.

[137] In current times companies whom military expenditure goes to take Profits and remove money from circulation through the taking of these Profits. In a non-exploitative system, the government would fulfil this role of removing currency from circulation. The difference between the two being we don't have to concern ourselves with some fictitious national debt that means absolutely nothing. The supplier of currency cannot be in debt, it is impossible, what the debt actually means is the level by which the Labourers are getting screwed over by Capitalists. We can see the value that has been taken away. Profits are utilized to buy security bonds which the government must then pay back. Paying them back is never the issue, the issue is that the Profits taken by the Capitalist to purchase these security bonds were taken via the exploitation described in this book. As a result, the national debt becomes a way to at least wag at the levels by which Capitalists have exploited Labour.

Therefore, the goal of government is to provide services which the society needs while utilizing taxation to manage the money supply. The critical difference in this understanding is that if the government fails at its taxation portion, the only thing that happens is that Labour value is re-monetized. Prices change, that's it. The work to make all those services happen was still performed, and the products they created are still there. The only tangible difference in the system that remains is the amount of circulating money.

It is this understanding of taxation that is so important to internalize. It is for this reason that the government has the capability of pursuing all of the policy examples I am about to lay out in the following pages. From Energy to Education, Healthcare, Infrastructure, and beyond. The question of "affordability" should never even come up for all the reasons outlined above. The only questions that matters are "do we have the Labour Power to perform it?", and "does it benefit society?" If we can say yes to both of those questions. There is no logical reason to not pursue.

CHAPTER 16:
STRUCTURAL POLICY GOALS: ENERGY[138]

Hands down the goal that will have the most significant impact on the human condition is Energy. Energy is the most critical resource we have. It is what powers innovation, and drives prosperity. It lifts us up out of poverty and gives us the ability to produce far beyond our normal means. One of the claims of Capitalism is that it has overseen the most significant growth in human history and has lifted more people out of poverty than any other period. It claims that it has accomplished this due to the efficiency of the system. But to make this claim inherently neglects the importance of Energy. It applies credit where credit is not deserved. Capitalism was lucky that its existence coincided with the largest discovery of Energy in human history. It oversaw the discovery of Steam, Coal, Oil, Renewable, and Nuclear. It is Energy which has lifted us up and human ingenuity that has harnessed it. Capitalism is not essential for human Ingenuity, Copernicus and Newton can attest to that. It is, therefore, Energy, which is the most crucial policy goal we can set, because it is Energy which has allowed for growth and prosperity to occur more so than any other factor.

The United States currently believe this. In fact, securing Energy is our #1 priority, and we pursue that policy with such vigor that should any source of Energy be stopped from becoming ours we view it as a threat to national security. It is, however, this very mindset which this book aims to undermine. We pursue Energy for Profit in this system, not for the betterment of all. This is evident by our lack of pursuit forward into the science of Energy.

Oil and Coal are great, and they have a large energy density, but they are outdated. We have run through our peak supplies and are travelling down the mountain. Besides that, our emissions of CO_2 into the atmosphere are at catastrophic levels and need to be brought down for the sake of the planet. The only option is to start vigorously researching new energy alternatives.

Research into Solar and Wind need to continue, but we must be honest with ourselves. These are not viable options to replace the energy dependence

---

[138] https://andrewplotner.com/Nuclear & https://andrewplotner.com/Energy

that we have on oil and gas. One of the big reasons is that the production of Solar and Wind energy requires significant usages of oil and gas. Therefore, we must first break that dependence. Continue to research, but laser focus our time and resources into a specific direction.

That direction is Nuclear. Now before you go apocalyptic and freak out, let me provide some education on the topic of Nuclear Energy to wash away all the fear-mongering that has surrounded it.

What is Nuclear Energy?

It is the Energy which is released from the fusion or fission of atoms. Everything around you is made up of atoms, and at the center of those atoms is a concentration of mass called the nucleus. The nucleus is composed of protons and neutrons. It is held together through Nuclear forces. These forces are vital because Protons act like magnets of the same polarity. They like to repel. As the number of protons increases disproportionately to the number of neutrons needed, the stability of the atom becomes harder to maintain.

1																	18
1 H 1.008	2											13	14	15	16	17	2 He 4.0026
3 Li 6.94	4 Be 9.0122											5 B 10.81	6 C 12.011	7 N 14.007	8 O 15.999	9 F 18.998	10 Ne 20.180
11 Na 22.990	12 Mg 24.305	3	4	5	6	7	8	9	10	11	12	13 Al 26.982	14 Si 28.085	15 P 30.974	16 S 32.06	17 Cl 35.45	18 Ar 39.948
19 K 39.098	20 Ca 40.078	21 Sc 44.956	22 Ti 47.867	23 V 50.942	24 Cr 51.996	25 Mn 54.938	26 Fe 55.845	27 Co 58.933	28 Ni 58.693	29 Cu 63.546	30 Zn 65.38	31 Ga 69.723	32 Ge 72.630	33 As 74.922	34 Se 78.97	35 Br 79.904	36 Kr 83.798
37 Rb 85.468	38 Sr 87.62	39 Y 88.906	40 Zr 91.224	41 Nb 92.906	42 Mo 95.95	43 Tc (98)	44 Ru 101.07	45 Rh 102.91	46 Pd 106.42	47 Ag 107.87	48 Cd 112.41	49 In 114.82	50 Sn 118.71	51 Sb 121.76	52 Te 127.60	53 I 126.90	54 Xe 131.29
55 Cs 132.91	56 Ba 137.33	57-71 *	72 Hf 178.49	73 Ta 180.95	74 W 183.84	75 Re 186.21	76 Os 190.23	77 Ir 192.22	78 Pt 195.08	79 Au 196.97	80 Hg 200.59	81 Tl 204.38	82 Pb 207.2	83 Bi 208.98	84 Po (209)	85 At (210)	86 Rn (222)
87 Fr (223)	88 Ra (226)	89-103 #	104 Rf (265)	105 Db (268)	106 Sg (271)	107 Bh (270)	108 Hs (277)	109 Mt (276)	110 Ds (281)	111 Rg (280)	112 Cn (285)	113 Nh (286)	114 Fl (289)	115 Mc (289)	116 Lv (293)	117 Ts (294)	118 Og (294)

* Lanthanide series	57 La 138.91	58 Ce 140.12	59 Pr 140.91	60 Nd 144.24	61 Pm (145)	62 Sm 150.36	63 Eu 151.96	64 Gd 157.25	65 Tb 158.93	66 Dy 162.50	67 Ho 164.93	68 Er 167.26	69 Tm 168.93	70 Yb 173.05	71 Lu 174.97
# Actinide series	89 Ac (227)	90 Th 232.04	91 Pa 231.04	92 U 238.03	93 Np (237)	94 Pu (244)	95 Am (243)	96 Cm (247)	97 Bk (247)	98 Cf (251)	99 Es (252)	100 Fm (257)	101 Md (258)	102 No (259)	103 Lr (262)

For example, let us understand Uranium #92. The 92 stands for the number of protons in the nucleus. The number underneath it is the combined protons and neutrons of the nucleus. This version of Uranium, U^{238}, simply means that the most abundant form of Uranium is the version of Uranium that has 92 Protons and 146 Neutrons. That is, however, a lot of protons bunched together in the nucleus of a single atom, all of whom are trying to repel each other. This means that Uranium is going to experience radiation to try and make itself more stable.

What is Radiation?

Radiation is the spontaneous release of Energy. The release of this Energy occurs through the emission of Alpha particles (2 protons and 2 electrons), Beta particles (electrons or positrons), and Gamma rays (Photons). Each of these forms of radiation contains a different amount of Energy. For example, Alpha particle radiation can be blocked by a piece of paper[139] While Beta particles can be blocked by a sheet of aluminum foil, and gamma particles require a block of lead. With that being said, it must be noted that radiation is not really all that dangerous, once you understand it. You see, the body has a tremendous ability to repair itself from radiation. The danger comes from receiving radiation amounts that are beyond the body's ability to repair. Radiation is measured in Micro-Sieverts (μSv) or 1/1000th of a Milli-Sievert (mSv). The human body experiences a steady state of background radiation of around 0.15 μSv/hour. Natural items such as bananas have higher than average background radiation. So, you can see that merely saying that something is radioactive is not very informative. For example, I can say that bananas are radioactive for 1.3 billion years, yet you know bananas are not dangerous.[140] What is helpful is to understand how much radiation is being emitted per hour, and to look and see if you are receiving more than what is considered to be a safe dose of radiation (typically an accepted range is less than 50 millisieverts a year, or 50,000 μSv/year). To give you an idea of what would lead to this, reference the chart below for comparison.

---

[139] This is mainly due to it having the largest mass of the emissions types. It actually does the most damage, but because it is so large, it has next to no penetrating power. Throw a boulder (alpha particles) at a wooden wall, and then it will stop. The wall will be destroyed, but the boulder will have stopped. Now shoot a bullet at that same wall (gamma), the wall won't be destroyed, but it will have sustained damage, as will anything behind it since the bullet kept on going.

[140] Unless you're the indigenous population being exploited by United Fruit.

Material/Activity	µSv/hour
X-Ray/ 2 packs of cigarettes	50-100 (single dose)
Uranium (4.5 billion year half-life)	75-160
Flying on a Plane	200
3-Mile Island	1000
Sun Bathing(no sunscreen)	3,650
CT Scan (Head-Heart)	2,000-16,000 (single dose)

The rate of emission or decay is measured in what is called a half-life. A half-life is the time it takes for half of the material to undergo radioactive decay. If I have 10 grams of Uranium, after 4.5 billion years I will then have 5 grams of Uranium since half of it has undergone radioactive decay. It is for this reason that a long half-life should not breed fear. It merely means that there is only so much Energy contained within a material and that Energy is being released very slowly. Thus, its µSv/hour is small and it is not all that dangerous. It is the shorter half-life radioactive elements which are truly dangerous (elements such as Cesium-137 with a half-life of 30 years). This is because they release their Energy at a rate which is greater than our bodies ability to repair. If you hear that something will be radioactive for millions of years, I want you to recognize that this is a good thing, because it is not releasing a lot of Energy and therefore it is safer than something that is releasing Energy for only a couple years or even a couple seconds. This is because the more radiation you receive in a single dose, the more dangerous it is, because your body cannot keep up with the repair.

Those are the principles behind why radiation can be dangerous. But within those principles are the reasons as to how we can hack nature for Energy. It allows us to utilize the instability of these large atomic nuclei to generate a continuous process of energy release.

This is done through Nuclear fission, which is the process of shooting a neutron at one of these unstable nuclei, giving it just enough Energy to cause it to burst apart. This explosion results in two new atoms of different mass and the release of Energy. This Energy is in the form of heat, light, and sometimes particles. If the explosion releases more than 2 neutrons consistently, this allows a chain reaction to occur where one atom bursts apart sending out multiple neutrons that then collide with other atoms causing them to do the same. This releases a massive amount of heat which we then utilize to create electricity through the generation of steam and the funneling of that steam through high and low-pressure steam turbines.

This release of Energy is what led to the Manhattan Project in the '40s. This is because whenever you contain the release of Energy, you can capture the dispersed force and release it in a single instant. That instant is the moment the container holding back that force is breached. If you light a whole bunch of sparklers, nothing happens, but if you bind them in duct tape and then light them all together that builds up force and releases it all at once.

This is the very reason why the first uses of Nuclear Energy were as weapons. But that reality should not limit us to pigeonholing it into just that category. Nuclear Energy is but a natural phenomenon that we can utilize for the benefit of humanity. We know that oil can be used as a weapon, yet we recognize it is also beneficial. It is all dependent on how it is used. Let's first understand the potential benefits of Nuclear, then look at its detriments, and the risks associated with it to discover how we can reduce those risks while still allowing us to capture the largest amount of benefit possible.

Benefits of Nuclear Energy

Material	Energy Density (MJ/Kg)	100W light Bulb time
Wood	10	1.2 days
Petroleum	41.9	4.8 days
Uranium (LWR)	$5.7*10^5$	182 years
Uranium (Breeder)	$5.7*10^7$	25,700 years

The energy density, while immensely higher than oil is, isn't the only benefit that Nuclear provides in comparison to petroleum. It is more sustainable, it is more ecological, and it can produce more than just Energy as a byproduct.

As far as sustainability goes. By the U.N. IAEA's 2005 Uranium Reserves "Red Book" there are over 200 years' worth of Uranium at current demand.[141]

Uranium, however, is not the only atom that can be utilized as Nuclear fuel. Thorium can be utilized, as well. There is about 3-4 times as much Thorium as there is Uranium, and of that Uranium, which is mostly U^{238}, only 0.5% of it is fissionable, the U^{235} variety. Meanwhile, Thorium can be decayed into U^{233}, which is also fissionable. This means that while we may only have 200 years' worth of U^{235} on the planet left at current demand, we have well over 12,000+ years of Thorium. It is for this reason that Nuclear fuel is vastly more abundant than petroleum, which may only last us another 50 years or so.

Nuclear Energy is not only more sustainable than oil, but it is also more ecological; In operation, Nuclear power plants emit no CO_2 into the atmosphere. The only thing they emit to the environment is water vapor. As for radiation, the environment surrounding a Nuclear power plant is the same as standard background radiation. In contrast to this, coal plants have radiation levels at 100 times the standard background radiation. This is due to Nuclear power plants consuming radioactive materials in a contained process whereas Coal burns its fuel, which contains minute levels of Nuclear materials and thus releases them into the atmosphere. More than that, given our abundance of Nuclear fuel, if we pursued Nuclear Energy with the enthusiasm that we pursued Nuclear weapons, we could actually begin to reverse climate change. This is because, given enough Energy, you can actually pull CO_2 out of the atmosphere and generate petroleum-like products from it.

Imagine it, being able to clean up the CO_2 levels of the atmosphere while generating products that can be used as gasoline. This means that all of our infrastructure that is built upon petroleum would not have to be wasted, that they could be used, and they could be used in a renewable fashion. This technology already exists.[142] The only problem with its utilization is the energy demand that is required. With clean Nuclear Energy, this atmospheric carbon recycling could be realized to avert the damaging effects of climate change while also allowing us to recapture some of that Energy as usable hydrocarbons.[143]

---

[141] There are also substantial amounts of Uranium dissolved in seawater which can be harvested once technology discovers a method to do so. Perhaps this harvesting can be combined with other utilization of seawater, such as salt harvesting, and production of potable water.

[142] https://carbonengineering.com/

[143] Since heat is being utilized in this process if you placed this atmospheric carbon recycling plant near sea water you could at the same time combine a water processing plant into the structure to generate clean drinkable water for your societies population without

The other benefit of Nuclear power is the potential of creating more than just Energy as a byproduct. The fission of Nuclear atoms creates what is typically termed Nuclear waste. But to call that "waste" is so short-sighted that it is actually infuriating. The potential goes far beyond what we have limited ourselves to. By fissioning atomic nuclei, we create brand new elements. Elements which can be of use if only we decided to research their potentials instead of calling them waste and throwing them away. For example, one such element that can be created via this process is Molybdenum-99 which is already used in the medical community as a Nuclear isotope for imaging of myocardial perfusions, bone scans, even finding tumors. With more research, other elements that reside on the decay chain of these reactions may find commercial use as well.

Nuclear Energy allows us to employ the principle of recycling to the maximum advantage. It allows us to create a society whose consumption and waste products can then be turned back into necessary raw materials to begin the process anew. Plentiful and cheap Energy affords us the ability to massively increase our consumption without endangering our supply since the waste created by that consumption is recycled. Regardless of the system, Capitalism or socialism, this emphasis on recycling is an absolute necessity when there is a finite amount of resources.[144]

Risks of Nuclear Energy

There are several risks associated with Nuclear Energy. The two big ones are safety and proliferation. Safety concerns about Nuclear Energy come down primarily to three historical incidents: Three-Mile Island, Chernobyl,

---

needing any additional energy to be produced.

[144] Recycling by principle, however, is not Profitable. It can only ever be Profitable if what it creates through waste is cheaper than what it would take to extract the same amount through normal means. Under socialism, however, the benefits of recycling to society become the reason for its pursuit. Society as a whole chooses to recycle because that is what is best for us. Capitalism is structurally incapable of doing this. It requires the state to place restrictions on natural Capitalism, to regulate them, to conduct these processes itself. For example, consider the waste of a Capitalist corporation owned by one individual who lives divorced from the community that the business resides in. Will he choose to dump or recycle the waste? If Profit is the motivation, then he will choose to dump it, of course, it's cheaper; regardless of how it will affect the community. If the community has a say even though it is less Profitable to recycle it, by recycling, they avoid the detriment to the community from dumping it. As a result, the structural outcomes of Capitalist vs Socialist can be seen.

and Fukushima. The proliferation concerns come down to the devastating effects of Nuclear weapons themselves.

The Three-Mile Island incident was a partial meltdown that occurred in reactor number 2. This was due to a malfunction of pumps which shut off the steam generators. Without those functioning, the heat continued to build up in the reactor, causing the pressure to rise. To relieve it, a release valve opened and got stuck in the process, allowing more water to escape than was needed. This led to a partial meltdown of the exposed core. This facilitated the formation of steam in the core which when it came in contact with the zirconium cladding of the reactor vessel while in the presence of radiation, broke the covalent bonds of water allowing the oxygen to react with the zirconium to produce zirconium dioxide and hydrogen gas. When the Nuclear reaction continues past this point, you end up with heat continually being generated, which melts the containment and causes the solid fuel pellets to crack and release radioactive isotopes into the coolant water. Since the valve was still open, allowing coolant to escape, this is how the radiation got funneled into the surrounding environment. Fortunately, the reaction was eventually contained before it got too far out of control. The hydrogen gas did cause a small explosion. But partially thanks to the design of the building this did not result in harmful levels of radiation leaking into the environment. The two million people surrounding Three-Mile Island ended up with only 14 μSv of radiation exposure.

Chernobyl was the largest of the disasters. It resulted in a massive power increase in the core, which led to the boiling of the coolant. Steam absorbs heat less than liquid water does which led to a rise in the temperature of the reactor, which caused even more water to flash into steam. This increase in temperature eventually led the fuel rods to fracture, which prevented the containment rods from encasing them to stop the reaction. This led to the reactor producing 10X more heat than it would normally output. This caused all the water to turn into steam. Steam has 1000 times more volume than water does. The increase in volume caused pressure to rise more than the container could handle, resulting in a massive steam explosion that spread Nuclear isotopes from the cracked fuel rods all over the surrounding area. This led to radiation levels of the reactor building to be too high to measure, though it was estimated at 300Sv/hour or 300,000,000 μSv per hour (a fatal dose would occur in less than a minute). The average exposure of the residents was about 100,000 μSv, or twice what is to be considered a "safe" annual dose.[145]

---

[145] To provide perspective, a yearly dosage of 1,000,000 μSv (10 times what the Chernobyl residents received) based on studies performed suggests that 5% of the individuals who

Fukushima occurred in much the same way. A power failure caused by a tsunami led to an increase of heat buildup in the core, causing water to turn into steam, that steam then explodes and showers the surrounding area with radioactive isotopes. Fukushima, unlike Chernobyl, had a containment building which prevented a lot of radioactive material from spreading. Safety mechanisms also prevented the reaction from getting too far out of control, and as a result, a max radiation level of 400,000 μSv was recorded.[146] The average citizen was exposed to around 10,000 μSv, radiation levels equivalent to a CT scan. Thanks to efforts by the Japanese Government, scraping away the topsoil immediately afterward (Cs^{137} rests on top of it after being dispersed by the explosion) the area is far less radioactive than it otherwise would have been.

The other risk associated with Nuclear Energy is the worry about proliferation. This requires us to look into what is necessary for an atomic bomb. The main requirement is that you need to have a large enough mass of fissile material (U^{235}, or Pu^{239}) compacted to the point where when one atom is bombarded by a neutron it creates a quick chain reaction that releases a ton of Energy instantaneously. That is the essential mechanism of a Nuclear explosion. But it requires very pure and compact fissile material.

Remember that U^{235} is only present in 0.5% of Uranium. It is mixed together with U^{238}, which isn't able to be utilized in Nuclear weapons since its fissile behavior does not allow for the quick chain reaction to occur. This means that U^{235} has to be isolated and refined. Nuclear fuel, however, is only refined to being 3-5%. This means a Nuclear pellet is 95% U^{238} and 5% U^{235}. Atomic bombs require a nearly pure sample of U^{235}.[147] The only difference between U^{235} and U^{238} are those three neutrons, aka the weight is the only difference. Everything else about these two isotopes is the same. This makes separating them extremely difficult since their difference in weight is only 5.025×10^{-25}g or 0.0000000000000000000005025 grams.

---

experience these levels of radiation develop a fatal form of cancer. A single dose of this level of radiation is not lethal but will lower white blood cell count, and cause nausea. The residents of Chernobyl were relatively safe and unharmed, though only moderately since it must also be noted that there is a statistical increase of cancer at the 100,000 μSv dose, the vast majority of which is not fatal, however.

[146] It has been estimated that the core itself reached levels of about 530 Sv. But thanks to the containment building. This was retained in the core and did not leak into the environment.

[147] Fuel Grade <20%, Weapons Grade >90% & less than 1 ppm U^{232} contamination

This is done by turning Uranium into a gas by fluorinating it into uranium hexafluoride and then speeding up that gas to incredible speeds. This allows the smaller U^{235} to travel slightly faster. This is what centrifuges are used for. But each pass through a centrifuge is only able to refine the uranium gas a tiny amount. What was say 99.5% U^{238} gets turned into 99.2% U^{238}. With each subsequent pass through the centrifuge, the change in refinement gets smaller and smaller. This means getting a material that is 3-5% U^{235} is reasonably easy. But getting a sample that is at least 90%, U^{235} becomes enormously difficult. Not only that, but you need enough to reach what is called critical mass. Which for U^{235} is roughly 33 lbs. This is well over what any plant would ever be allowed to have and would take a normal plant a significant amount of time to produce. With proper monitoring and regulatory standards these concerns about proliferation can be adequately addressed.

Addressing the Risks

After learning about the risks of Nuclear Energy, we see that proliferation is not really a concern as it can easily be mitigated through ensuring facilities which produce the solid form of Nuclear fuel are small enough that they cannot provide weapons-grade levels of U^{235} easily, and monitor them in a manner that mitigates the remaining concern.[148]

As for the risk associated with the safety of Nuclear facilities. We can see that the primary risk is the use of pressurized water as either the coolant or the moderator.[149] Pressurized water is needed because water boils at 100 degrees Celsius when it is unpressurized. But we need larger amounts of heat to generate electricity. This requires the reactor to run at much higher temperatures than the 100 degrees Celsius. To get water to these temperatures, we need to increase the pressure.

---

[148] For example, if they require 7 months to generate the critical mass for a nuclear weapon then require an inspection every 7 months with a random inspection thrown in somewhere before that. Or just have an inspector sit at each site, with their sole job be to randomly take samples to test and ensure compliance with each of them on a rotation schedule to minimize corruptibility. There are plenty of potential solution to mitigate proliferation.

[149] The moderator is needed to slow down the Neutrons that are released. Thermal reactors require a moderator, Fast reactors do not. This has to do with the cross-section of the fissile material. An ejected Neutron must collide with a nucleus to make molecule fission. The faster the neutron, the more likely more neutrons will be ejected; however, the faster the neutron, the less likely it is to hit its target. Either way, water plays the role of controlling the reaction and is present in both systems of PWR's.

The design of this way of developing a Nuclear reactor comes straight from Capitalism. You see the design was first engineered for the Navy in the production of a Nuclear submarine. At the size that was needed for the reactor, the strength of the pressurized vessel was absolute, and even if all the water within it turned to steam, the vessel would not rupture. The Navy paid the first mover cost in the development of this newer technology. The research was done, we knew it worked, but we also knew it was risky if it got larger. Capitalism didn't want to pay to research a better way of doing things for commercial applications. The work had already been done for them. They just had to increase the size. Why pay the first mover cost, aka why take the risk when they can invest in a proven design despite the safety concerns.

Well, the inventor of the pressurized water reactor (PWR) Alvin Weinberg didn't necessarily think this was a good idea. It was perfectly acceptable on a submarine, but once you start making the size bigger the security of the pressure vessel is no longer absolute. It is for this reason he advocated against the PWR in commercial use. He wanted to pursue a different method of creating Nuclear Energy. One that got rid of the safety concerns that come with a pressurized system.

We can see this in his quote.

"In these early days, we explored all sorts of power reactors, comparing the advantages and disadvantages of each type. The number of possibilities was enormous since there are many possibilities for each component of a reactor—fuel, coolant, moderator. The fissile material may be ^{233}U, ^{235}U, or ^{239}Pu; the coolant may be: water, heavy water, gas, or liquid metal; the moderator may be: water, heavy water, beryllium, graphite—or, in a fast- neutron reactor, no moderator. I have calculated that, if one counted all the combinations of fuel, coolant, and moderator, one could identify about a thousand distinct reactors. Thus, at the very beginning of Nuclear power, we had to choose which possibilities to pursue, which to ignore" -Alvin Weinberg, Nuclear Chemist

He earnestly believed that a better reactor design could be created. In fact, he got his chance to prove this. The Navy brought to life the PWR, but the Air Force brought to life the Molten Salt Reactor (MSR). The Air Force wanted a Nuclear-powered airplane. As a result, the concept that was created was the use of fissile material dissolved in a salt to produce a liquid fuel, while utilizing a solid moderator to slow down the neutrons. This offered the distinct advantage of not having to have a pressurized system. It also provided two other unique benefits.

Whereas PWRs had to be monitored, and their reactivity controlled, the MSR was self-regulating. Because the Nuclear fuel was dissolved in the molten salt. The more reactive the core got, the hotter the salt got as well. But the hotter the salt gets, the more its volume expands and the farther apart the Nuclear fuel becomes. As a result, reactivity then decreases. It is self-regulating. Even though it is self-regulating, the idea of letting a Nuclear reaction proceed without any control over it is still scary. As a result, the MSR has an ingenious and passive safety mechanism in place in case of a loss of power. But before we can fully understand and appreciate this safety mechanism, we must first understand the difference between a fast and a thermal spectrum.

Fast spectrum reactors are ones which do not need a moderator but need a lot more fuel. This is because when Nuclear fission results and neutrons are released, they leave the atom at incredible speeds. The benefit that is afforded to a fast spectrum reactor is that this speed if it hits another nucleus, will with near 100% probability cause fission to result and even more neutrons to be released. Usually on the order of as little as 2 neutrons to as much as even 5 neutrons. The downside to this reactor type is that the faster the neutron is moving, the less likely it is to hit another nucleus. It is for this reason that a lot more fuel needs to be added to the reactor to increase that possibility.

Thermal spectrum reactors do utilize a moderator. What a moderator does is slow down the speed of the neutron that is released. The benefit of slowing down the neutron is that it dramatically increases the chances of it hitting another atom. The downside is that this collision does not always result in fission and its collisions that result in fission release fewer neutrons, an average of just above 2 for U^{233} and U^{235}.

Since the MSR was a thermal spectrum reactor, this means that the presence of the moderator is essential for reactivity to occur since, without it, there is not enough fuel to allow for a fast spectrum reaction to take place. The safety mechanism relied on the use of a frozen plug down at the bottom of the tank. The frozen plug connected the reactor vessel with a drain tank. Cold gas was blown on the plug to keep it frozen. As long as it was frozen, then the fuel would remain in the reactor vessel, and the Nuclear reaction could continue. However, if power was lost, then the gas blowing on the frozen plug would also stop. The heat of the reactor vessel would melt the plug, and that would cause all of the fuel to drain into the drain tank. This would stop the reaction since the moderator is a solid that is only present in the reaction vessel. Remove the fuel from the moderator, the neutrons are no longer being slowed down, and their probability of hitting a nucleus dramatically decreases.

This completely passive safety mechanism combined with the self-regulating nature of the liquid fuel reaction mitigates every risk associated with the safety of Nuclear Energy.

But this type of reactor offers us some additional benefits which PWR reactors do not, and it comes from the utilization of liquid fuel.

Benefits of an MSR

The benefits of an MSR besides the safety increase come from the use of liquid fuel. This allows us to clean the fuel as we go.

You see one of the downsides of PWRs is that they use solid fuel. This means that as the Uranium is fissioned its fissioned products stay within the fuel pellet. This causes damage to the pellet and leads to the buildup of neutron sinks. Neutron sinks are fissioned byproducts which absorb neutrons. It is for this reason that Nuclear fuel has to be replaced after only 1-4% of it has been used. Because the buildup of neutron sinks steals neutrons and prevent the chain reaction from continuing. This means the majority of Nuclear waste (96-99%) we have just sitting around is prime recycling material to become Nuclear fuel for an MSR.

The MSR, because its fuel is liquid, has an advantage when it comes to these neutron sinks. The liquid can be passed through a series of chemical reactions to remove and isolate each of the fission products. This can be thought of as the reactor's kidney. With a properly functioning kidney, we can achieve near 100% fuel utilization rates as opposed to the 1-4% we get from conventional PWRs.

MSRs also allow us the ability to utilize Thorium as a fuel. This greatly increases the availability and supply of fuel. Thorium, however, requires a breeder reactor to be utilized. Thorium will absorb a neutron and decay over 30 days into U^{233}. U^{233} is fertile fissioning material that yields more than two neutrons when it is fissioned. This means we can build a reactor that utilizes some of its neutrons to turn Thorium into U^{233} and some of its neutrons to fission the U^{233} that is already present. Since we already will have a kidney that serves to remove neutron sinks, we can easily add an additional step to filter out the Thorium that will take 30 days to decay into U^{233}. Once decayed, we simply combine it with the molten salt and add it back into the reaction vessel.[150]

---

[150] Fluorinating is how you turn these into salts. For example, Sodium and Chlorine ionically bond to each other to produce a salt. Salt is a solid at room temperature, which

Proliferation with this method is possible but just as tricky. Not only is the amount of Thorium you would need to power an MSR for a year is far below the critical mass needed to turn U^{233} into a Nuclear bomb you end up with natural adulteration from U^{232}, which you absolutely do not want in a nuclear bomb. To cure this filtration would need to occur similar to how uranium is filtered.[151] Additionally, thanks to the liquid fuel, it makes the chemistry predictable. If a country decides to add extra or remove some uranium from the fuel cycle in an attempt to siphon off U^{233} to be utilized for weapons, this alters the composition of the fuel which is then detectable. One can measure the amount of Thorium in the reactor vessel and see how much should be getting generated. One can look into the decay vessel where its kept until it turns into U^{233} and see how much of it is present. One can also look to see the concentration of U^{233} in the reaction vessel to see what levels exists and determine proliferation that way. At all steps of the process, from storage to reactor it can be measured and any siphoning that occurs will result in a deviation of concentrations which are measurable and therefore enforceable.

To give an example, let's say a country wishes to procure a Nuclear weapon and agrees to non-proliferation terms. This means that they are only allowed to keep so much unused Nuclear fuel on hand. Let's say 1Kg of Thorium per sight. They are also only allowed to have a specified concentration of thorium present in the reactor vessel at any given time. This accepted concentration yields a constant generation of decaying Thorium, which is kept in a decay vessel. You can measure the concentration of U^{233} and Thorium in the decay vessel to ensure this level has been kept. If more Thorium was added to the reaction vessel than was allowed, a different concentration of U^{233} to total Thorium will then be present in the decay vessel, and it will be detectable that nefarious actions are occurring. If one decides not to add more Thorium to the reaction vessel and instead siphon off from the decay vessel and just add in less U^{233} back in, then there will be less fissile material to absorb the released neutrons, leading to more Thorium in the reactor vessel to absorb those neutrons instead, leading to an alteration in the concentration of the decay vessel once again.

---

means you can melt it. You can add fluorine to Uranium or Thorium and turn either of those into salts too.

[151] If you say, no we will not allow filtration plants and focus solely on allowing thorium to be the nuclear fuel that is acceptable, then centrifuges become unnecessary and this makes proliferation significantly more difficult. One of the byproducts of U^{233} production is U^{232} which is a strong gamma ray emitter which decays into Thallium-208 which is extremely difficult to handle and easy to detect.

The regulation of this material becomes far easier and makes proliferation that much harder. This is only for the Thorium fuel cycle, though. Regular U^{235} fuel must still be produced the usual method and would fall under current proliferation checks.

The pursuit of Nuclear Energy is of the utmost importance as its presence allows for us to continue increasing in productivity, while simultaneously helping us with climate change, and providing us with the means to be good stewards of our resources through increased capabilities in recycling.

CHAPTER 17:
STRUCTURAL POLICY GOALS: NECESSITIES & HEALTHCARE

Structural policy changes surrounding necessities such as health care, food, and protection need to have the Capitalist circuit removed from them entirely. The reason being is that exploitation in these areas offers the largest power imbalance. It crosses the line from exploitation to extortion. If they don't pay, then they die. This should be unacceptable in a democracy. It is for this reason that the necessity sector be the first to completely and utterly abolish the M-C-M' circuit of exchange.[152]

Health Care

Fortunately, public support for this trend today is well above the 50% acceptance mark. Universal Health Care is already a rallying cry amidst the progressives of our society. The public recognizes that Profit above people is wrong. The solution of providing government competition to the private sector in this realm ultimately falls in line with the goal of eliminating the M-C-M' cycle.[153] The reason this is being accepted without much resistance is that it's doing so without removing anyone's freedoms. It merely changes who and how payments occur. But this is just the start. The call for universal health care only covers how the payments are made. It does not eliminate the M-C-M' circuit that exists within the pharmaceutical industry, and also does not eliminate it within the hospitals themselves.

---

[152] This is not saying completely eliminate the choice for Capitalism in this sector, but it is saying that the dependency on Capitalists needs to be abolished. "Government options" would be the modern language that would be utilized. Government options is all things necessary to life. Healthcare, housing, food, water, utilities. If a Capitalist can provide it better, great, pay for the perk, but under no circumstance should you have to pay for life.

[153] Preferred method is to get rid of private insurance all together and not worry about the competition. Otherwise we risk private insurance covering all healthy applicants and then claiming it is far more efficient than the public system since the cost of the denied sick people will obviously be higher than the accepted healthy ones. That will be the rhetoric used to attack Medicare for all should private insurance be allowed to exist in competition.

To combat this, we must first combat the pharmaceuticals. The best way to do that is by attacking the patents. We have already gone over how the concept of ownership should not entitle you to perpetual gain, especially if that "intellectual property" is a natural chemical formula. Calls that you can't patent nature should be sufficient enough to change the dialogue surrounding price justification. That is Big Pharma's defense that prices are high because of research and development. For every successful drug, there are thousands of failed ones. But that's not a defense at all; short term risk does not yield perpetual gain.

Big Pharma is exceptionally Profitable, so obviously, the prices for their drugs have paid for the R&D many times over. Enough is enough. We must alter the patent laws to do a couple things:

1. Limit the length of reward
2. Prevent patents from being able to be bought and sold
    a. Intellectual property is only the intellectual creation of the person who thought it up. You shouldn't be able to buy or own someone else's thoughts. That is a grossly unjust benefit to the rich by allowing them to purchase and own the ideas of the masses. It allows the rich to steal benefit solely for themselves instead of cooperating with producer of that idea and allowing them to reap the reward of its implementation.
3. Instead of outright ownership implement a reasonable royalty system.
    a. If it is a company who is claiming the patent, then half of the royalty belongs to the research team who discovered it.
        i. Add a harsh punishment to this that any corporation trying to remove this stipulation loses all rights to the royalty and it goes to the team as a whole instead.
        ii. The reason for this is to overcome the hurdle of Profit. Emphasizing that it must be shared with those who do work.[154]

Doing this opens up the pharmaceutical industry to competition. Competition by government, and competition by others who can now utilize those patents to produce the drugs. If the government can pay good wages to steal the pharmaceutical industries employees from them and have them implement their expertise for the public good instead. This public sector drug

---

[154] We want to Westinghouse this, not Edison it.

company can then provide the public with drugs at near the cost of raw materials and Labour. Thereby eliminating the extortion that Big Pharma currently uses to make its massive Profits. This serves to force the private industries to increase their productivity and ingenuity to stay ahead of the state or die.[155]

Lastly, for hospitals, since everything is being paid for through universal healthcare, there needs to be a countrywide patient registry. All medical files are available in a protected cloud able to be pulled by any doctor whom the patient wishes to see. There should be no reason to have a primary physician if the patient doesn't wish to have one.[156]

If a patient feels they need an X-Ray, they should be able to go to a radiology clinic and not be turned away because they do not have a referral. If they want a test done, they should be able to go to a lab and request those tests without a referral. These minor inconveniences that are present in privatized healthcare as well as the military public healthcare annoy the general public and are ultimately pointless hurdles that need not exist. The general physician will write a recommendation if the patient is forceful enough about getting what they want. Let's Capitalize on this. When implementing a public sector hospital, you have your departments: Emergency Care, Urgent Care, Family Health, Radiology, Laboratory, etc. Except that once you are enrolled and your file is present in the cloud you can go to whomever you want, whenever you want.

Sure, you might think you have broken your foot and go get an X-ray and when it turns out that nothing is broken you then go to a general practitioner. Maybe you wasted some time, that is a possibility. But what is essential is that it was the person's choice to operate in that order. People prefer choice. Does it mean that more work was done in the medical sector? Yes. Does that mean anything significant? No. It just means that consumer choices have influenced the demand in the sector. Whether or not that demand was necessary or not means nothing. We staff to demand, and demand equilibrates over time. If we know that 20% of the people who show up get an x-ray don't need one, then fine, plan for that extra 20%.

Implementing public sector hospitals that grant people that freedom of choice also serves another benefit. It makes their experience with healthcare

---

[155] This is real competition.

[156] This seems to be one of the downfalls of both military medicine as well as Canadian medicine. Giving patients a choice is what is truly important.

much more streamlined. They don't have rules that they have to follow, they don't get bogged down with red tape. They know that they can simply walk up to any section and get taken care of then and there. Having that capability will far outstrip any private sector competition. That's a guarantee! Doesn't that sound like something you want? If we can implement this then we are one step closer to removing the M-C-M' circuit from our system as a whole. [157]

Food

Removing the M-C-M' circuit from food production is another necessary step. The reason being is that food is necessary for the very survival of the population. As such, it should be a right to have access to cheap, nutritious, and plentiful food. Not as a commodity but as a right.[158] There are a couple steps we must take to first get there.

Meat

Having the government overtake the meat industry practices of these corporations would be a difficult political argument to make. But there are ways around this. The farming industry is cruel. There is no avoiding that fact. It's also a challenging sector to get rid of as the mass of people love to eat meat. As such, the strategy for tackling these issues and removing the M-C-M' cycle is a threefold attack.

- First is building up cooperative free-range industries by providing subsidies and tax benefits while removing those very same benefits from the unwanted practices of the likes of the privatized companies.

---

[157] You will be challenged with the skill and wages argument. Reiterating the point that wages are different from Profit is essential here. It means you can still pay doctors a lot because that is what their Labour is worth without extracting Profit.

[158] There will always be some private industry offering niche commodities that are food. Things like veal, etc. But for the majority of food items, what is currently in supermarket stores can be replaced with public sector goods. Think of the great value brand. Each and every one of those great value brand items can be replaced with a public sector equivalent and provided to the population for free, or initially at little cost. There would have to be some regulatory rules on how many items you could take at one time etc. A test run in a city for a prolonged period could be used to discover pre-implementation purchasing habits with post-implementation habits. This would provide data with which to gauge these policies effects on demand.

- Second is regulations on the treatment of animals must be implemented and enforced. This will cut into the Profit of the private sector food companies by making them treat their animals more humanely.[159]
- Third, is the focus on researching and developing lab-grown meat. Having the ability to create and grow laboratory meat synthetically means far cheaper and more sustainable production in the long run. Getting the nutrition and flavor right is of the highest priority or else it will not be competitive.

Being able to accomplish those three objectives will ensure ethical sources of living meat, while also providing a cheap, sustainable, and nutritious alternative.

Non-Meat

This area is similar to the meat with the exception that the public sector can directly compete against private companies. It also has the added benefit that we can take the same approach as universal health care. Where universal health care doesn't replace the doctors, it merely changes how they are paid the same too can be done with food. Most of the farmers who produce food sell them to big agriculture. By merely changing the buyer and the distribution, will net a massive win against the private companies. As their Profits fall, they can be purchased by the public sector to provide all the food that is needed. Direct state competition is the method by which we combat the M-C-M' circuit of the agriculture industry.

Now a small word on GMOs. We must continue research into them. Genetically Modified Organisms are not harmful. Yes, there has been a successful marketing campaign to scare the public into believing otherwise, but genetically modifying an organism ranges from selective breeding techniques all the way to gene splicing. At the end of the day, science knows enough about these systems to do this. Furthermore, it is highly beneficial that we continue to do this. By continuing our research into GMOs, we can produce more resistant, more varied, and more productive crops.

In addition to this, with the public sector acquisition, we can also begin to focus on creating pro-recycling and biologically cooperative environments. That is, we can focus on sustainable agriculture.

---

[159] This will increase cost of meat.

Water

Water is an exciting topic. It never receives much attention or even gets thought about until something has gone wrong; like Flint, Michigan. Water is primarily a public resource in the United States, and legislation needs to focus on keeping it that way. It needs to remain a right, not a commodity. To ensure this it needs to be added to the constitution.

Our goals towards Water, therefore, should be first protecting it and second finding ways to make more of it, either pulling it out of the atmosphere or out of the ocean. Both of which are possible with abundant energy that can be obtained through Nuclear.

Obtaining that lab-grown meat would also save a ton of Water. 1lb of meat takes an average of 1900 gallons of Water to be produced. Being able to lab grow meat would free up that Water to then be directed to other uses.

Protection

We are already really good at funding our Military. Our Military is also in the public sector. What changes should we implement? The first change to implement is to get out of utilizing private businesses to produce weapons for us. This leads to a war for Profit motive. This motive generates lobbyists and fear mongers who create enemies out of nothing to sell weapons. Instead, we should create public sector mirrors of these companies to do just what they are doing.[160]

The Military is also perfect as a testing ground for new capabilities. The Military is all about national security. As such, it only makes sense that technological advancement is a part of that mantra.

"Why of course, the people don't want war. Why would some poor slob on a farm want to risk his life in a war when the best that he can get out of it is to come back to his farm in one piece. Naturally, the common people don't want war; neither in Russia nor in England nor in America, nor for that matter Germany. That is understood. But, after all it is the leaders of the country who determine the policy and it is always a simple matter to drag the people along, whether it is a

---

[160] There is a case to be made about private corporations producing military weaponry. State seizure in this instance has a strong case for the protection of national security. Afterall if the state doesn't buy the weapons, who will they then sell them to?

Structure

democracy or a fascist dictatorship or a parliament or a communist dictatorship.

Voice or no voice, the people can always be brought to the bidding of the leaders. That is easy. All you have to do is tell them they are being attacked and denounce the pacifists for lack of patriotism and exposing the country to danger. It works the same in any country."
Hermann Goring, Nazi Military Commander, Nuremburg Trials 1946

The military therefore is the organization whose job is to avoid war at all costs. This is both through making war extremely inadvisable and unwanted, but also through the perpetuation of peace. The military should be focused as a peace organization who is capable of waging war. Not as a war organization who is tasked with maintaining the peace. Promoting peace focuses on enhancing living conditions of all those around the world, and respecting the rights of sovereign nations. We should lead by example, not by force.

Here is a scenario to help illustrate this point. Look at Okinawa, Japan. Every year the population there has voted to have the American Military Base removed. Year after year the mainland of Japan shoots down that possibility. We should be respectful of another people's land. They don't want us there; we shouldn't be there. But at the same time, that is a very strategic location. We can take a note from China and create artificial islands. Or move to one of the islands that have no inhabitants. This where technological advancement needs in the military R&D sector can really shine.

We need a global presence to secure our trade routes, to provide global defense for ballistic missiles, to acquire a plethora of global readings for science, and most likely a ton of other benefits that are not available for public consumption. Bottom line, global presence is a good thing, if used properly. But we must also respect the wishes of the people whom our presence is near. If they don't want us there, then we move to someplace we are allowed.

Having research to provide abundant energy, sustainable agriculture, clean water, and the like is essential to remote bases. If you don't have a civilized place to stay then terraform one instead. If you want to be near civilization, then make your presence beneficial to the people. For example, for island bases that are surrounded by poor populations, go ahead and create an electricity source that can not only power your base but also provide it to the local population for free. Need plumbing, go ahead and combine it with the local populations and do all the treatment on the base. Provide services back to the communities in which we stay. This is important because it helps foster a global community of cooperation.

Our Military has a global presence, so let's use it to spread the ideals of cooperation. Let's use it to set good examples around the world on how a cooperative structure can work. Put in each base an expert on forming, managing, and dealing with the logistics of cooperatives. Have our bases become trading centers with these cooperatives all over the world. We have to fly planes between bases anyway. Why not throw traded goods on them as cheap transportation.

The point I am making with this section is that we need a culture change with how we utilize the Military. It exists to protect our national security. Let's use it for that. When you were a kid, you were afraid of the class bully, they were bigger, badder, and they were in charge. But this meant they were not liked, and the moment the class had the chance to turn on them, they did.

Meanwhile, everyone in the class wanted to be friends with the nice kid, the saint, and had their back through thick and thin. Everyone would go out of their way to spend time with that person, to help out that person. If there were a chance to turn on them, no one would do it. Instead of being the biggest and the baddest, we should instead be the best. Lead by example, be the nicest.

We need to stop invading other countries, we need to utilize the security council how it is supposed to be utilized and stop going against it. We need to submit ourselves to the law of the international court by becoming a ratifying signatory on the Rome Statute. We should stop sanctioning countries we disagree with and instead make a point to be a shining example in the right way to do things. If the goal is to change people's minds. You definitely don't achieve it by killing the people whose minds you are trying to change through sanctions or war. You do it by giving them an example to aspire to and a clear path to get there.

That is what the purpose of our Military should be. An excellent example to whom everyone else can look toward to foster relations of peace and prosperity throughout the world; resorting to physical self-defense only if we should ever need it. We should always strive to never act forcefully unless provoked through attack, and hold ourselves with the upmost dignity obtaining and maintaining the acceptance of the world's population.

CHAPTER 18:
STRUCTURAL POLICY GOALS: INFRASTRUCTURE

It is no secret that our infrastructure is ageing and is in desperate need of repair. Dams, roads, bridges, railways, energy grids, water pipes, and even the telecommunication infrastructure. These are all fundamental structures which are all too often taken for granted. Without a nationalized refresh program, we have let them age past the point the point of acceptance, performing break-fix repair only when necessary and neglecting the structural maintenance to keep them up to standards.

We have already touched upon how the government can fund these projects. If the Labour force is there, and the supply of materials is there, it is entirely possible. So then how should we go about implementing these changes and what infrastructure upgrades should be performed?

All of them. Massive overhaul. To understand what needs to be done, let's start underground.

- We need to dig up and replace water lines ($1-2 trillion) and maintain them (another trillion over 25 years before replacing again).
- Since this is going to require digging massive holes in the ground lets go ahead and plan appropriately. Have an encasement and a way to sectionally replace it in the future without having to dig it up again.
- While we do that, we can implement vast telecommunication pathways as well, run them adjacent to the water lines in a second sealed off, watertight compartment with plenty of room for growth.
    - Plan this out so that in the future we don't have to dig the stuff up again. This part is of the utmost importance because one of the most significant costs with maintenance is the construction which shuts down everyday life.

- - If you plan for a replacement, you can incorporate a construction-free method into the design.
  - We can also make a sizeable 3rd compartment for electricity transfer instead of having the wires above ground.

Now that we have telecommunications water and potentially the electrical grid as well out of the way. About a total of 5 trillion in cost; next, we need to implement high-speed rail to act as transport all over the United States. China can do 2500 miles of track for 118 billion. It will probably cost us three times that since our logistics are a tad more complicated than those in China. We know they are looking to have close to 23,000 miles of high-speed rail in the future. We should implement the same. Enough track to connect every major city and all of its surrounding medium-sized towns etc. We are looking at around 3 trillion for all that.

We know all of our roads, bridges, and dams are in desperate need of repair as well. Roads and bridges come in at about 2 trillion, and dams come in at a respectable 100 billion.[161]

In total, for a complete overhaul of the United States infrastructure, we are looking at roughly 10 trillion dollars. Which is completely doable. The implementation of which can be used to further all of the policy goals set about in Chapter 14. This will be the boom that drives the rise of the worker cooperative.

We accomplish this through a phased approach. Bring the world experts in from each of the areas (roads, water, rail, etc.) here to start the projects. Have them work side by side with groups of engineers and workers so that once they have completed a project, our working base now understands how to accomplish the task. We then take those engineers and workers and send them out on another project while repeating the process once again training up a new group. This produces a slew of skilled and knowledgeable workers to help us undertake the massive problem that is our infrastructure.

Once this work is complete, there will be a massive demand for expansion. A demand, which the workers who were working for the government can now fulfil as a part of the market supply of Labour. We can provide those groups of individuals the means of production. The tools and equipment used to build all of our infrastructures can be added to the worker cooperative pool of resources. We can give each group a chance to form into their own

---

[161] All of these numbers are taken from civil engineer societies and inflated to the larger order of magnitude.

cooperative company with access to that pool of resources and with access to interest-free financing as a sort of severance package since the need for all of them as government workers will no longer be needed. This is how we will make cooperatives competitive against private industry, and this is how we will structurally start to overtake the hurdles that stand in the way of removing the M-C-M' cycle from the system.

We need to do this and do this in a way that is forward thinking. Walt Disney was a fantastic visionary, forward thinker, and achiever. We have many more of them lying about our country, unnoticed, and underutilized, and we need those visionaries on these infrastructure projects to help us plan for and propel us into the future.

Other countries around the world are already doing this. Take a look at Singapore. How innovative they are and how much power they give to their startups and what that has led to. We need to take note. The rest of the world is moving ahead and planning for multiple decades into the future. China, for example, is building massive megacities in its drive for prosperity. Meanwhile, we are sitting on half a century old technology getting farther and farther behind the curve.

If for some reason, the prospect of "payment" still invades your brain. Remember, we are a larger economy than China, we are the world reserve currency, we are smaller population wise and land wise than China is. And yet, China can perform all of this building without the cost being a factor. It's because the government doesn't have to pay for anything. China devalues the yuan when it prints massive amounts of money into the economy, aka it re-monetizes its Labour.[162] If it wants to decrease the supply of the yuan and increase its value, it can do that through taxation or charging more for government services. Ultimately it comes down to what is best for the country: International trade (the strength of your currency to others) or the wellbeing of your Labour force and infrastructure. No nation on earth is going to stop trading with the United States because of massive government spending, just as no country on earth is going to stop trading with China. To think so is absolutely absurd because Labour is Labour. That is the real value.

We are the largest consuming economy in the world today. As a result of this fact, the only repercussion flooding our economy with dollars will have in increasing the consumptive capacity of our citizens. Besides, we will recuperate the value through the increase in productivity down the line

---

[162] But even with the devalued Labour the rest of the world still pays for that Labour. They pay for the Labour at the rate which they agreed to pay for it, regardless of the yuan's value.

anyway by improving our infrastructure. That is what it means to spend on Productive Labour. Spending on Productive Labour is never a bad thing. This increase in current worker consumption capacity and future productivity gains means that countries are going to be more willing to trade with us, not less. This won't lead to a devaluation of the dollar so long as the productive capacity is there. The productive capacity of the consumptive market is the world market. We are nowhere near the productive capacity, and as such, we can print and print just like China is doing, and it doesn't matter. We can increase demand as much as the supply can handle. By doing so, we are benefitting ourselves in the long run, we are becoming forward thinkers. We need to start improving the very foundations on which we stand or prepare to fall as they crumble beneath us.

CHAPTER 19: STRUCTURAL POLICY GOALS: EDUCATION

Today's model of schooling was started in the early 19th-century Prussia. Primarily to service the industrial interests of the time. The Prussian education system would eventually come to be adopted by the West.[163] There was some controversy surrounding the Prussian system, but not the kind you would think today. Some believed that kids were inherently dumb, and were like empty vessels, needing to have information placed into them while others thought that the masses of people were incapable of learning to read and write at all. Those were the beliefs at the time, and we recognize them to be inherently false in modern society. However, today's system evolved from it and for all intents and purposes is essentially the same type and structure as it was back then.

The most influential proponents of the Prussian system saw humanity, not as a whole, each with their own abilities, but rather as raw material that could be molded for use in the market. They saw it in a hierarchy and structured their method of education to perpetuate that world view.

"The higher classes constitute the mind of the single large whole of humanity; the lower classes constitute its limbs."

"The schools must fashion the person, and fashion him in such a way that he simply cannot will otherwise than what you wish him to will."

"The new education must consist essentially in this, that it completely destroys freedom of will in the soil which it undertakes to cultivate, and produces on the contrary strict necessity in the decisions of the will, the opposite being impossible. Such a will can henceforth be

---

[163] There is an excellent book from 1920s Russia called the Road to Life by Anton Makarenko. It depicts the struggles Makarenko went through with the formation of the Gorky colony and how by empowering the children in his charge to think, act, and do for themselves, and hold each other accountable out of respect for one another they were able to form a wonderfully successful collective.

relied on with confidence and certainty." -Johann Fichte, addresses to the German Nation (1807) "The General Nature of the New Education"

Others who saw more of a middle ground adopted elements of the above but reformed the idea. Alexander James Inglis is one such man who explored this middle ground. So much so, he outlined 6 primary principles/function that every school should strive to accomplish.[164]

6 principles are
1. The adjustive or adaptive function.
    a. "Schools are to establish fixed habits of reaction to authority."
    b. "establishment of certain fixed habits of reaction, certain fixed standards and ideals, but also the development of a capacity to readjust adequately to the changing demands of life."
    c. This serves the purpose of creating a populous accepting of authority.
2. The integrating function
    a. The demands made of secondary education are "Development of like-mindedness, of unity in thought, habits, ideals, and standards."
    b. This is done to create social cohesion and conformity. To create a population which is alike.[165]
3. The differentiating function
    a. "Failure to recognize this fact [people's natural differences] ...must mean failure to do justice to the individual and failure to develop the highest social efficiency out of the raw material available."
    b. People have differences, and school need to Capitalize on that.
4. The propaedeutic function
    a. This function is just the preparation for higher education (college).
5. The selective function
    a. The schools should identify and eliminate individuals who cannot carry out the necessary capacities while rewarding those who can.

---

[164] Principles of Secondary Education by Alexander Inglis (1918) 367, 375-384.

[165] The problem is that they dictate what "alike" means instead of allowing society to mix naturally.

       b. "In contrast to selection by elimination, the second aspect of the selective function emphasizes selection by differentiation."
       c. Differentiation is allowing a student to focus on areas in which they are stronger and be eliminated from areas they are not
6. The directive function.
       a. Students must be given a wide range of subjects to try to find what best suits their needs.

These may sound like decent principles. However, as Sir Ken Robinson and Paulo Freire both point out, these notions are based on an outdated system. In this way, the Prussian model of education was built to service the needs of the industrial revolution structurally. Thus, it was made to service Capitalism through the fundamental culture it promotes.

Capitalist education promotes:
- Conformity
- Compliance
- Competition
- Obedience to Authority

These sectors can be seen in the narration sickness that our educational system suffers from. How subjects such as math, science, and history are taught as if they are motionless, static, compartmentalized and predictable is wholly divorced from reality and by extension the natural human experience. A narrative structure to education simply leads to memorization and regurgitation instead of the internalization of understanding that is needed. As a result of this, the goal of Capitalist education becomes more about filling the containers as they pass by on the assembly line. Measuring them to see how much is in the containers and tossing out the ones that aren't full enough.

This model of education is what Paulo Freire termed the banking concept of education. Where the student is only permitted in this structure of education to the role of receiving, filling, and storing deposits.[166] We can then see how this follows the ideological structure of oppression.

The teacher's word is law, their power absolute. Students in this dynamic are the ignorant who must be taught, who don't know better. In Hegelian

---

[166] This is not to say that students cannot become self-actualized learners. Oh no. This is a capability that is available to every student; however, it must come from within the student. It is a process that is dependent solely upon the student. This is because, in banking education, teachers are narrators and not facilitators or nurturers.

terms, the teachers are the masters and the students the slaves.[167] By teaching in this type of authoritarian structure in the educational system, it only serves to perpetuate and enforce conformity and obedience in the master/slave relationship that exists within the economy.

- Teachers know everything/ students nothing
- Teachers think/ students are thought about
- Teachers talk/ students listen
- Teacher lead/ students follow
- Teachers say/ students do
- Teachers choose content/ students adapt
- Teachers discipline/ students are disciplined

The problem that arises out of this is that the more students remain passive receptacles, the less they develop the critical understanding that they are active movers of the world. That by merely being in it, and interacting with it, they can transform it.

Banking education represses the student's creative power through its very structure and serves to promote their credulity[168] Which in turn only serves the interests of the oppressors who wish to maintain the status quo. [169]

---

[167] Hegel's dialectic of the master and slave show how in authoritarian structure the master is dependent on the slaves for without them he is nothing. In this way, the teacher is the master, but without the students, what good is being a teacher. Their existence is only validated in the presence of the students. The analysis of this means that the slaves are capable all their own, they can survive without the master, but the master cannot survive without the slaves. Students can still be students without a teacher, they can self-actualize, but the teacher cannot be a teacher without students.

[168]. Credulity: The willingness to believe that something is right. In this sense, the willingness to believe what the authority source says is right must be right without a second thought or question.

[169] This is why individuals like Betsy DeVos react almost instinctively to an experiment in education that stimulates a promotion of critical faculties. The very act of questioning the underlying factors to some new bit of knowledge received, the asking of why and connecting the dots is viewed as dangerous. This is why passivity in the education system is so dangerous because by passively accepting what a teacher narrates to you as accurate, leads to passive acceptance of whatever the "authority" narrates to you, later on, is also true. This is one of the contributing factors to why Fox News and the rest of the mainstream media can be in opposition, all while having their base never question what they are told and passively accepting it as the truth.

The underlying issue with Banking Education is that it enforces (not through the intention of the teachers, but through the structure of the system) the interests of the oppressors.

"Indeed, the interests of the oppressors lie in 'changing the consciousness of the oppressed, not the situation which oppresses them'; the more easily the oppressed can be led to adapt to a situation the easier their domination." -Paulo Freire quoting Simone de Beauvoir

It is this control that we can see throughout our society, even in the way that education is talked about. More often than not, it is used as a sort of slander. That if those receiving it do not fit into the mold of the system, it is not the fault of the system, it is the fault of the recipient. That anyone who does not fit within society simply lacks education. That they are lazy, incompetent, in need of integration or have given up.

But this slander lacks the understanding that an individual is incapable of failing a society. This is because they are not divorced from society and that they are a product of it. That if an individual is failing, it is a flaw of the society failing to incorporate all parts of itself within itself. On a more primal level, for an individual to deem another insufficient is to acknowledge that they are ignorant of understanding. An ignorance that arises out of a lack of perspective. They lack the knowledge of "why doesn't the individual understand?" and "Why is the individual failing?". To declare the individual ignorant is admitting their own inability to identify the root of the problem.

- Student drops out of high school
- Student then commits a crime like selling drugs
- Student goes to jail
- Society then claims that the student is insufficient and lacks education.

This outcome ignores the critical perspective of the "insufficient". It ignores how the environment contributed to the creation of this insufficiency. It ignores the Why.

- By narrating in schools, the teacher is always projecting and never receiving.
- By not receiving they don't learn of the student's experience
- By not learning of the student's experience they alienate the student
- The structure has created the "insufficiency" of the student by not learning itself.

"There are innumerable well-intentioned bank clerk teachers who do not realize they are serving only to dehumanize" - Paulo Freire.

To only deposit knowledge does not match reality, as reality is a process. Only those students who recognize when reality and deposits contradict, do they begin to truly learn. That when the narration and their own experiences collide, do they then begin to finally question. But by then, the narrators have often changed and the process of discovering the contradictions must begin anew. It is no longer the teachers but the media who inform. The oppressed having already been conditioned to the structure of being a receptacle and lacking the critical consciousness to question simply accept the authority's narrative. They believe the narrative to be right since there is opposing narrative, such is the effect when the interests of the oppressors are in conflict. Often times, the narrative chosen to accept is based solely on emotion stemming from their personal experience and upbringing.[170]

Education, therefore, must expand the humanism present within it. To expose to the student that a person is not merely in a world but one with the world. That history is the outcome of desires, and the people of those times had the same motivations we do. That the literature evokes the same emotions, that the science was pursued with the same curiosity, the art sprang from the same passion. We must receive actively, not passively. Think critically, not thoughtlessly regurgitate. We must own our understanding of the world, not be owned by the narration of it.

Education, as a result of not doing these things, has become necrophilic. It serves to focus on:
- Turning organic into inorganic
- Memory rather than experience
- Having rather than being
- Gathering rather than understanding
- Listening rather than questioning
- Obedience rather than creativity
- Approach life mechanically as if living beings were things, or where raw materials

"Education as an exercise of domination stimulates the credulity of students, with the ideological intent (often not perceived by the

---

[170] Our culture is that of democracy and Capitalism. Both can be boiled down to the fundamental principles of individualism and collectivism. The narrative you choose is mainly dependent I suspect on which way you lean. If you lean toward the individual, then fox news will be the authority on narrative, if you lean toward collectivism, then CNN will be the authority. But neither authority, much like the banking clerk teacher, promotes the development of critical consciousness, they simply narrate from a position of authority to you, the ignorant subject.

educators) of indoctrinating them to adapt to a world of oppression."
Paulo Freire

To illustrate this point. In this very moment, I, the author, am narrating to you. You are a passive receiver with no ability to interact with me. A teacher could facilitate discussion, could ask you about your experience, listen to your thoughts, even have you analyze the meaning and implications of what I have said so far. But I am not a teacher, I am an author and my role with you is limited. It requires your critical consciousness to digest, analyze, and understand the content. Not merely memorize and regurgitate it. Education is more than just imparting knowledge. It is a process, one that not only accumulates knowledge but also one that empowers the pursuit of it. Empowers people to question and search for answers, the think inquisitively and creatively. A system that does not promote this, is oppressive. Students are not receptacles; they are not merely receivers. They are the future, they are the change, they deserve empowerment.

When education is empowering, it is also liberating, and can even be revolutionary. But for it to be so, its structure must reflect that. Its structure must focus on the fact that teachers are at the same time students and students at the same time teachers. In this way, authority is no longer an answer to a question, its use in arguments is no longer valid. Instead, only truth and what is right matter, and people can teach each other, mediated by the world.

Look at the picture. What do you see?

I'll bet if you are from the West you said a Tiger. If you are from the East, you will most likely have mentioned the jungle.[171] The reason for this is the cultural importance we place on objects. People in the West tend to focus on the focal point of the picture. In this case, a tiger. Whereas people in the East tend to take in the image as a whole. This breeds two different perspectives to the same piece of information.

This is the underlying premise of why banking education is so faulty and why education through narration is terrible. It ignores the perspectives. The difference in perspectives from teacher and student allows for multiple viewpoints of the same question. It breeds mutual understanding of problems. This further engages both parties in an exploration of meaning.

> "As women and men, simultaneously reflecting on themselves and the world, increase the scope of their perception, they begin to direct their observations toward previously inconspicuous phenomena."
> Paulo Freire

A teacher in this case, therefore, continually reforms his reflections in reflection with the student's reflections. Both student and teacher grow together. This process I daresay is how you promote creativity. A creative solution is but one solution that is approached uniquely. Original/creative merely means that the one who is judging it to be so hadn't considered that perspective before. That the solution was approached from an angle that differed from the standard. Creativity is the changing of perceptions of reality and the adjustment of observations on that reality to breed new understanding.

To increase creativity, then, means to expand the perspectives in which information is analyzed. This is done through constant reflection, dialogue, evaluation, consideration, and re-reflection. This is termed by Paulo Freire as the problem-posing educator.

The problem-posing educator is one which:
- Is always cognitive; not sometimes cognitive, sometimes narrative
- Does not regard thoughts and information as private property but as an object of reflection for themselves and the student
- Students are critical co-investigators in dialogue with the teacher
- Promotes the emergence of consciousness and critical intervention in reality

Students who are challenged in this way begin to inter-relate problems together within a total context. Approaching it not as a theoretical question but as one with direct and real impacts upon the world. This removes one of

---

[171] Proceedings of the National Academy of Sciences (vol 102, p 12629)

the most significant problems associated with Banking Education, and that is the alienation. By removing the alienation, you begin to encourage the student to take on new challenges, ask new questions, both of which are followed by new understanding which then breeds within the student a feeling of commitment.

This is a natural process. You are doing it right now by reading this book. You have searched out answers and analysis to questions you have had. You have taken in new information and increased your understanding by adding a new perspective to your repertoire. This new perspective now provides you with a tool by which you can re-evaluate previous information that you have collected. This further increases your understanding. And that understanding breeds a feeling of accomplishment as well as a commitment to continue learning.

Looking back at school, at least for me, learning was tedious; it was a barrier. Once I was free to pursue it how I saw fit, I blossomed. By focusing on areas, I wanted to focus on when I wanted to focus on them, I obtained my own free will. Started gathering different perspectives, and even began to enjoy the process of learning. This is self-actualization, it is this hunger, this desire for knowledge which education needs to promote.

Sir Ken Robinson has written several incredible books on the topic of education. "Creative schools" is the book which I would recommend the most. It serves to change the educational system structurally from what it is now. It asks several critical questions that challenge the dynamic of the school structure. For example, why do we have distinct periods for different subjects ordered like an assembly line process? 40 minutes of education here, get up move and go to the next subject. He also questions why we have classes divided up by age groups. Yes, it's convenient in a logistical sense, but does it make a lot of sense beyond that? Why not instead structure the classes to be more adaptive to the children's needs? Why limit a 7-year-old who is fantastic in math to the math classes of a 2nd grader. Allow them to progress forward. Why force a teenager through physics when they clearly do not enjoy it. Will they ever honestly use it again even if you force it down their throats? Why have a class structured the way it is? In his book, they explore many examples of most public schools who are changing up the way education is done.

Each of those schools serves to incorporate the intent of Paulo Freire's problem-posing educator. But one of the critical elements of the book is that this is a fluid process. The national level needs to give freedom to the state level, who needs to provide freedom to the local level, whose boards need to give freedom to the principles, who need then, to give freedom to the teachers.

The way this is done at the national level is to:
1. Eliminate the notion of standardization.
    a. It turns testing into a 12-16 billion dollar a year industry which only serves to inject corporate interests more monetarily into the school's structure instead of just ideologically.
    b. This includes common core. It's nice to have a standard, but the standard still acts as a restriction upon the freedom of the schools to teach how they see fit. It imposes that authoritarian structure upon the schools and therefore upon the students.
        i. I also find it hard to believe that if given a choice, schools would opt out of teaching the common core.
        ii. Eliminating the common core simply gives schools the freedom to choose at what pace they would like to teach certain things. Maybe their population has a hard time with math, the parents can't help out the kids. Instead of ordering the schools "you shall teach this by this time", you leave it up to the discretion of the schools on how they will educate the population they reside in.
2. Increase teacher pay
    a. Good pay promotes better quality teachers. It removes a barrier of having to sacrifice your well-being for a passion you hold.
    b. Increases in education pay off in the long term anyway. More education and more creativity will result in more productivity down the line.
3. Give school and teachers the freedom to experiment.
    a. This includes the evaluations of students.
    b. For example, one such method of evaluations is peer evaluations. Much like a scientific review. In science, if you pass peer review, then you are published.
    c. Another example would be the elimination of a grading standard altogether. Simply have a progressive program where students progress at their own pace through the subjects and teacher recommendations allow them to move up to the next level in that subject.

Structure

These may not be many in terms of policies. They are also not as specific as some of the other sections. The reason for this is that the path forward is not as clear. Energy is quite simple as there is an obvious path forward, which I prefer and advocate for. Education is so vast, and there are so many examples of successful implementations that to choose and advocate for any one over the others I feel would be unwise at this moment. Experimentation needs to occur and a lot of it. Through trial and error, we will discover what works and what doesn't. The only thing that is for sure now is that the system we have right now…isn't working. It alienates far too many kids and promotes a cultural apathy to and acceptance of the power dynamic within Capitalism as well as credulity toward the narration of the Capitalist class's mouthpieces.

CHAPTER 20
STRUCTURAL POLICY GOALS: THE CRIMINAL JUSTICE SYSTEM

Perhaps one of the most colossal failures of our society is our abysmal Criminal Justice system. More specifically, the systemic violence it perpetuates, the draconian laws it espouses, and the utter failure of our prisons to accomplish their supposed intent. As a result, both our justice system, as well as our prison systems, need to be overhauled completely.

Let's start first with the intent of the law. This is a free society, meant for people within it to have as much freedom as possible. But in this expression of freedom, we run into conflicts with the values that we place on rights. For example, someone in a state of nature has the right to do whatever they want, even kill. However, when they enter into society, they must surrender certain rights, certain freedoms. The reason they surrender these rights is that their right to do some action is in direct conflict with another's right. Law, by its structure, comes about as a limitation of one person's right to protect the right of another. In other words, it is the limitation of personal freedoms to protect the rights valued by society.

Laws, therefore, serve to balance the rights of society and create a hierarchy of importance. For example, your right to kill is not greater than my right to life. Thus, it becomes illegal to kill. My right to own is more significant than your right to take. Therefore, it becomes unlawful to steal. Etc. It is when we begin to divorce ourselves from this basic understanding of the law that their intent changes from that of protection to that of control as we see with the definition of what a law is today.

Law: the system of rules which a particular country or community recognizes as regulating the actions of its members and which it may enforce by the imposition of penalties.

This definition has nothing to do with the intent of the laws, it's a nuance but an important one to notice. By removing the intent from the definition (to protect the rights valued by society) and only define it by its action (regulation of actions enforced through penalties) you then permit its misuse. When it is defined this way, it allows the class which is in power to control the outcome.

Structure

To utilize the justice system as a Profit-making venture. As a way to maintain its power. As a way to continuously keep the economically downtrodden in a state of submission. How does it do this? Through structural violence.

Drugs

Brief History[172]
- Throughout most of American, History Drugs have been entirely legal.
    - There were some specific drug prohibition laws, but the reasons for those were racial, not scientific, and their enforcement was not nationwide.
        - 1870's anti-opium law directed at Chinese immigrants
        - 1900's anti-cocaine laws directed at black southerners
            - Coca Cola had cocaine in it up until 1929 to provide context as to how racially motivated these laws were.
        - 1910's anti-marijuana laws directed at Mexican immigrants.
            - The immigrants used it as a medicine and as a relaxant.
    - It wasn't until 1914 we had any definitive nationwide law, and it was aimed at narcotics.
        - Harrison Narcotic act- intended to regulate the commerce of opioid-containing substances.
    - Of course, 1919, we had Alcohol prohibition, which was anything but successful and was eliminated in 1933.
    - 1937 marijuana tax act- which was passed as a result of Testimony by then-Commissioner Anslinger who testified "Marijuana is an addictive drug which produces in its user's insanity, criminality, and death."
        - We all know how factual this statement really was. Truth is that Hemp threatened a Profit line of certain companies. Dupont to be exact.[173]

---

[172] The History of the Non-Medical Use of Drugs in the United States by Charles Whitebeard, Professor of Law, USC Law School

[173] Huffington Post- Dr David Bearman.

- o 1951&56 saw the Boggs act and the Daniels act. More fear mongering from that very same man. Mr. Anslinger. No scientific proof presented. In fact, he contacted 30 scientists looking for help testifying, 29 told him that cannabis was not dangerous in the slightest.[174]
    - ■ This same man was the racist who argued that Jazz music was of the devil and fueled by marijuana.
- o Then it wasn't until 1970 that the controlled substances Act was passed by Nixon and the war on drugs as we have known it began.
    - ■ As you can see, most drugs were entirely legal for the majority of U.S. history and the one which was attacked the most, marijuana, was done so out of racial intentions and against scientific advice.
- o We can see the effect this has had:

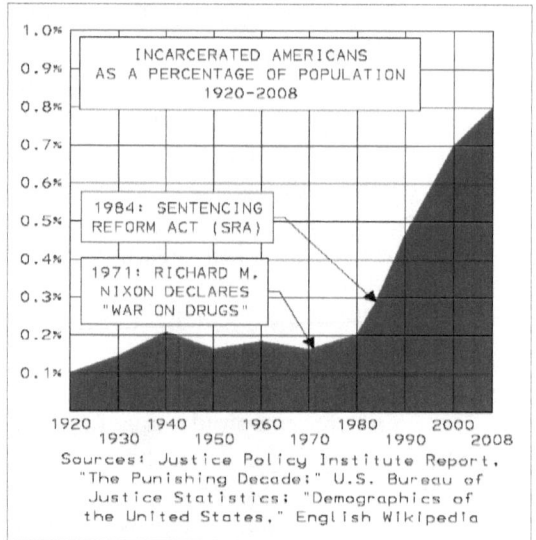

- • Today 40% of people in federal prison are there for drugs. 15% in state penitentiaries are there for drugs. [175]
    - o Systemically racist since both black and whites use at the same rates yet blacks are incarcerated at 5-7 times the rate.[176]

---

[174] Johann Hari- Chasing the Scream

[175] Prison Policy Initiative 2019 stats.

[176] Carson EA, Sabol WJ. Prisoners in 2011. U.S. Department of Justice: Bureau of Justice

Structure

The big questions that need to be asked are: "why did we initiate the war on drugs?" And "why do we continue to do so?" Fortunately, we have from the April 2016 issue of Harper's Magazine an interview that Dan Baum conducted with John Ehrlichman who was the Council and Assistance to the president for Domestic Affairs under President Richard Nixon.

"The Nixon campaign in 1968, and the Nixon White House after that had two enemies: the antiwar left and black people. You understand what I'm saying? We knew we couldn't make it illegal to be either against the war or black, but by getting the public to associate the hippies with marijuana and blacks with heroin, and then criminalizing both heavily, we could disrupt those communities. We could arrest their leaders, raid their homes, break up their meetings, and vilify them night after night on the evening news. Did we know we were lying about the drugs? Of course, we did." -John Ehrlichman

With this, I hope you can see how real class warfare is, and how interconnected this entire book is with policies that matter. What are we supposed to do with this knowledge now that we have it? Rewrite the drug policies, of course!

    a. We need to base drug policies, classifications, and punishments off of the scientific literature, not off of fear mongering and propaganda.

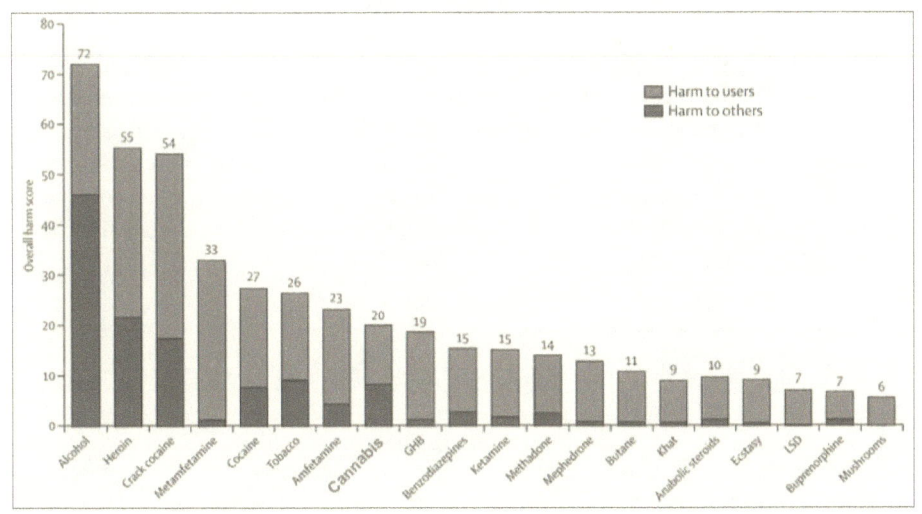

Statistics;

[199]

Lancet published a study titled "Drug Harms in the U.K.: A Multicriteria Decision Analysis" on Nov 1, 2010

    b. Arbitrary laws for substances that are less harmful than legal ones simply serve to undermine the validity of the justice system and perpetuate class violence.
        i. Mushrooms, LSD, Ecstasy, and Marijuana are by far much safer to both the user and society as a whole when compared to alcohol and cigarettes.[177]
    c. This provides an excellent way for the government to be the sole providers of these substances, while adjusting their costs based on the safety of use to control consumption (just as we do with cigarettes).
        i. This removes the drugs from the black market since they are now readily available on the regular market.
        ii. It makes them far safer since their purities can be ensured eliminating the harm that is present to the user in the unregulated black market.[178]
        iii. It acknowledges that where there is demand, there will always be a supply. If there is no moral or scientific objection toward providing that supply, then it should be legal.
        iv. Drugs can be priced to curb demand and the "Profits" made from that pricing can be utilized to balance money available in the market.

Sound drug regulation and the treatment of addictions as a medical issue instead of a crime is how we begin to move away from class violence and into a scientific understanding of drug policy. Also, it allows us to get back to the intent of what a law is.[179] Utilizing a drug should be your right. You should be free to do so, so long as you do not infringe upon the right of another. Drinking alcohol is legal, so long as you don't get in a car where your actions now endanger the public's right to life. Any drug laws we have should focus

---

[177] David Nutt- Drugs without the Hot Air. Explicitly referencing the ISCD's 2010 report of overall drug harm.

[178] The majority of harm that comes from drug use is the adulterants that are present from impure manufacturing techniques. Heroin for example has a lot of damage caused more so by the remaining solvents like kerosene than from the actual effects of the drug itself.

[179] We don't want to outlaw equestry because it is more dangerous than ecstasy do we?

on the principle of maintaining individual rights while protecting public rights, and they should focus on that principle alone. [180]

For-Profit Prisons

Our Prison System needs to be overhauled completely. Unfortunately, one of the solutions as of late has been to utilize private contractors, ones who own the prison completely or contracting out necessary services such as food and healthcare. The problem with this is that it puts Profit and human quality of life in direct competition with each other; we know who the victor in that matchup is.

For Profit prisons create perverse incentives to lock people up. They structurally work to keep rates of recidivism high, lower quality of care for human life, and reduce necessary services to the cheapest cost possible. We can see the effects of this in the following statistics:

- 6% of prisoners report being sexually assaulted, and the problem is rising[181]
- Private subcontractors for food like Aramark have failed on multiple occasions to provide decent food for prisoners. In one case maggots had even been found.[182]
- Privatization of healthcare is leading to a reduction in the standard of care.
    - This leads to a reduction in medical spending at the prisons. Because now a Profit motive exists that is in direct conflict with the well-being of human life. Care declines with privatization.[183]

---

[180] One implication of Drugs would be the utilization of LSD in studies. Dr David Nutt has found that LSD and Psilocybin more or less shut off the controlled operation of the brain. It allows the brain to operate more flexibly. Talk to portions it had not talked to before. It would be interesting to see if LSD could be utilized then to break out of learned habits. Break out of the socially conditioned narrative structure our current education has brought us up to follow, or if LSD could be utilized medicinally as a treatment for addiction. These are the types of questions that need to be asked. These are the legitimate scientific explorations that Capitalism, through the utilization of class warfare has prevented us from exploring, this is a specific situation where it has hindered human progress and understanding because of self-interest, because of Profit.

[181] BJS- sexual victimization reports 2012-2015

[182] PBS- Prison Strike organizers to Protest Food Giant Aramark

- Recidivism is only getting worse.
    - Private Prison companies advertise it as a sound business model to their investors.
    - The stats show that within 6 years of release, 79% of prisoners were re-arrested. With the majority of the re-arrests (92% or more) being non-violent: Property crimes, drugs, or public order. [184]

We need to remove the Profit incentive from the prison industry and actually focus our solutions to a more constructive and creative way of dealing with the intent behind prisons. Are they reformation or punishing institutions? What is the objective that they are supposed to meet? Because if that objective is anything but creating a culture of violence, lowering the quality of life, and wasting a whole lot of money, then they are failing.

Mandatory minimum sentencing

These laws require judges to punish criminals with a minimum number of years regardless of circumstances. They were quite popular in the '80s with the Reagan and Bush Presidencies. But Clinton did his fair share of harm too. Combine these draconian mandatory minimums with the class warfare on drugs, and you see more than a quadrupling of our prison population. One horrible example of this is In Kingsland, a man with an oz of meth was sentenced to life in prison in 2015. This isn't the mandatory minimum; the mandatory minimum is 10 years for anything over 50 grams. But you can see how insanely unjust these laws are as they redefine the baseline leading to harsher punishments. [185]

The effects of these mandatory minimums are not only ruining of lives, wasting of money, tearing apart of families, increasing the ever-widening gap of inequality in this country, but it also serves to disenfranchise entire pockets of the population. It serves to remove the voting rights from the members of the class whom the wealthy steal from the most. This process serves to harm the people of this country who do not have any economic rights by removing their political rights as well all while protecting the economic elite. Their

---

[183] 39 New Eng. J. on Crim. & Civ. Confinement 407 (2013) The Privatization of Prisons and Prisoner Healthcare: Addressing the Extent of Prisoners' Right to Healthcare

[184] Mariel Alper, and Joshua Markman, US Department of Justice Special Report: 2018 Update on Prisoner Recidivism.

[185] Bush and Reagan and Clinton were the principal promoters of these laws.

existence might as well be that of slaves. No say political and dominated economically. They work just to survive and the fruits of their Labour, forcibly taken from them by the structure of the system.

Bail

One of the most nefarious aspects of our justice system is the system of bail, which does excessive amounts of harm to the economically downtrodden compared to their wealthy counterparts. The bail system is relatively simple to understand. If you are suspected of committing a crime you can be arrested,[186] and once arrested if you are charged with a crime, you must remain in jail until your hearing. By posting bail you're allowed to buy your way out of jail, an option which the poor cannot afford. As a result, they must instead spend that time in jail waiting for their hearing to occur which can take weeks. This only serves to disrupt their life and makes their situation worse.

The frequency and cost of bails are rising, which only result in further systemic harm done to the impoverished. This increase in frequency and cost can in no way be justified as being for the safety of society either, because it must be noted that we are not talking about bail for violent crimes, no, we are talking about bail for minor offenses. For example, driving with a suspended license can yield a $1000 bail. We know that 63% of American families can't afford a $500 emergency.[187] How then are they to afford bail for non-violent crimes? They simply can't.

It means that violent criminals who are wealthy are able to avoid jail altogether while the non-violent poor are forced to stay in jail for weeks to months while they wait for their hearing. This leads to termination of employment, eviction from housing, and the overall destruction of their lives. Wealthy murders get to walk while the innocent poor have to suffer. The cost of bail is simply too high, and the consequences of staying in jail to wait for the trial are too great.

As a result of this, many poor admit guilt so that they can avoid that damage. They don't want to lose their job, their house, and destroy their lives

---

[186] Even though we claim innocent until proven guilty, this bail system proves that notion incorrect. I could buy an argument that for violent crime suspects it is moral to temporarily suppress an individual's rights to guarantee the rights of the public, but for non-violent crimes, this assertion of bail or having to remain in jail until the court date is an absolute bastardization of the notion of innocent until proven guilty.

[187] According to a survey done by Bankrate through Princeton Research associates.

because they can no longer pay their bills. But by doing this, not only do they become subject to whatever crimes they as innocent citizens now have to pay for, but they also become the target of systemic violence. By pleading guilty, they lock themselves into a downward spiral as any future jobs require they disclose the fact that they are guilty of committing a crime. A crime which they never committed, but a crime for which they will be harshly and unjustly persecuted for. This is sick.

A straightforward solution we can implement now is to not allow bail to be set for non-violent crimes. To follow the principle of our justice system, which is innocent until proven guilty. Or if you want to take a middle ground approach to account for those drug lords and big wall street financiers who commit property crimes and fraud, then simply do not allow the setting of bail beyond what a person can afford for non-violent crimes. It's as simple as that.

Municipal violations

Another aspect of our justice system that is inherent in systemic violence against the poor are municipal violations. These are those little tickets like parking, speeding, failing to signal, jaywalking. Etc.

These tickets come with a fine. These fines are often far more devastating on the impoverished of the society as the proportion of their wealth that it takes is far greater. For example, speeding tickets range from $100-200, which can be a crippling expense for most individuals. In most cases, the fines themselves are not all that bad. Failure to obey a traffic sign in Virginia results in a $97 offense. But after surcharges and fees, the final ticket ends up around $180. In California, the same offense is $35, but with the additional surcharges and fees, the final ticket is $238.

The problems with these offenses and extra fees are that if you are making just over minimum wage at $10/hour, then a quarter to half of your week's pay is suddenly gone. For people living paycheck to paycheck, this means that sometimes they cannot pay. If you cannot pay, punishments range from increased fines, to license suspension, all the way to jail. These punishments only serve to worsen the conditions the victim is already in.[188]

If you do not want to experience any of the punishments above, you can opt to be on a payment plan. But the problem with this is that 44 out of the

---

[188] You can't pay, then you must pay more. Oh, you cannot pay, let me take away your license and remove your ability to transport yourself to work. Oh, you cannot pay for this minor civil infraction, let me send you to jail and completely ruin your life.

50 states charge you a fee to do so. Which only exacerbates the problem. Eric Holder, the Attorney General of Ferguson, was on C-Span recounting how unjust this is. He recalled a case where:

> "a woman had two parking tickets that together totaled $152. To date, she has paid $552 in fines and fees to the city of Ferguson. Yet today, she still inexplicably owes Ferguson $541." -Eric Holder, Attorney General

These citations only get worse if the institutions that enforce them become corrupt. Stories of quotas for tickets and competitions between cops to see who can write the most tickets become a reality. This only serves to shackle the population to everlasting poverty further.

The underlying cause of many of these practices from quotas and surcharges, to excessive fees. Is that many of these budgets are funded by municipal violations. This creates an environment where the ones who are upholding public order now are being rewarded when there is less public order. The violations are beneficial to them. This goes against the whole intent of the police and justice system, which is to maintain public order, not systematically destroy the lives of the citizens through municipal violations.

Municipal violations have their place, but they are meant to be an inconvenience and a deterrent. Not a money maker. They are not meant to enslave the poor through debt. They are not meant to ruin lives.

Solutions to the Prison Problem

To find a solution to the prison problem, we must first ask what the intent of the prisons are, how are they designed, and do these designs meet the intent or objective. If they do not, then they need to be overhauled.

As far as I can tell, the prison has two primary objectives. Reformation and Punishment. I see these two things as completely separate.

Reformation prisons are for criminals whom education can help. Who drew a lousy lot in life and whose circumstances must be understood and internalized by the society. These sorts of prisons are for criminals whom the Judge, Jury, or even the individual pressing the charges, believe the offender should go because they have a chance at reform. Society has failed them in some way, and this is how society provides that second chance at redemption.

Reformation prisons, therefore, do not serve to punish, they help to educate by providing a community within the prison itself. A community which performs productive work for society and the inmates get paid a living wage as a result of that work.

- Reformation prisons teach the principles of cooperation
- They teach technical skills as well as provide environments for creativity and self-reflection to occur.
    - Prisons are actually a perfect place to harness creativity. There are perspectives from all walks of life within a prison, and by exploring those perspectives, they gain new insights into life and in understanding different groups of people.
- Reformation prisons are also an excellent place to help train groups of people in how to create and run a cooperative.
    - You start by allowing cooperatives to run within the prison itself. You create mini economies which trade with the outside world and whose income from those products is divvied up amongst the inmates by Labour hours worked.
        - By creating a functioning society within the prison, itself, the inmates are naturally reformed to the outer society as well.
        - The added benefit of this is that we can utilize reformation prisons as cooperative creating factories.

Punishment prisons are for those criminals whom education can't help, or for those whose crimes are so egregious justice demands they pay the price.

- Things like murder would land you in a punishment prison.
    - Even if it is apparent that you drew a lousy lot in life, the end result is that you still took away someone's life.
    - It is up to the loved ones of the lost to determine your fate. Do they forgive you, or do they want to see you punished? Your future lies in their hands because their loved one's life was taken by yours.
- More controversially would be which system would individuals like Martin Shkreli and the bankers who nose-dived the economy in 2008 end up?
    - I would advocate that these individuals had benefited from the system. That their transgressions were not forced on them by the system but solely through their own actions

and greed. That they knowingly and without external provocation invaded the rights of others for personal gain.
- Because of this lack of systemic pressure against their basic human needs, they were of their own free will and require punishment, not reformation.
    - No, greed is not a basic human need. Yes, the system pressures you to increase Profits, but no that is not a justification.
    - Martin Shkreli, for example, was Profitable regardless of the price increase and his decision cost people their lives.
    - Drug dealers, for example, depending upon the situation, could be either or:
        - Are they selling drugs to get by? If so reformation.
        - Are they drug lord and wealthy? If so, Punishment.
- This isn't to say that Punishment prisons solely revolve around punishment. If you are not there for life, then punishment prison should have a similar aim as reformation prison. That is that it should aim to prepare you to enter back into society.
    - For individuals like Martin Shkreli, that means empathy education and forcing him to experience the many different perspectives of the people who make up our wonderful society.

This means that the fundamental aspects of Prisons, therefore, is concerned with what actions did they perform, and did those actions infringe upon another's rights? If not, then no crime has been committed. If they did, then what kind of sentencing do they need? Are they in need of reformation, or are they in need of punishment?

CHAPTER 21:
STRUCTURAL POLICY GOALS: DIRECT DEMOCRACY

We saw back in Chapter 10 how representative democracy is structurally flawed as a tool of liberation for the masses. Instead, by its very design and operation, it becomes a tool of societal obstruction and the perpetuation of class interest. To overcome this flaw of representative democracy, we must first ask ourselves how we can achieve direct democracy. To do this, we must look around the world for examples on where it is practiced, to what extent, and the pros and cons associated with its implementation. After considering the current examples we can then hypothesis on how improvements can be made and thus true democracy achieved.

Switzerland's direct democracy

- Oldest form in Switzerland is the Landsgemeinde which is an event where all residents gather every spring to decide on laws and on expenditure.
    - This is, however, only in two regions (cantons) of the country.
- Country wide Residents gather 4 times a year to vote on local, state, and country wide issues.
    - They do this through a combination of a representative democracy in which their parliament (their house and senate) passes laws. These laws can be overturned by the populous through a referendum by collecting 50,000 signatures within 100 days of the law being passed.
    - Once this is done, the bill must then be voted on by the public.
    - Only about 3 in 5 people vote in these sections.
- There is also a thing called the people's initiative which allows people to make changes to the constitution or to propose a law. 100,000 signatures must be collected within 18 months.

This is very powerful in that it provides a check by direct democracy on representative democracy, but it also leads to a lengthy decision-making process. But Switzerland isn't the only country to implement a direct form of democracy. There is another country that does as well.

Liechtenstein

- It is a constitutional monarchy, but the majority of its decision-making processes are done through referendums.
- All decisions are left up to the residents themselves.
    - Of the 11 parishes, each parish has referendum control by its population on all matters.
    - They can even choose to leave the country if they desire.
    - The entire country, however, is only about 38,000 people.
- The process starts when the Public starts an initiative and then holds a referendum if they can get 1,000 signatures.

There is a book out called the state in the 3rd millennium that outlines how to implement the Liechtenstein model in a larger country. It features a few key points.

1. The state as a service provider (things the state can do better than local communities or local businesses)[189]
2. Giving each of the municipalities the ability to withdraw if they so choose via a referendum is a way of ensuring the state does a good job at providing the services.
3. Each of the villages makes determinations on how they will tax, what industries they want to go there, what they will give the industries to go there, and even Immigration.[190]

The right to self-sovereignty allows the country to make every decision they can imagine if they can bring it to a referendum. With such a small population getting the signatures needed for the referendum is 1/38th of its country's population. Translating that to say the United States would require roughly nine million signatures. This poses a logistical problem. Nine million

---

[189] Here in this book, we have defined this as the state providing necessities and taking over natural monopolies. The necessities sector is entirely the state, the productivity sector is a combination of the state and private, and the luxury sector is entirely private. Needs- state, wants-private, and getting better- both.

[190] This served to educate the population on the need for immigration. Each village was unable to supply the manpower for manufacturing as they were. They needed to allow immigration in to also bring manufacturing in. As a result, it educated the population on the benefits and detriments of immigration. The population is then more informed as to the effects of their decisions when compared to the United States.

is far harder to validate and gather than one thousand. With appropriate technology however it is achievable.

Another of the difficulties with upscaling this model is that the large countries no longer operate as a monoculture like Liechtenstein is. Even within an average city in the United States, you have socioeconomic differences, cultural differences, and ethnic differences to consider. How do you implement the direct democracy without apocalyptic outcomes? To quell those fears before we address them lets tuck away the initiative and referendum in our back pocket and take a look at this thing called liquid democracy.

Liquid Democracy

- A mixture between representative and direct democracy.
- A representative's vote holds the weight of X number of voters who are registered in their geographical area of representation.
- Citizens who disagree with how their representative will vote can remove their vote from their representative and cast it how they see fit.
    - For individuals who reside in a state or city where they disagree with their representative, they can cast their vote on the issues directly.
- This is done electronically. If any of the voters that are assigned underneath that representative cast a vote, the system recognizes it and their vote is removed from that representative's total.
- This requires voting IDs to be given out to individuals and those voting IDs attached to a geographical area. The representative of that geographic area automatically represents the people of that area.
- People can choose how to vote on specific issues.
    - At a national level, this could manifest as a drop-down menu in each category, and you would be able to place default votes in each category.
    - Apps such as vote spotter already do similar things; the difference is that by placing your vote your voice then matters at all levels of the society.
- This also eliminates the disproportionality of different state's votes having a different say. This means that the most total votes at the end is how the legislation is decided.
    - For example, in the current system for the house of representatives, a state like West Virginia has a voting

power of 4.15 while a state like Nebraska has a voting power of 2.08.
- Based on the representatives allocated to those states. The individual's vote from Nebraska, in the end, has half as much influence in Congress as the individual's vote from West Virginia.
- This system eliminates that by changing to a popular vote system where the representatives don't stand for an arbitrary 1/435, but rather their vote counts for the total number of voters they represent.
- This can then lead to alterations to the number of representatives in the house, to make each representative more even in total amounts of votes they represent.

Combining the strengths of these three systems is the first step toward restoring democratic power back to the masses. The downfall of representative democracy is the formation of class and the development of the party where the focus becomes winning power for the party instead of focusing on the betterment of society.

Adding a pinch of direct democracy into this system may prevent or limit that from happening. Winning is no longer the thing that matters since:

- You don't automatically get representation over the voters.
    - The losing parties' voters can still cast their vote if they disagree with you.
    - Additionally, you must keep your own base happy since they have the option of voting against you at any time.
- The security of the party's power then lies in winning over the mass of people not merely undermining the opposing party.
- Class influence gets reduced as direct democracy input into the representative democracy system removes total class control from how voting occurs.
    - The majority can make their voices heard even after a representative has been elected.

Additionally, to prevent the people from merely being plebiscites having to accept via a yes or no vote the legislation that is presented to them, they can utilize initiatives and referendums to bring their ideas to the table. This is an excellent way to introduce democratic control over state and national issues. We see Colorado is very successful with this type of democracy, but they are one of the few states who allow their citizens that luxury. This needs to apply universally to the local, state, and national level.

That means direct ballot initiatives that are voted on every two years at all levels of government. These are the top issues facing the country. Gathered through queries of the people to determine what it is they want to see on these direct ballots. The issues will be announced with plenty of time for public debate. 6 months to a year prior. And should a desired issue not appear on that ballot, the people can form their own immediate initiative to gather enough signatures to get it added to the ballot before it goes to vote. If we take Switzerland's example that is enough signatures need to be collected within 100 days of the initial announcement.

As for how many signatures would be needed to initiate the referendum. Using Lichtenstein as the marker if the 1/38 or 2.6% of the local level, the state, or the nation agree through signatures on an initiative, then that referendum must be placed on the ballot.[191] This is actually quite promising, since studies suggest that if you can get 3.5% of the population to agree on something AND take action, that usually translates into a revolutionary change.[192]

There does exist a legitimate critique of the initiative and referendum model. It focuses around how it can be hijacked by the wealthy and used as a tool against the masses.

John Diaz in the San Francisco chronicle 2008 wrote the following:

"There is no big secret to the formula for manipulating California's initiative process. Find a billionaire benefactor with the ideological motivation or crass self-interest to spend the $1-million plus to get something on the ballot with mercenary signature gatherers. Stretch as far as required to link it to the issue of the ages (this is *for the children*, Prop. 3) or the cause of the day (this is about *energy independence and renewable resources*, Props. 7 and 10). If it's a tough sell on the facts, give it a sympathetic face and name such as "Marsy's Law" (Prop. 9, victims' rights and parole) or "Sarah's Law" (Prop. 4, parental notification on abortion). Prepare to spend a bundle on soft-focus television advertising and hope voters don't notice the fine print or the independent analyses of good-government groups or newspaper editorial boards ... Today, the initiative process is no longer the antidote to special interests and the moneyed class; it is their vehicle of choice to

---

[191] Currently, national initiatives and referendums are not done in the United States. This must be one of the changes to implement.

[192] This comes from the book "Why Civil Resistance Works".

attempt to get their way without having to endure the scrutiny and compromise of the legislative process." -John Diaz

The problem to this system can also be seen in the many internet spoof videos where signatures are obtained to ban dihydrogen monoxide or ban women's suffrage. [193]

These are indeed issues to be dealt with. However, this is where informing the public and implementing positive control is recommended. For example, having a safe universal method by which referendums can be voted on. Let's say an app on the phone. Since the wealthy are going to utilize the media to spread misinformation, the app on the phone must require the voter to watch a short 1-2-minute video explaining each side of the issue. There must also be options provided to the voter to do additional research should that video spark concern that they were misinformed by the media.

Historical examples also exist that the above concerns are minor. In cases where the public has passed referendums that they didn't actually pay attention to, they were quickly overturned. This ability to test and re-vote is a critical aspect of experimentation and democracy. Running a country is an experiment, growth is an experiment. As such you have to propose hypothesis, see how they go and be willing to abandon them if they don't turn out the way you thought.

Another aspect to consider about initiatives is that the legislature might change them before sending them out to the public as a referendum. That has the potential of stealing the voice away from the public. Colorado has found a way past this through a referendum called Colorado O that requires the Colorado legislature to have a 2/3rds majority to make changes to proposed initiatives before they are sent to the public for a referendum. This makes it easy to make uncontroversial changes, and at the same time when combined with the liquid democracy model prevents a class from stripping out revolutionary content that the ruling class doesn't like.

So how would this proposed model of democracy work?

First steps will include policies such as:

- Eliminating the electoral college, the system being advocated for is one person one vote.

---

[193] Most likely a cultural change will happen if people are given actual agency and power.

- - No reason to be giving someone in Wyoming multiple times the voting power compared to someone in Florida.
- Eliminating superdelegates.
  - no reason to give the wealthy any more power than they already wield. The existence of these delegates simply robs voting power from the people and provides it to the establishment.
- Eliminating Gerrymandering and making the geographical locations of representatives intuitive.
- Introducing a new type of voting system built off of the principles of block chain technology. This means that multiple copies are checked, that everyone's votes are public and at the same time everyone's votes are anonymous. This allows for elections to be verifiable and tamper proof.
  - By introducing a voting method via a cryptologically secure digital means, you also serve to reduce the inconvenience of voting and make it more accessible to everyone.
  - This method is already better than current voting means since existing methods of voting are non-verifiable by the public. This aspect of our current voting system has led to critiques that our elections are rigged and tampered with.
- Introducing an updated voter registration service where individuals receive a voter-ID.
  - This ID is unique to them and is their public facing vote. When they cast their ballot, their vote is listed next to their voter ID in the public space. This allows the voters to go back in and verify that their vote was cast for the correct candidate.
  - You can acquire this voter ID online or in person.
- Introducing the liquid democracy concept redefines how the government roles play out. It changes it from a one representative one vote system to a one person one vote system.
  - Utilizing the same voting system, we can see all the voter IDs that a member of Congress represents.
  - If one of those voter IDs votes on an issue, then their voter ID is removed from the total number of votes that member of Congress's vote can represent on that issue.
    - They can't speak for people who have already spoken for themselves.
- Introduce the 2-year direct ballot initiative process

- Query the population to discover the top issues they wish to see on the ballot.
- In conjunction with immediate initiatives process.
  - If the public doesn't see an issue, they wish to see they have 100 days to gather the required signatures to get it added to the ballot.
- Give ample time between the announcement of the direct ballot to allow for public debate.

Thought experiment:

A voting block of 10 people want a specific policy passed. They elect a representative and verify that their votes were indeed cast for the individual they said they cast it for. That individual gets into Congress and starts blocking the progressive reforms that the people wanted to see. Instead of Universal health care, the representative starts pushing health insurance for all or "accessible" healthcare. The people utilize liquid democracy to make sure that their voice is heard by removing power from the representative. They begin to speak for themselves so the representative cannot speak for them. But without a representative willing to put forth a universal healthcare bill, the people never get a chance to exercise their newfound voting power.[194]

A year after the election they answer the national direct ballot query. Filling in the top 10 policies, they would most like to see added to the direct ballot initiative.[195] This query is compiled, and the winning initiatives (any that are over 2.6% of the total population) chosen for a referendum and then announced. Some of the people don't see their initiative on the ballot. So, they move for an immediate initiative. They have 100 days to gather the signatures of 2.6% of the population to get their policy added to the ballot. If they succeed, that initiative is added to the direct ballot. The people then vote directly on the referendums.

This is the type of system that this book is advocating for. It is the transitional system to direct democracy by changing the aspects of the old which don't work while introducing some aspects of the new to discover their operational benefit. The left tends to like collectivization while the right tends to like individualization. These policies above give power to both and as such, make it far more appealing to the entire mass of people. The only ones who

---

[194] In this state they are nothing more than the plebiscite.

[195] This elevates them from plebiscite to an active participant in the political process, this gives them true democracy.

will dislike this system are the class of people whom it removes power from. The parties and the elite.

CHAPTER 22:
FINAL WORD
THE INFINITE GAME[196]

We go through our lives playing games, and so do companies and even nations. Each new chapter is a new challenge, a new set of winners and a new set of losers. But it is the leaders who dictate how the game is going to be played.

You are the leader of your own life. Beach season is coming up, and you need to get in shape. It's February and if you can rock that six pack by June then you won the game. The boss is the leader of the company. The annual metrics are coming up, and his business is currently lagging behind its competitor by just a few sales. He's going to sprint for the finish to try to come out on top. The countries president declares we are number one and makes grand gestures to ensure people think so.

These are all games. But are they the right games? That is the question we need to be asking. America amid Vietnam had the superior forces, had the superior tactics, won every battle they came across, and for all intents and purposes kicked the North Vietnamese ass.... yet we still lost. The leaders did everything they could, they played the game to win, made the right decisions to win the battles, but they still lost the war. How can that be?

It comes down to the concept of winning. What was winning for us? Did we define that? We had metrics by which we measured our success, and we met them. We had objectives and goals set forth, and we achieved them...but we still lost. The reason is simple. We were a finite player in an infinite game

The Infinite game is the one which one can never stop playing. If you are playing an infinite game, then it is the one which you will sacrifice for over and over again. It's one where there is no winning and losing, there is only surviving. To keep the game going is the only objective, nothing else matters. That was the difference in Vietnam, that is the difference now in the Middle

---

[196] Based on the talk from Simon Sinek- "The Infinite Game" and applied to the principles of what so far have been discussed to provide the moral and intuitive argument as to why a country should strive to provide for its people's desires.

East. We were/are the finite players playing an infinite game. That's dangerous.

Finite players blow through resources, make short-sighted decisions, wear themselves out, and eventually must drop out of the game when they are playing against an infinite player. That's because we are trying to win, they are playing to survive. The North Vietnamese didn't have any other objective than to fight and fight and fight until we left. They were fighting for their lives, their friends, their family, their culture, and their society. Why were we fighting? Were our reasons as just? No, of course, they weren't, that's why we left, we quit the game. We couldn't win, and it was no longer fun to play.

This becomes a valuable lesson, especially for leaders. Play the infinite game! Do not worry about winning and losing. That's short-sighted. Focus on what matters, focus on the things that you would sacrifice for over and over and over again instead of the things you think will "win" you the game.

You are the leader of yourself, don't focus on the beach bod, focus on a healthy life. Don't win the diet, make eating healthy your lifestyle. If you own a company don't focus on catching up to competitors, don't try and think about how you can surpass them, or stay ahead of them. Focus on the reasons as to why you started the business in the first place. Focus on the betterment of your company for the sake of being better.

The United States keeps focusing on making sure we are number one. Making sure that all the countries of the world think that. We should be focusing on the principles of what made the United States so great to begin with. We should be focusing on the people who make up the country. When you worry about games that aren't infinite, games that deal with emotions such as pride, greed, envy, and the like. Your focus is turned away from what is truly important. Turned away from the things that inspire and drive you. To be a good leader, you must figure out the infinite game. To be a great country, you must play an infinite game.

Infinite players seek an ideal vision, their achievements are always in pursuit of a just cause. A just cause is one that is worth it no matter how many sacrifices you make, it won't always feel good, it might even be painful, but it feels right. Finite games are games played to feel good that don't always feel right. Is our invading of Iraq to capture control of their oil fields an infinite game? Does it feel like a just cause? Does it feel right? No, of course not, because we are a finite player participating in an infinite game. That is their land, their home, their people. There is a good percentage of those people who feel so strongly that we shouldn't be there that they are willing to die for it, and to keep dying for it. That's not a game we can win. What is a game that we can win? Following our principles of life liberty and the pursuit of happiness, applying that to every man woman and child on earth and respecting their unalienable rights. Building a country that meets and exceeds those rights. Producing a country where you can look at every activity we engage in and say without a sliver of doubt, "we are just".

This means that you have to have a vision for the future, not a metric. You must have an ideal that you can never reach, that you will perpetually work toward and each small progress toward it, helps motivate it along and inspire those around you and under you that it is possible. Martin Luther King had a vision. He had a dream. He pushed for that dream, he fought for that dream, and he died for that dream. When people feel that they connect with it, they get inspired by it, follow it, and then they contribute to it. The first thing we, as a country have to do is define our vision, define our dream. My dream is a world without exploitation, where people don't work because they have to, but work because they want to. All their needs are taken care of. They achieve their wants without much strain. That if you want to travel around the world, done, no problem. If you want to take up a new skill, that's great! do it! Yes, it's an ideal, it seems impossible, it may very well never be reached, but that's what makes it an infinite game. You set forth the ideal, and then you work step by step to achieve it. Much to your surprise you just might.

"The US should commit itself to achieve the goal, before this decade is out, of putting a man on the moon and returning him safely to earth." - John F Kennedy.

Was that an infinite game? In a way, it was. At the time, it seemed like an impossible goal. It had many doubters. But it also inspired many people, it got them hopeful, and it got them contributing. The infinite game is the one which you will continue to sacrifice for because you believe in it.

This brings us to an aspect of the infinite game, and that is teamwork. An infinite game isn't accomplished alone. The vision is adopted, people join in, they believe it in their bones. The effort of everyone combines to further the collective dream. When people's beliefs combine, they accomplish the impossible.

Weak leaders are the ones who do just the opposite. They play a finite game, they set rules for themselves and work to accomplish those rules. Weak leaders are those individuals like Martin Shkreli who do not inspire, who make short termed decisions which no one buys into except for the people that benefit. Sacrificing people's lives for Profit by hiking up the price of the drug

Final Word: The Infinite Game

Daraprim by more than 5,000%. Weak leaders do not earn the admiration of those around them, what they receive are distrust and hatred. Donald Trump is another such leader. Lawsuit after lawsuit in his business adventures, never playing the long game always the finite. One after the next going bankrupt[197], lying about his wealth so that he may get on the list of the Forbes 400. Sure these two examples are of successful people, but what is the measure of "success"? What about the people they had to trample on to get where they are at? Did their success come with a raising up of society as well? Or did they push others down so they may be on top?

Good leaders don't do that, good leaders lift people up, good leaders passionately speak of a dream, speak of a vision, inspire people to buy into it, and facilitate an environment that allows for the dream and vision to prosper. In the case of a country whose vision is a utopia for its people, that means creating a system whose structure allows for that to occur. An environment where companies synergize instead of competing. Where they work on advancing the betterment of society for the sake of society. Where the government, the company, and the people treat each other in such a way that they lift each other up. When people are asked if they like their government or work or neighbor, they don't answer in disgust. Instead, they answer with excitement, they answer with joy, and they answer with love.

This is only accomplished through having morals, having a dream, and having a conviction to pursue it. The only way we can ever make a socialist society reality is to pursue it with all our hearts, even when it's hard, even when we don't like the struggle. We will pursue it because it is worth it.

---

[197] In each Bankruptcy, Trump was able to avoid having to pay back his debts, while passing that burden onto the insolvent company and leaving with millions in Profit for himself. Abandoning the individuals who relied upon the income those jobs provided to fend for themselves. What risk did Trump take? None, whatsoever.
https://www.nytimes.com/2016/06/12/nyregion/donald-trump-atlantic-city.html

ACKNOWLEDGMENT

No one deserves more acknowledgment than you for picking up this book. Whether you agree with the words I have written or not; I thank you from the bottom of my heart for adding my perspective to your repertoire of knowledge

www.ingramcontent.com/pod-product-compliance
Lightning Source LLC
Chambersburg PA
CBHW021813170526
45157CB00007B/2565